Legal Responses to Domestic Violence

This book aims to examine legal responses to domestic violence in a holistic way. In England and Wales, as in other jurisdictions, much attention has been paid to the criminal justice response to domestic violence. The response of the civil justice system has not been ignored, but has been somewhat marginalised. *Legal Responses to Domestic Violence* takes a systematic approach to examining legal responses, encompassing the full range of decision makers within the legal system to analyse developments in substantive law and practice, in particular the movement towards an integrated justice approach.

Mandy Burton is currently a Senior Lecturer in Law at the University of Leicester. She has carried out numerous empirical studies for UK Government departments, including a study of the effectiveness of the civil remedies for domestic violence under the Family Law Act 1996 and two studies of specialist domestic violence courts.

D1355126

Legal Responses to Domestic Violence

Mandy Burton

 Routledge·Cavendish
Taylor & Francis Group
LONDON AND NEW YORK

First published 2008 by Cavendish Publishing

Transferred to digital printing 2009
by Routledge-Cavendish
2 Park Square, Milton Park, Abingdon, Oxon, OX14 4RN

Simultaneously published in the USA and Canada
by Routledge-Cavendish
270 Madison Avenue, New York, NY 10016

*Routledge-Cavendish is an imprint of the Taylor & Francis Group,
an informa business*

© 2008 Mandy Burton

Typeset in Times New Roman by
RefineCatch Limited, Bungay, Suffolk

British Library Cataloguing in Publication Data
A catalogue record for this book is available from the British Library

Library of Congress Cataloging in Publication Data
A catalog record for this book has been requested

ISBN10: 0–415–45423–9 (hbk)
ISBN13: 978–0–415–45423–0 (hbk)

ISBN10: 1–84472–026–8 (pbk)
ISBN13: 978–1–84472–026–2 (pbk)

ISBN10: 0–203–92775–3 (ebook)
ISBN13: 978–0–203–92775–5 (ebook)

Contents

Table of Cases   vii
Table of Statutes   ix

1 Domestic violence: what has the law got to do with it?   1

Defining domestic violence 1
Extent and nature of the problem 4
The role of law 6

2 The civil law: social change and legal change   11

The civil remedies in the 1970s and 1980s 11
The Family Law Act 1996 14
Child contact proceedings under the Children Act 1989 29
Conclusion 32

3 The civil justice response: protection in practice?   33

*The implementation of remedies before the Family Law Act
     1996 33*
  Relationship with solicitor 33
  The court process 35
Implementing the Family Law Act 1996 36
Child contact 42
Conclusion 45

4 Improving the civil justice response   47

Obtaining an order—time for third party applications? 47
Enforcing orders—criminalisation of breach 52
Civil protective orders in criminal proceedings 56
Conclusion 57

5   The criminal law: slow or no recognition   59

Non-fatal offences against the person 60
   Sentencing domestic violence 63
   Is a special offence of domestic violence needed? 66
Rape 68
Homicide 74
   The provocation defence 75
   Sentencing domestic homicide 85
Conclusion 86

6   The criminal justice system: justice for victims?   89

Police response 89
   Early failings: policing domestic violence in the 1970s and
      1980s 89
   Policy changes: policing domestic violence in the 1990s 91
   Policing domestic violence in the twenty-first century 94
Crown prosecution service 97
   Prosecution of domestic violence in context 97
   Prosecution policy 98
   CPS practice 99
Criminal courts 104
The criminal justice response to rape 107
Conclusion 108

7   Improving the criminal justice response   109

Background to domestic violence court specialisation 109
Domestic violence courts in England and Wales 112
Do specialist courts benefit victims? 117
Conclusion 122

8   Are legal interventions effective?   123

Victims' perspectives 123
Victims' perspectives on the criminal justice system 124
Victims' perspectives on the civil justice response 128
Are legal interventions changing violent men? 130
Conclusion 132

Bibliography   135
Index   149

Table of Cases

AG of Jersey v Holley [2005] 2 AC 580 .... 82, 83, 84
Ansah v Ansah [1977] 2 All ER 638 26

B v B (Occupation Order) [1999] 1 FLR 715 .... 22, 23

C v C (Non-Molestation Order: Jurisdiction) [1988] 2 WLR 599 15
Chalmers v Johns [1999] 1 FLR 392 .... 22, 23
Chechi v Bashier and others [1999] Fam 528 27

G v F (Non-Molestation Order: Jurisdiction) (2000) 2 FCR 638 .... 17, 18
G v G (Occupation Order: Conduct) [2000] 2 FLR 36 .... 24, 25

H v H [2001] 3 FCR 628 28
Hale v Tanner [2000] 2 FLR 879 .... 28, 53
Hipgrave v Jones [2005] 2 FLR 174 55
Horner v Horner [1982] 2 All ER 495 15

Johnson v Walton [1990] 1 FLR 350 15

Lee v Lee [1984] FLR 243 13
Lomas v Parle [2004] 1 FLR 812 .... 28, 29
Luc Thiet Thuan v Queen, The [1997] AC 131 80

R v Ahluwalia [1992] 4 ALL ER 889 .... 76, 78, 80
R v Bedder [1954] 1 WLR 1119 77
R v Camplin [1978] AC 705 .... 77, 79, 80
R v Chan-Fook [1994] 1 WLR 689 .... 61, 62
R v Clarence [1889] QBD 23 68
R v Clarke [1949] 2 All ER 448 68
R v D (2006) 2 Cr App R 24 61
R v Duffy [1949] 1 All ER 932 .... 75, 76
R v E (Keith) [2005] 1 Cr App R (S) 59 72
R v F (Davis Nigel) [2006] EWCA Crim 2305 73
R v Humphreys [1995] 4 All ER 1008 .... 78, 79
R v Ireland v Burstow [1997] 4 All ER 225 .... 60, 62
R v James [2006] EWCA Crim 14 82

R v Julkowinksi [2006] EWCA Crim 3077 74
R v M (1995) 16 Cr App R (S) 770 69
R v Milberry [2003] 1 WLR 546 .... 70, 71, 72, 74
R v Morhall [1996] 1 AC 90 77
R v Newell (1980) 71 Cr App R 331 77
R v O'Brien [1974] 3 All ER 663 68
R v Price [2003] 2 Cr App R (S) 73 71
R v R [1991] 2 All ER 257 .... 68, 69
R v Smith [20000] 3 WLR 645 .... 80, 81, 83
R v Suratan, R v Humes and R v Wilkinson [2003] 2 Cr App R (S) 42 .... 81, 85
R v Thornton (no 2) [1996] 2 All ER 1023 79
R v W (1993) 14 Cr App R (S) 256 .... 69, 70
R v Weller [2004] 1 Cr App R 1 81
Re BJ (A Child) (Non-Molestation Order: Power of Arrest) [2000]
    2 FLR 443 .... 19, 27
Re L (Contact: Domestic Violence) [2000] 2 FLR 334 .... 30, 31, 32
Re H (A child) (Contact: Domestic Violence) [2006] 1 FCR 102 .... 31, 32
Re Y (Children) (Occupation Order) (2000) 2 FCR 470 .... 24, 25
Richards v Richards [1984] AC 174 .... 13, 21

Thorpe v Thorpe [1988] 2 FLR 127 53

Vaughan v Vaughan [1973] 3 All ER 499 15

Table of Statutes

Bail Act 1976 103

Civil Partnership Act 2004 .... 20, 21
Children Act 1989 .... 29, 30,
43, 44
County Court Act 1984 11
Criminal Justice Act 1988 60
Criminal Justice Act 2003 .... 101, 104
Criminal Justice and Public Order
Act 1994 69

Domestic Violence and Magistrates
Court Act 1978 12
Domestic Violence and Matrimonial
Proceedings Act 1976 .... 2, 12
Domestic Violence Crime and Victims
Act 2004 .... 18, 20, 39, 47, 53,
54, 55, 57, 74

Family Law Act 1996 .... 2, 3, 11, 14,
15, 16, 17, 18, 19, 20, 21, 22, 23, 24, 25,
26, 27, 28, 29, 32, 33, 36, 37, 38, 39, 40,
41, 42, 45, 47, 48, 51, 52, 55, 56, 63, 129

Homicide Act 1957 .... 75, 77, 80

Magistrates Court Act 1980 105
Matrimonial Homes Act 1983 ..... 12, 13

Offences Against the Person Act
1861 .... 60, 61, 105

Protection from Harassment
Act 1997 .... 17, 18, 29, 55, 56,
57, 60, 62, 63, 64

Supreme Court Act 1981 11

1   Domestic violence

What has the law got to do with it?

An account of legal interventions in domestic violence must begin with an examination of what domestic violence is and an attempt to assess the scope of the problem. It is also important to explore the reasons for legal intervention and whether the law has a meaningful role to play in addressing what some might regard as essentially a social problem rather than a legal problem. The focus of this book will be legal responses to domestic violence in England and Wales. However the law or practices of law enforcement agencies in England and Wales has sometimes been developed to take into account approaches in other countries. Thus it can be contextually illuminating to compare legal interventions in domestic violence in other jurisdictions. Many of the theoretical debates about the role of law in domestic violence cases are not jurisdiction specific and consequently there is a rich international debate to be drawn upon in this respect.

This is not the first book to examine legal responses to domestic violence in England and Wales. There have been books that have looked at the law relating to domestic violence in some detail (Bird, 2006). Others have taken a more socio-legal approach of examining how discretion is exercised by particular actors within the legal system in domestic violence cases (Hoyle, 1998). The approach of this book will be to combine an analysis of the law with an examination of the socio-legal research on decision-making in practice. This book will not confine itself to one area of law or to a single set of actors, for example police or judges. The objective is to examine different areas of the law relating to domestic violence and critically review interventions at all levels of the legal system by a variety of different legal actors. Inevitably areas of weakness, as well as strength, in the existing legal response will be identified. In recent years there has been considerable effort to change the way that the legal system works in domestic violence cases. This book will provide a commentary on this process of change and the policy dynamic underpinning it.

Defining domestic violence

Defining domestic violence is not easy, given that the term has a multiplicity of meanings to different people in different contexts. In responding to domestic violence different parts of the legal system have often produced different definitions of both 'domestic' and 'violence'. Multiple definitions have become a well-recognised obstacle to effective responses to domestic violence across the legal system (Home Office, 2003 p 8; Paradine and Wikinson, 2004; Radford, 2003). Legal definitions of domestic violence, or those used by agencies involved in the administration of justice, may bear little resemblance to those used by other statutory agencies (e.g. health, social services) or voluntary sector support agencies, potentially undermining any efforts to achieve a coordinated response. Agency definitions of domestic violence may vary significantly from how individuals in society, including those who fall within those agency definitions, understand and interpret their own experiences.

Legal definitions of domestic violence have shifted over time. Until the 1970s there was little recognition of domestic violence as an issue that ought to be tackled by the legal system (Dobash and Dobash, 1992). Neither the civil or criminal law had evolved to provide specific remedies for domestic violence. It was in the mid-1970s that the first statutory civil remedies were developed and a definition of the 'domestic' relationships to be afforded specific protection against violence was developed. The Domestic Violence and Matrimonial Proceedings Act 1976 provided injunctive relief in the county courts to parties to a marriage or men and women living together in the same household as husband and wife. 'Domestic' in this context meant spouses or heterosexual cohabitants, although a subsequent piece of legislation of the same decade restricted the injunctive relief available in the magistrates courts to spouses only (see Chapter 2). It was not until the 1990s that a much broader concept of 'domestic' relationships found its way into the legal definitions of domestic violence. In the area of civil law this was through the concept of 'associated persons' in the Family Law Act 1996. The category of persons entitled to seek injunctive relief was extended beyond spouses and heterosexual cohabitants to a wider range of relationships. However the inclusiveness of the definition was still a matter of debate: certain relationships which some felt should be recognised as 'domestic', such as long-term non-cohabiting couples, were not originally included in this particular legal definition. Very recently the definition of domestic violence in civil law has been expanded further (see Reece, 2006, and the discussion in Chapter 2). While definitions of 'domestic violence' were evolving in the civil law, various definitions were being developed by criminal justice agencies. Domestic violence was not, and still is not, a specific criminal offence in England and Wales (see Chapter 5), so agencies such as the police and Crown Prosecution Service (CPS) developed definitions to identify cases which they should apply their emergent domestic violence policies to when enforcing the general criminal law. Government departments also started to produce various definitions for use in policy development in this area. It is useful to examine some of these definitions to demonstrate the confusion and disagreement about what constitutes domestic violence. The Home Office adopted a definition of domestic violence as: 'Any violence between current and former partners in an intimate relationship, wherever and whenever the violence occurs. The violence may include physical, emotional and financial abuse' (Home Office, 2003). This definition confines 'domestic' to intimate relationships between partners and excludes other family relationships. The CPS definition of domestic violence at the same time applied to: 'Any criminal offence arising out of physical, sexual, psychological, emotional or financial abuse by one person against a current or former partner in a close relationship, or against a current or former family member' (CPS, 2005). Although the CPS is more inclusive than the Home Office definition, in so far as it extends to a range of family members beyond intimate partners, both definitions recognise that 'violence' is broader than physical assault and can encompass a range of other behaviour including 'emotional' abuse. However the CPS definition specifically confines itself to the criminal law and this potentially creates difficulties for prosecutors trying to accommodate emotional and financial abuse within the range of offences that can be charged in domestic violence situations (see Chapter 6). Actual violence and threats of violence are much easier to fit within the scope of the existing criminal law than emotional abuse, although there are some offences that can be used where the relationship has been mainly characterised by non-physical abuse (see Chapter 5). On the whole it might appear that the civil law copes better than the criminal law with a broad definition of 'violence'. The report that proceeded the Family Law Act 1996 (Law Commission, 2002) made clear that various forms of non-physical abuse were to be covered by the civil legislation and defined violence as: '. . . any form of physical, sexual or psychological molestation or harassment which has serious detrimental effect on the health and well being of the victim, albeit that there is no "violence" involved in the sense of physical force' (Law Commission, 2002, para 2.3). Although the Family Law Act 1996 does not include a definition of domestic violence, case law demonstrates that the concept of molestation fulfils the Law Commission's intention that it should be interpreted wider than violence to encompass any form of serious pestering or harassment (see Chapter 2).

Compared to a few decades ago the law now recognises a wider range of relationships, and abusive behaviour as 'domestic violence'. For government purposes the 'common definition' of domestic violence agreed by the inter-ministerial group for domestic violence is 'Any incident of threatening behaviour, violence or abuse (psychological, physical, sexual, financial or emotional) between adults who are or have been intimate partners or family members, regardless of gender or sexuality' (Home Office, 2005). Legal definitions of domestic violence may have shifted to the extent that victim's definitions of domestic violence may be more restrictive than those used by the legal system. These disparate definitions present a problem for those attempting to capture the extent of the problem that they are seeking to address. If those who fall within official and legal definitions of domestic violence do not identify with them they may not disclose themselves as experiencing abuse that the legal system could potentially tackle. This has traditionally proved a problem in the context of sexual assault where, for example, victims of marital rape have not recognised their experience of violent non-consensual intercourse with their husbands as 'rape' (Russell, 1990). This poses the question of how much we really know about the extent of domestic violence and how willing victims are to reveal abuse in all its various forms.

Extent and nature of the problem

Estimating the extent of domestic violence is not easy. Information can be gleaned from a variety of different sources and although none is entirely reliable some do appear to be more robust than others. Statistics from the legal system are unlikely to provide a reliable estimate of the extent of domestic violence. Judicial statistics on the number of non-molestation and occupation orders made under the Family Law Act 1996 are unlikely to be very illuminating since many victims of domestic violence will not, for a variety of reasons, seek a civil remedy for the abuse they are suffering. There is considerable cause for scepticism about whether the criminal statistics reveal more than a small proportion of domestic violence given reporting and recording practices to be discussed in more detail in Chapter 6. A snapshot of domestic violence in the UK revealed that one incident is reported to the police every minute (Stanko, 2001). For what the criminal statistics are worth (Maguire, 2002), they reveal that approximately 15 per cent of violent incidents are domestic violence, but that violent crime is declining (Walker, Kershaw, Nicholas, 2006) and there was a 64 per cent decrease in the number of incidents of domestic violence between 1995 and 2004/5. The homicide statistics show that on average two women a week are killed by a partner or former partner; in 2004/5 45 per cent of all female homicide victims were killed by their current or ex-partner compared with 6 per cent of male homicide victims (Coleman, Hird and Povey, 2006) A number of studies have examined the gendered nature of homicide and concluded that when men kill intimate women it is normally part of an escalating pattern of domestic violence, but when women kill intimate men it is typically in self-defence (Cavanagh et al, 2002; Brookman and Maguire, 2003; Dobash et al, 2004).

More accurate estimates of the extent of domestic violence can perhaps be established from victimisation surveys, although these raise their own methodological issues (Maguire, 2002). The 1996 British Crime Survey found that one in four women and one in seven men reported being subjected to domestic violence during their lifetime (Mirrlees Black, 1999). The British Crime Survey has attempted in recent years to adopt innovative research methods to try to capture the extent of domestic violence hidden in other official statistics (Walby and Myhill, 2001). The 2001 British Crime Survey contained a detailed self-completion questionnaire designed to ascertain the extent of interpersonal violence in England and Wales. A nationally representative sample of 22,463 men and women aged between 16 and 59 were asked whether they had been subject to domestic violence, sexual assault or stalking during their lifetime and during the preceding year (Walby and Allen, 2004). The self-completion questionnaire was administered via computer with every effort made to try to ensure that no one else was in the room when completion took place. These precautions were designed to overcome some of the obstacles to disclosing abuse, such as embarrassment or fear of retribution, however interviewers were not always able to ensure that no one else was present. Despite some of the methodological limitations of the self-completion module (discussed by Walby and Allen (2004) in Annex A of the report), it can be argued that it offered a more reliable means of estimating the extent of domestic violence in England and Wales than previous surveys.

The survey estimated that one in five women (21 per cent) and one in ten men had experienced at least one incident of non-sexual domestic threat or force since they were 16 years old. Four per cent of women and two per cent of men had been subject to domestic violence during the year preceding the interview. The survey examined the impact and meaning of domestic violence to the respondents. It found that 25 per cent of women and 59 per cent of men who had experienced abuse, that met a definition more restrictive than the Home Office definition of domestic violence, did not themselves call it 'domestic violence'. It also found that 64 per cent of women and 94 per cent of men subjected to domestic violence in the last year did not consider that what had happened to them was a crime. The above findings suggest that self-definition of domestic violence is more limited than official and legal definitions of domestic violence.

The findings from the latest BCS self-completion interpersonal violence module suggest that estimates of the prevalence of domestic violence are in the same order of magnitude for 2004/05 as they were for the 2001 survey (Finney, 2006). The latest survey suggests that approximately 1 in 4 women and 1 in 6 men had been a victim of violence by a partner or ex-partner since the age of 16 and 6 per cent of women and 4 per cent of men had experienced domestic violence during the preceding year. Like earlier surveys the latest one revealed that the experience of domestic violence is different for women than men.

It would be wrong to deny that there are incidents of female on male domestic violence which are non-defensive in nature (Grady, 2002). However, women are much more likely than men to sustain some physical or mental injury in incidents of domestic violence (Walby and Allen, 2004, pp 33–34). This undermines the argument advanced by some (Gelles and Loseke, 1993) that there is gender symmetry in domestic violence. Contradictory views about whether women are as likely as men to perpetrate violence against an intimate partner abound in the literature. The disagreement may be largely attributable to the different measures of domestic violence used by 'family violence' researchers who focus on discrete acts and do not look at the context in which they occur and the consequences (Dobash et al, 1992; Dobash and Dobash, 2004). Dobash and Dobash (2004) argue that serious intimate partner violence is asymmetrical; women's violence against men differs significantly in terms of the context and consequences. The context of women's violence is often self-defence and the consequences for men are less severe. Women's violence towards male intimate partners does not occur with the same frequency or ferocity as men's violence towards female intimate partners. This conclusion has significant implications for developing responses to domestic violence, including legal responses. Thus Dobash and Dobash (2004) argue that priority should be given to policies that aim to effectively tackle men's violence against women and to support female victims of domestic violence. Male and female violence to same sex partners has only recently been given significant research attention (Donovan, 2007). As the nature of abuse in same sex relationships becomes better understood the pressure for appropriate services and legal interventions increases. Same sex partners are, like ethnic minorities (Mama, 1989; Kewley, 2000), 'hard to reach' groups so far as accessing legal remedies are concerned. However, in terms of legal responses to domestic violence the fundamental question remains; how, if at all, can legal interventions help to address the significant problem of domestic violence?

The role of law

Recognising domestic violence as a significant social problem does not necessarily entail legal recognition of the problem. The process of feminist legal advocacy and scholarship has been a critical component in legal recognition of domestic violence (Schneider, 2000). The process of feminist law making gave visibility to violence against women in the United States and advocates and scholars in that jurisdiction continue to formulate new legal approaches to domestic violence. However, as Schneider (2000) notes, the process of change has been complex; one of partial inroads and sometimes deep resistance. Feminists in the US and UK have also been ambivalent about focusing on legal 'solutions' to the problem of domestic violence, some arguing the limited possibilities for social change through legal reform (Smart, 1989). One danger of focusing on legal interventions in domestic violence is that it may become decontextualised from the wider issue of gender subordination. Schneider for example has observed: 'Domestic violence is now treated as a problem in isolation, with neither history nor social context. It is viewed as though it can be "solved" or "treated" through legal remedies' (Schneider, 2000, p 27). It is, she argues, important that the role of law does not become divorced from the political context because winning legal rights for victims of domestic violence will not in itself be enough: 'The assertion of rights claims may assist in the growth of legal and political consciousness and simultaneously reveal the limitations of legal change ... Lawmaking in general and claims of rights in particular can be part of a larger process of political struggle' (Schneider, 2000, pp 34–35). Law is but one element in advancing a vision of ending violence against women.

Although the limitations of law making in the context of domestic violence must be acknowledged, it is also useful to identify what role the law may play. The role of law is arguably multifaceted: 'First there is its concrete and material impact – the actual effect it has on people's lives. Then there is its symbolic level – the role that law plays in expressing, embodying, and shaping social messages' (Schneider, 2002, p 37). Law has a role in shaping public consciousness, giving a 'voice' to individual experiences and allowing individuals and groups to see themselves in new ways. 'Rights claims not only define women's individual and collective experience, they also actively shape public discourse . . . The public nature of women's rights assertion is especially significant because of the private nature of discrimination against women' (Schneider, 2002, pp 39–40).

In the classic public/private dichotomy intimate relationships are seen as part of the 'private' sphere not suitable for public regulation (Lacey, 1998, Ch 3). It can be argued that one of the roles of law in responding to domestic violence is to open up private relationships to public scrutiny and state intervention; to make private violence a public matter (Fineman and Myktiuk, 1994). Legal intervention implies that aspects of life that are removed from public view should be regulated. The public/private dichotomy is however a contentious concept (Thornton, 1995). Some have argued that the search for a division between the two spheres, in terms of the presence or absence of state regulation or legal intervention, is flawed (Olsen, 1983). Although there may be a great deal of rhetoric about intimate relationships being private, many aspects of those relationships are subject to legal and state regulation. It may be a mistake to see failure to regulate as non-intervention. Lacey (1998) also makes the important point that the state is not monolithic but made up of diverse institutions which give rise to complexities in identifying regulation and non-regulation. Thus she asks: 'What are we to say of issues such as wife-battering – always "regulated" in the sense of being within the purview of the criminal law, but frequently "unregulated" because of the decisions of law enforcement agencies' (Lacey, 1998, p 76). At a descriptive level the public/private dichotomy as applied to family relationships is unsustainable when subjected to scrutiny. When analysing legal responses to domestic violence it is therefore crucial to give weight to the concrete practices of law at the same time as considering the ideological role of the public/private dichotomy. The public/private dichotomy has sometimes failed to provide useful insights into the role of law in relation to domestic violence when considered empirically. There are occasions when the dichotomy does provide a useful analytical tool, but it is useful to remember that domestic violence is always a public problem whether it occurs on the street or in the home (Burton, forthcoming). The cost of domestic violence to society (Walby, 2004) highlights one of the public dimensions of the problem (Mackinnon, 2005).

An alternative, or perhaps supplementary, theoretical approach is to see the law as gendered. Smart has argued that the law works to produce gendered identities (Smart, 1989). The construction of 'woman'/'victim'/ 'mother' in the law relating to domestic violence shows how some women are denied protection whilst, at the same time, others are granted it, and this continues to define and reinforce gender roles. This can be seen for example in the law of homicide and the defence of provocation in particular (discussed fully in Chapter 5). Some women who experience domestic violence are treated as more problematic than others and not all women's experiences are incorporated into the legal constructions of the 'battered woman'. The argument that law is gendered shows how the process of constitution of women as legal subjects and the legal construction of a problem of domestic violence faces hurdles of containment and subversion in legal discourse (Schneider, 2002). The role of law in relation to domestic violence is partly to reinforce cultural values about abused women. Whilst law may struggle to take into account the range of experiences in this area, it can be argued that law has the potential to undermine established understandings if judges can be persuaded to modify it.

Domestic violence is a legal problem as well as a social problem because the legal system plays a part in constituting the problem (Freeman, 1984). Within the English legal 'system' there are a variety of different courts that can hear disputes involving domestic violence matters according to their restricted jurisdiction in different areas of substantive law and their position in the court hierarchy. Although the courts are traditionally seen as the most important part of the legal system, the reality is that they are not central to most legal interventions and focusing on the courts would overestimate their importance in terms of evaluating the legal response to domestic violence. Courts can make a significant contribution to law making. In interpreting statutes and developing the common law the courts have the power to set a precedent that may influence outcomes in future domestic violence cases. Thus at one level it is valuable to analyse the decisions of appellate courts in domestic violence cases. A ruling of the House of Lords on the meaning of rape for example may indicate how far judges are prepared to go (or not) in modifying the law to take into account women's experiences of domestic violence. However the work of legal actors outside the courts is just as important for evaluating the legal response to domestic violence, although it may be less visible. Empirical studies of street-level actors, such as the police, have sought to make the practices of law more visible, showing the successes and failures of the legal system in protecting victims of domestic violence.

A holistic approach to understanding legal responses to domestic violence needs to be able to move between different parts of the legal system, whilst recognising that they are still part of the same phenomenon. The aim of this book is to examine how the English legal system responds to domestic violence by examining different levels of decision making and different areas of law. The first half of this book will concentrate on the civil law and responses of actors in the civil justice system. The second part will focus upon the criminal law and criminal justice actors. The book will conclude by examining victims' and perpetrators' perspectives on legal interventions and asking the crucial question: are legal interventions in domestic violence really effective?

2 The civil law

Social change and legal change

The changing political and social environment of the 1970s resulted in new laws to respond to domestic violence (Dobash and Dobash, 1992, p 174). In this chapter the development of the civil law remedies for domestic violence will be examined. The purpose of the new laws was to provide speedy and effective relief to victims of domestic violence, if necessary by excluding the perpetrator of the abuse from the family home. However the scope of the legislation fell to be determined by judiciary, which was conservative in relation to preserving male property rights. Judicial interpretation of the civil laws thus considerably undermined the effectiveness of the civil law remedies in the 1970s and 1980s. However, further legislative reforms took place in the 1990s, the most significant of these being Part IV of the Family Law Act 1996, which completely overhauled the protective orders available to victims of domestic violence under the civil law. Of course the provisions of the Family Law Act 1996 also fell to be interpreted by the judiciary and it may be questioned whether the purposes of the legislation have been fully achieved given the case law developments. This chapter will consider the extent to which the civil laws, old and new, provided a legislative framework for effective protection of victims of domestic violence, and the extent to which judicial interpretation of the legislation at appellate level has supported or undermined the protection available. It will also examine the issue of child contact under the Children Act 1989 and the extent to which judicial interpretation of that legislation has provided effective protection for women and children experiencing domestic violence post-separation.

The civil remedies in the 1970s and 1980s

In the 1970s, when domestic violence was first being recognised as a significant social problem in Britain, a number of legislative measures were introduced to respond to domestic violence under the civil law. The High Court had always had jurisdiction to grant injunctions where just and expedient to do so, and this power was put on a statutory footing by the Supreme Court Act 1981, s 37(1). The County Court Act 1984, s 38(1) gave the County Courts the same powers, but these remedies were not tailored specifically to victims of domestic violence. The first legislation designed with domestic violence specifically in mind was the Domestic Violence and Matrimonial Proceedings Act 1976 (DVMPA) which gave the County Courts powers to grant injunctions to spouses and heterosexual cohabitants. The injunctions could prohibit molestation of the applicant or any child living with the applicant, and orders were also potentially available to exclude the respondent from the matrimonial home or the area surrounding it. If the courts were satisfied that the respondent had used actual bodily harm, and was likely to do so again, they could attach a power of arrest to injunctions or exclusion orders.

Shortly after the introduction of the DVMPA another piece of domestic violence specific legislation was enacted, the Domestic Violence and Magistrates' Courts Act 1978 (DVMCA), but this only applied to spouses. The DVMCA gave magistrates' courts powers to grant orders of protection where satisfied that the respondent had used, or threatened to use, violence against the person of the applicant or a child of the family and the court was satisfied that it was necessary for the protection of the applicant or child of the family that an order be made. The court was empowered to make orders that the respondent should not use, or threaten to use, violence against the applicant or a child of the family. If the court was satisfied that the applicant or a child was in danger of physical violence by the respondent it could make an order requiring him to leave the matrimonial home or prohibiting him from entering it, but the grounds for making such orders were limited. Exclusion orders could only be made if the respondent had used violence towards the applicant or a child of the family, or he had threatened such violence and already used violence against a third party, or he was in breach of an order made under the DVMCA not to use or threaten violence. Powers of arrest could only be attached to orders once the court was satisfied that the respondent had physically injured the applicant or a child of the family and was likely to do so again.

Even by examining these two pieces of legislation it can be seen that the civil remedies for domestic violence varied according to the status of the parties and the court in which the remedy was being sought. The civil protection available to victims of domestic violence was significantly defined by another piece of legislation; the Matrimonial Homes Act 1983 (MHA). Although not specifically a piece of domestic violence legislation, the MHA became the principle legislation governing ouster orders. The MHA, which incorporated and amended the 1967 legislation of the same title, gave wives rights of occupation which could be registered and enforced against third parties. It also gave the courts powers to regulate occupation of the family home. When considering whether to exercise any of its powers to regulate occupation of the matrimonial home under the MHA the court could make such order as it thought just and reasonable having regard to a list of factors in s 1(3) of the legislation. The specified factors were the conduct of the parties in relation to each other and otherwise, the respective needs and financial resources of the parties, the needs of any children and all the circumstances of the case. The judicial interpretation of these criteria became highly problematic for women seeking protection from domestic violence.

In *Richards v Richards* [1984] AC 174 a wife applied for a divorce on the basis that her husband's behaviour was such that it was not reasonable to expect her to live with him. The allegations of behaviour centred upon him showing little regard for her feelings and not taking an interest in her pregnancies. During one of the pregnancies it was alleged that he had thrown a book at her stomach when she had asked him to feel the baby kicking. She said that he had not shown any affection or regard for her after the birth and complained that he did not take her out socially. The husband did not want a divorce and denied the allegations. The wife left the marital home, taking with her the couple's two children (both under 5). Eventually she exhausted the hospitality of her friends and obtained an injunction to exclude the husband from the matrimonial home so that she could return there with the children. Although the Court of Appeal felt that the wife did not have reasonable grounds for refusing to return to the marital home whilst her husband was there, and regarded her allegations against him as 'flimsy and rubbishy', they concluded that the needs of the children (who would otherwise be accommodated in a caravan over the winter) were determinative. The husband's appeal was allowed by the House of Lords who decided that whenever an application was made to exclude a spouse from the matrimonial home, be it under the MHA or some other jurisdiction, the criteria in MHA, s 1(3) applied. The House of Lords stated that no priority was given to the needs of the children under the MHA criteria. The conduct of the parties was specifically enacted as one of the matters to be taken into consideration and thus the wife's conduct in *Richards* ought to be taken into account. Lord Hailsham asserted: 'on any view she has had a number of affairs in the course of the marriage, whereas nothing adverse to the husband has been found . . . It has never been found or suggested that [the wife] needed protection.' He concluded that a wife should not be able to get an injunction simply because she was bored with her husband and she had care of children. Lord Brandon agreed that conduct was an important factor to be weighed in with the other criteria, and that in a substantial number of cases would be a factor of such weight it would lead the court to think that it would not be just and reasonable to allow an application for exclusion.

This emphasis on the conduct of the parties, rather than their needs and the interests of the children and applicant, came to be particularly problematic in the interpretation of the legislation specifically enacted to provide protection for victims of domestic violence. In *Lee v Lee* [1984] FLR 243 it was confirmed the criteria in MHA, s 1(3) applied to applications made by cohabitants for exclusion orders. Thus it was not only the conduct of spouses that was scrutinised but also the conduct of cohabitants who were seeking protection from domestic violence.

The operation of the civil remedies for domestic violence was reviewed by the Law Commission in 1992 (Law Commission Report No. 207, 1992). The

Commission concluded that: 'The fact that different remedies are available to different applicants on different criteria in different courts with different enforcement procedures has resulted in a vastly complicated system, made even more confusing by the complex interrelationship between the statutory remedies and the general principles of property and tort law' (Law Commission, 1992, para 2.24). The Commission identified a number of problems with the regime: significantly it concluded that too much weight was being given to the conduct of the parties. It also noted that the law provided no protection for a range of people who might need it, for example former spouses and former cohabitants. Thus the Commission proposed removing the 'gaps, anomalies and inconsistencies' in the existing law by providing for two kinds of order, a non-molestation order and an occupation order, available in all courts. A first attempt was made to implement these proposals in the Family Homes and Domestic Violence Bill, introduced into Parliament in 1995 but withdrawn at a late stage because of a media led campaign by a minority of Conservative MPs who said it threatened 'traditional family values'. The Commission's recommendations, with some modifications, were finally enacted as Part IV of the Family Law Act 1996 (Murphy, 1996).

The Family Law Act 1996

Part IV of the Family Law Act 1996 (FLA) came into force October 1997 and is now the key piece of legislation providing remedies under the civil law for victims of domestic violence (Bird, 2006; Ministry of Justice, 2007). The two orders available under the legislation, occupation and non-molestation orders, may be granted in the high court, county courts and magistrates' courts; all the courts have jurisdiction to grant the orders although the magistrates' courts have no power to determine disputes as to a party's entitlement to occupy any property (FLA, ss 57 and 59). A non-molestation order is an order prohibiting the respondent from molesting an associated person and/or a relevant child (FLA, s 41(1)). A 'relevant child' is a child who is living with or might reasonably be expected to live with either party to the proceedings, a child to whom an order under the Adoption Act 1976 or Children Act 1989 is in question, or any other child whose interests the court considers relevant (FLA, s 62(2)). The last 'catch all' provision makes clear that the legislation was intended to have wide scope insofar as protecting children by non-molestation orders is concerned. Typically the children to be protected will be living with their mother, the respondent's partner or former partner, who will be seeking protection for both herself and them. A non-molestation order can be made in free-standing proceedings, or any family proceedings either on application, or of the court's own motion if it considers the order should be made for the benefit of any party to the proceedings or any relevant child (FLA, s 42(2)). The Law Commission (1992) was of the view that it would be useful for the court to have a power to make orders of its own motion, for example in divorce proceedings, where the victim was being subjected to threats or intimidation or for some other reasons reluctant to make an application herself. There is no statutory definition of molestation, but the Law Commission envisaged that the term would be interpreted broadly, observing:

> Molestation is an umbrella term which covers a wide range of behaviour
> . . . the concept is well established and recognised by the courts. Molestation includes, but is wider than violence. It encompasses any form of serious pestering or harassment and applies to any conduct which could properly be regarded as such a degree of harassment as to call for the intervention of the court.
>
> (Law Commission, 1992)

The Commission referred to examples of 'molestation' under the pre-FLA law to illustrate the range of behaviours that might be encompassed by the term. In *Vaughan v Vaughan* [1973] 3 All ER 449 the respondent followed his estranged wife to and from work in the mornings and evenings, constantly asking her out, even though she repeatedly refused and he knew that she was frightened of him. Davis LJ concluded that the respondent knew that he was making a 'perfect nuisance of himself the whole time', and the effect of being constantly pestered by a man who had been previously violent to her and of whom she was frightened must have been damaging to the victim's health. Taking into account the effect on the victim's health, of which the husband was to a degree at least aware, he found molestation was plainly made out. Stephenson LJ agreed, adding ' "Molest" is a wide, plain word which . . . If I had to find one synonym for it, I should select "pester" '. He noted that whether communication amounted to molestation would be a question of fact and degree but, given the parties' respective knowledge of past conduct, was clearly made out on the facts of the case. In *Horner v Horner* [1982] 2 All ER 495 it was held that handing the plaintiff menacing letters and intercepting her on the way to work amounted to molestation. Ormrod LJ observed that molestation did 'not imply necessarily either violence of threats of violence. It applies to any conduct which can properly be regarded as such a degree of harassment as to call for the intervention of the court.' The circulatory nature of this definition is unhelpful but illustrates the ultimate flexibility of the concept. In *Johnson v Walton* [1990] 1 FLR 350 the respondent sent partially nude photographs of the plaintiff to a national newspaper for publication. Lord Donaldson referred to the *Horner v Horner* definition of molestation but went on to say molestation includes within it an element of intent to cause distress or harm. He concluded that by sending the photos to the paper with the intent to cause distress to the plaintiff the defendant came within the prohibition against molesting.

There has been some case law on the meaning of molestation since the FLA came into force. It is clear that the concept of molestation continues to be flexible, as the Law Commission desired, but it is not limitless. In *C v C (Non-Molestation Order: Jurisdiction)* [1988] 2 WLR 599 a husband sought a non-molestation order against his wife under the Family Law Act 1996, s 42. The wife had divorced him on grounds of his adultery and had given details to national newspapers about her complaints regarding her husband's behaviour during their marriage. At first instance a non-molestation order was granted but the wife appealed on the basis that there was no molestation. Sir Stephen Brown stated molestation 'is a matter which has to be considered in relation to the particular facts of particular cases. It implies some quite deliberate conduct which is aimed at a high degree of harassment of the other party, so as to justify the intervention of the court'. He concluded that the conduct complained of in this case came nowhere near the molestation envisaged by the FLA, s 42. The husband was concerned about damage to his reputation and was seeking to protect that. The meaning of molestation under the Family Law Act 1996 does not include the protection of privacy.

The Family Law Act enables 'associated persons' to apply for non-molestation orders. The categories of persons who are 'associated' was controversial during the passage of the legislation and has continued to be so post-implementation (Reece, 2006). The Act greatly enlarged the categories of people entitled to apply for domestic violence remedies under the civil law which, as noted above, was previously confined to spouses and heterosexual cohabitees. Under the Family Law Act 1996, s 62(3) a person is associated with another person if they are spouses or former spouses, cohabitants or former cohabitants, live or have lived in the same household, are relatives, have agreed to marry, are parents or have parental responsibility for a relevant child or are parties to the same family proceedings. The original definition of cohabitants in s 62(1) was 'a man and a woman living together as husband and wife'. This gender specific definition excluded same sex couples but for the purposes of obtaining non-molestation orders same sex cohabitants were covered by the category of persons living together in the same household otherwise than merely by reason of one of them being the other's employee, tenant, lodger, or boarder. However the gender-specific definition of cohabitation remained problematic, mainly because it reduced the eligibility of same sex couples for occupation orders, and the definition was subsequently amended by the Domestic Violence, Crime and Victims Act 2004 which will be considered further below. The term 'relative' was very widely defined under the FLA, s 63(1) to include parents, step-parents, children, step-children, grandparents and grandchildren of a spouse or former spouse. It also includes siblings, aunts and uncles, nieces and nephews of a spouse or former spouse whether of full blood, half blood or by affinity. The Civil Partnership Act 2004 amends the FLA so that wherever reference is made to spouses (existing or former), or affinity by marriage, civil partners (existing or former) are included. If the application is being made by a child whilst under the age of 16 then leave of the court is required and may only be granted if the court is satisfied that the child has sufficient understanding to make the proposed application.

In respect of persons who are 'associated' by virtue of having agreed to marry one another the FLA provides that applications can only be brought within three years of the termination of the engagement and the applicant must adduce evidence of the agreement to marry. FLA, s 44 requires written evidence of agreement to marry although it also states that the gift of an engagement ring or a ceremony in the presence of one or more witnesses may suffice as evidence. Murphy (1996) has noted that an engagement ring is likely to be the most common way in which an engagement is evidenced but commented that this might militate against certain applicants; men who rarely receive rings, the less affluent who may not be able to afford them, and non-traditionalists who might deliberately eschew them. Unless the engagement is kept secret then it is likely to be marked by some public acknowledgement by friends and family which, depending on the interpretation of the word 'ceremony', would suffice for those who do not have rings. The provision for engaged couples now also extends to those who have agreed to enter into a civil partnership. The time limit of three years is probably of more consequence for victims than the requirement of proof of engagement. If the end of a relationship marks the beginning of abuse it may continue for longer than three years. In this type of situation the only remedy that the victim may have is under the Protection from Harassment Act 1997 (PHA), which does provide a civil remedy under s 3, but is mainly used for the criminal offences discussed in Chapter 5.

During the passage of the FLA there was a lively debate about whether people who had had a romantic relationship including some sexual involvement, but who had never cohabited or promised to marry, should be included in the definition of 'associated' persons. The Law Commission (1992) supported including boyfriend/girlfriend relationships where there was a degree of mutuality and participation in consensual activity, although not necessarily amounting to sexual intercourse. This, however, was resisted by the Government so the original definition of associated persons did not cover non-cohabiting girlfriends or boyfriends. However the courts showed that they were willing to take a purposive approach to interpreting cohabitation to maximise the number of relationships under which remedies for domestic violence were provided by the Family Law Act. In *G v F (Non-Molestation Order: Jurisdiction)* (2000) 2 FCR 638 a generous interpretation of 'cohabitation' provided remedies for a victim of violence under the FLA. In this case the parties had a sexual relationship but did not live together full-time; each initially retained their own home and they stayed at each others home two or three nights a week. The applicant said that early in their relationship the respondent had asked to marry her and said that he wanted to adopt her daughter from a previous relationship. The respondent said that in the later stages of their relationship they had talked about getting married and that he had sold his house with a view to setting up home with the applicant after they were married. The proceeds from the sale of the respondent's house were put into a joint bank account, the respondent moved into a rented flat and the money was spent on doing up the applicant's home. When their three-year relationship ended the applicant sought a non-molestation order alleging incidents of violence over more than two years. The justices refused to hear the application because they found that the parties were not 'associated' persons because, in their opinion, they were not cohabitants, they did not live together in the same household, nor was there was evidence of agreement to marry in the form required by the Family Law Act 1996. On appeal Wall J referred to six signposts of cohabitation identified in a social security case: membership of the same household, a stable relationship, financial support, a sexual relationship, children and public acknowledgement of the relationship. Whilst the parties in *G v F* had no children together Wall J concluded that there were plainly other indicators of cohabitation; evidence that they lived together in the same household, had a sexual relationship, provided financial support for each other (evidenced by the joint account) and received some public acknowledgement of their relationship. Although the relationship was not 'stable' it had lasted three years and so, viewed as a whole, Wall J concluded that the parties were 'cohabitants'. More importantly he was keen to send a message to justices that they should give a 'purposive construction' of the Family Law Act 1996 to ensure protective remedies were not denied to those in need of them. He stated that it would be most unfortunate if the legislation were 'narrowly construed so as to exclude borderline cases where shift and effective protection for victims of domestic violence is required'. He stated that it was arguable that the respondent's statements to the court about the agreement to marry constituted evidence in writing sufficient to satisfy the requirements of the Act, although technically these comments are obiter because the case was decided on the basis that the parties were cohabitants rather than an engaged couple.

G v F was an important case because it showed the willingness of the courts to stretch the definition of 'associated' persons as far as possible to accommodate people in a sexual relationship. However there was still concern that it left some people bereft of protection; those in a stable sexual relationship with no overnight staying and no other 'signposts' of cohabitation. Although such people would have protection under the PHA it was felt by many that they should have the domestic violence remedies available to them as well. The situation of 'dating' couples was considered again during the passage of the Domestic Violence, Crime and Victims Act 2004 (DVCVA). The DVCVA amended the definition of associated persons to include people who have or have had 'an intimate personal relationship with each other which is or was of significant duration'. The precise wording of this amendment was subject to considerable debate during the passage of the legislation, for example concerns were raised that it might by unduly restrictive if emphasis was given to how long the relationship lasted rather than its intensity. There was some support for a definition which would be wide enough to include even very short-lived relationships if they were very intense. However the government resisted this suggestion stating that the courts had a variety of other options for dealing with 'transient relationships' (Baroness Scotland, Hansard (HL)

19 January 2004). The expanded definition arguably gives the judiciary considerable discretion to provide protection to victims of violence in non-cohabiting boyfriend/girlfriend relationships. The limits of the definition remain to be defined by case law but the government at least was confident that with appropriate training in domestic violence the judiciary will be well placed to recognise those relationships which provide opportunities for abuse and control and ought to have a remedy under the FLA. The definition has been criticised by Reece (2006) who argues that the expansion of the definition of associated persons is misguided because it endangers the special category of domestic violence which turns on the isolation and inequality which are features of the spousal and quasi-spousal relationships which provided the impetus for the original protective legislation in the 1970s. However structural inequality is not just a feature of quasi-spousal relationships, and the expanded definition can therefore arguably overlap with Madden Dempsey's (2006) conceptualisation of domestic violence in its 'strong sense'; three intersecting spheres of illegitimate violence, domesticity and structural inequality.

Once applicants have cleared the hurdle of establishing that they are an associated person the court has a fairly wide discretion to grant non-molestation orders. In deciding whether to make the order the FLA provides that the court shall have regard to all the circumstances, including the need to secure the health safety and well-being of the applicant and any relevant child (FLA, s 42(5)). The rationale behind this provision is victim focused; the emphasis is on the victim's need for protection and the needs of the children, rather than the nature of the respondent's conduct. If it is emotional abuse that is presenting a threat to the mental health of the applicant or a child then the court can make an order because 'health' includes both physical and mental health. The terms of the non-molestation order can be general or specific. As molestation is not statutorily defined, a general prohibition against 'molestation' can cover a wide variety of behaviours. If the applicant is concerned about specific conduct, for example following to and from work, the non-molestation order can prohibit this. Non-molestation orders can be made for a specified or indefinite period, but to obtain non-molestation orders of unlimited duration it usually has to be shown that some special circumstances require an indefinite period of protection. However in *Re BJ (A Child) (Non-Molestation Order: Power of Arrest)* [2000] 2 FLR 443 the court seemed to suggest a more generous approach to granting orders for an indefinite period. The parties had been separated for sometime but had ongoing disputes about the father's contact with the child. The court of first instance granted an order of indefinite duration which the father challenged. It was held on appeal that in some cases orders of only limited and short duration would be needed because the purpose would be just to provide a bit of breathing space. However in cases like this, where there are continuing feelings, a long or indefinite order might be justified. The court concluded that it was wrong to say that long-term orders should be limited to unusual and exceptional cases. On the basis of this case the applicant should not have to show that her case is *exceptional* in order to obtain a long-term order, but empirical evidence, discussed in the next chapter, shows that in practice most orders are of limited duration.

The criteria for obtaining a non-molestation order under the FLA seem generous and certainly opened up this form of injunctive relief to a far wider range of persons than could have obtained a domestic violence remedy under the previous law; the same is not necessarily true of the other type of order available under the FLA, the occupation order. Whilst some of the case law relating to non-molestation orders suggests that the judiciary are willing to take a 'purposive' approach to the legislation in order to maximise protection the protection available, a much narrower approach has been taken to interpreting the requirements for occupation orders. The discussion will turn now to the criteria for occupation orders before returning to the issue of enforcement which is crucial to the effectiveness of both non-molestation and occupation orders.

There are two types of occupation orders, declaratory and regulatory. Most victims of domestic violence will be seeking both since an order which merely declares their interest in the family home is unlikely to be much use without an order which excludes the perpetrator of abuse from the home and the area surrounding it. The categories of persons eligible to apply for occupation orders are much more limited than the associated persons who can apply for non-molestation orders. When deciding who should be eligible to apply for occupation orders, the Law Commission (1992) was concerned about interference with the respondent's property rights, especially where the applicant for order had no property rights. The commission proposed a distinction between applicants with and without property rights and this distinction was incorporated in the FLA. An associated person who is an *entitled applicant* can apply for a more extensive remedy than a *non-entitled applicant* who can only seek a short-term order against a former spouse, a cohabitant or former cohabitant. It will be recalled that the definition of cohabitants was originally limited to heterosexual couples. This meant that the law discriminated against same sex couples in relation to occupation orders; they could only apply as entitled applicants. The extension of the definition of cohabitation under the Domestic Violence Act 2004 places same sex couples in the same position as heterosexual cohabitants insofar as occupation orders are concerned. If they are civil partners then the Civil Partnership Act 2004 places them in a similar position to spouses.

The basic distinction for the purposes of establishing eligibility for occupation orders is between entitled and non-entitled applicants. An entitled applicant, according to the Family Law Act 1996, s 33 is a person who has a right to occupy the home by virtue of the general law or matrimonial home rights. Section 30 provides where one spouse is entitled by virtue of the general law to occupy a dwelling house which is or has been intended to be the matrimonial home, and the other is not, that the other has matrimonial home rights. The matrimonial home rights are almost the same as the former rights of occupation under the Matrimonial Homes Act 1983, the key difference being that the rights exist in relation to property the parties merely intended to occupy. Under the Civil Partnership Act 2004 'matrimonial home rights' become 'home rights' and all references to spouses must be read to include civil partners.

An entitled applicant can seek an occupation order against anyone with whom she is associated provided the home has been or was intended to be their common home. The courts can make a declaratory or regulatory order. A declaratory order simply declares the nature of the interest from which the right to occupy flows. In order to enforce the right to occupy the applicant must seek a regulatory order. The criteria for regulatory orders for entitled applicants are contained in the Family Law Act 1996, s 33(6) which provides that the courts have discretion to grant an order taking into account all the circumstances—including four basic criteria. The four 'basic criteria', as they will be referred to hereafter, are; the housing needs and housing resources of each of the parties and any relevant child, the financial resources of each of the parties, the likely effect of any order, or any decision not to make an order on the health, safety or well-being of the parties or any relevant child and the conduct of the parties in relation to each other and otherwise.

This discretionary test with its list of four basic criteria was based on the Law Commission's (1992) recommendations for a test which is based more on the need for protection and less on the conduct of the parties. The Law Commission was keen to replace the test for ouster orders under the Matrimonial Homes Act 1983 which, as noted above, since the decision in *Richards v Richards* [1984] AC 174 had been interpreted in a way that focused too much on the conduct of the parties. Nevertheless, whether the FLA criteria do in fact tip the balance away from conduct and towards the welfare of applicant and child is debatable. In order to try and ensure more weight is given to the interests of victims and children there are mandatory provisions for making occupation orders in the FLA. In relation to entitled applicants, the FLA, s 33(7) provides that the court shall make an order if it appears that the applicant or any child is likely to suffer significant harm if an order is not made, unless it appears that the respondent or any child is likely to suffer as great or greater harm as a consequence of the order being made. This test is known as 'the balance of harm test'. Harm is defined in s 63(1) to mean ill-treatment or the impairment of health (and in relation to a child impair-ment of development). 'Significant harm' is not defined but, in the context of the Children Act 1989 the term, has been interpreted to mean 'consider-able, noteworthy or important'. The harm must be attributable to the conduct of the respondent. In the early days if the legislation it was suggested that the requirement of attribution of responsibility might cause problems (Douglas and Lowe, 1998). Douglas and Lowe (1998) posed the question: if a woman goes to a refuge to escape violence and is therefore living in cramped and unsuitable accommodation, is she suffering harm because of her violent partner's conduct or inadequate refuge facilities? They suggested that the best interpretation is that the harm is attributable to her partner's conduct because but for his conduct she would have no need for refuge facilities. Although subsequent case law suggests that some of the judiciary are aware of the inadequate alternative accommodation available to women and children escaping domestic violence it has not prevented them from refusing occupation orders that would allow them to return home.

The balance of harm test has been considered in a number of appellate cases which give some indication of the approach that the courts take to this provision. One of the earliest decided cases was *B v B (Occupation Order)* [1999] 1 FLR 715 which involved a married couple who had two children living with them; a boy, aged 6, from the husband's previous relationship and their own baby daughter. Before the girl's first birthday the wife left the marital home due to her husband's violence. She took her daughter with her but found that she was housed by the council in unsatisfactory bed and breakfast accommodation and so applied for an occupation order. The judge at first instance granted the order rejecting the husband's arguments that the occupation order was likely to cause significant harm to his son. The husband's appeal was allowed. The Court of Appeal acknowledged that the wife had suffered serious violence at the hands of the husband and that the judge was plainly entitled to find that she and her daughter were likely to suffer significant harm if the order were not made. Consequently, applying the balance of harm test, the court was obliged to make an order unless the husband and his son were likely to suffer as great or greater harm if an order were made. Turning to examine the harm likely to be suffered by the son the court noted that he would not only have to leave his home but also his school if the order were made. The Court of Appeal concluded that the harm that would be suffered by the son if an order were made outweighed the harm the applicant and her daughter were likely to suffer if an order were not made. Butler Sloss LJ said that she did not underestimate the difficulties of looking after a child in bed and breakfast accommodation but in her opinion the wife was unlikely to be there for long because she was not intentionally homeless and therefore the council had a duty to rehouse her under the Housing Act 1996. Victims of domestic violence may be treated as priority need because they have dependent children or are classified as vulnerable, but the practice of local authorities is variable (Levison and Harwin, 2001). The court in *B v B* however felt the husband's position was weaker because he would be treated as intentionally homeless (due to the domestic violence) and the council would only have limited duties to temporarily rehouse him.

It has been commented that the housing needs and resources of the parties seemed to play a significant, if not determinative, part in the decision in *B v B* (Kaganas, 1999). Furthermore the court seemed to apply the basic criteria in s 33(6) in assessing the balance of harm test in s 33(7). Should the two sets of criteria, one discretionary the other creating a duty to make an order, have been blurred in this way? In *Chalmers v Johns* [1999] 1 FLR 392 the Court of

Appeal clearly distinguished between s 33(6) and 33(7). Thorpe LJ suggested that the court should first consider whether it had a duty to make an order under s 33(7) and only if the balance of harm test did not apply should the court consider whether it should exercise its discretion to make an order under the criteria in s 33(6). Kaganas (1999), commenting on the two cases, suggests that the interpretation in *Chalmers* and *Johns* is correct: the checklist in s 33(6) is not intended to be invoked in applying the balance of harm test, although the lack of suitable alternative accommodation is something which can be taken into account in assessing significant harm in s 33(7).

The case of *Chalmers v Johns* [1999] involved cohabitants of 25 years who had two children, only one of whom was under 16 at the time of the application. The cohabitants' relationship had been marred by incidents of 'minor' violence towards each other. In the year before the couple separated the police were called to the home four times, on the last occasion following a complaint by the applicant who then left home taking her daughter with her. The respondent successfully appealed against the original decision to grant an occupation order. The Court of Appeal referred to a string of authorities under the previous domestic violence legislation which emphasised the draconian nature of ouster orders and noted that the FLA did not obliterate that authority. Thorpe LJ remarked that occupation orders remained 'draconian' and were only justified in exceptional circumstances. He noted that there would be cases where the character of the violence or the risk of violence was such that a draconian order must be made, but in his opinion this particular case was not 'in any ordinary forensic language a domestic violence case'. He concluded that the facts were nowhere near the level where the courts would have a duty to make an order on the balance of harm test. Furthermore the courts should be cautious of exercising their discretion under s 33(6) where it was yet to be decided who was going to get residence of a relevant child, in this case the parties' seven-year-old daughter. The parties were urged to attend mediation to settle their differences and one judge even suggested that attending mediation might be helpful with a view to resuming their relationship.

The combined effect of *B v B* and *Chalmers v Johns* does not suggest that under the FLA much more weight will be given to the applicant's need for the protection afforded by excluding the perpetrator from their shared home than was the case under the old law. *Chalmers v Johns* in particular suggests that the courts will take a restrictive approach and be reluctant to interfere with men's property rights. The needs and interests of the children were influential in *B v B* and the harm to applicant, attributable to the respondent's serious violence, did not weigh heavily in the balance. Kaganas (1999) speculated that it might have been different if the applicant had not left home because the harm to her and her daughter seemed to be assessed in the light of changed circumstances; because they had left the court felt that they are no longer at risk of significant harm. She argues that this is an incorrect application of the balance of harm test; significant harm should be judged at the time immediately before the applicant leaves home or on the basis of the risk if she returned home. Also by emphasising the draconian nature of occupation orders the Court of Appeal has set the tone that they should be used as a 'last resort' in 'exceptional cases'.

The opinion that occupation orders should be used as a 'last resort' was reaffirmed in *Re Y (Children) (Occupation Order)* (2000) 2 FCR 470. In this case the parties had been married for 20 years and had four children, including a boy aged 13 and a girl aged 16. During protracted divorce proceedings the husband applied for a residence order for the boy and an occupation order against his wife. At first instance the judge granted the occupation order because he felt that applying the balance of harm test the husband and boy would suffer greater harm than the wife and girl. The husband was diabetic and blind in one eye and had an appalling relationship with his 16-year-old pregnant daughter. The judge concluded that the council would have difficulty accommodating a partially blind man but no problem accommodating a pregnant 16-year-old. The Court of Appeal decided that the balance of harm test was not satisfied in this case. They were not sure that husband was in fact suffering significant harm because they felt that he may have overplayed his disabilities, but even if he was, it was not attributable to the wife's conduct. The husband had struck his wife some years previously but there was no evidence that she had been violent towards him except in a defensive way when she had intervened to protect her daughter. The Court of Appeal also commented that the judge had given insufficient weight to the harm likely to be suffered by the 16-year-old girl as a result of being rehoused. If anything they thought that the husband was more likely to be rehoused because of disability, leaving aside the question of whether he had made himself intentionally homeless. Ultimately however the court concluded that it was wrong to let housing matters to intrude so far into the balance of harm test. Having decided that the balance of harm test was not satisfied on the facts of the case the Court of Appeal went on to consider the discretion under s 33(6). In terms of financial resources; the wife was working but not earning enough to find other accommodation for herself and her daughter. The husband's well-being might have tipped the decision in his favour but for the fact he was not suffering as a result of his wife's conduct but because of his poor relationship with his daughter. In terms of conduct; the husband and wife were both as bad as each other. Taking into account the housing needs and resources of the parties it was concluded that these were adequately served by the existing arrangements. They were living in a four-bed house, having established separate camps within it, and the court concluded that there was nothing wrong with letting that continue until finances and property resolved on divorce.

A similar approach of refusing an occupation order, when divorce and ancillary proceedings were pending, was seen in *G v G (Occupation Order: Conduct)* (2000) 2 FLR 36. In this case the parties had two children and the wife applied for residence orders for them and for an occupation order against her husband. The occupation order was refused at first instance because the husband's conduct was not intentional. The Court of Appeal concluded that the judge had taken the wrong approach in looking at the intention of the husband; the court should not look at intentionality but well-being. However the judge was right to refuse the order because the wife had not suffered any violence at the hands of her husband; occupation orders are 'draconian' and should not be granted lightly. The Court of Appeal concluded that the parties could live together for a short time until divorce and ancillary matters were sorted. The combined effect of *Re Y* and *G v G* seems to indicate that occupation orders will be difficult to obtain in the absence of serious physical violence. Where a couple are married and divorce proceedings are pending the courts prefer not to make an occupation at all. This is perhaps unfortunate given that violence can escalate at the point of separation.

The cases discussed above all involved entitled applicants; spouses or persons entitled to occupy by virtue of the general property law. As noted above the Family Law Act 1996 also allows for non-entitled applicants to apply for an occupation order where the respondent is entitled to occupy. In these circumstances only limited classes of persons can apply; former spouses (which now includes civil partners), cohabitants and former cohabitants (including same sex cohabitants). Of the non-entitled applicants, former spouses/civil partners are in the most protected position. The court can make an order under s 33(5) that home rights should not come to an end on divorce, in which case they will be entitled applicants. But in the absence of such an order a former spouse/civil partner will be non-entitled and the court will go through a two stage process, first to decide whether to give occupation rights and then to decide whether to make a regulatory order. The criteria for deciding whether to make an occupation rights order in favour of a non-entitled former spouse include the four basic criteria discussed in relation to entitled applicants above. In addition to these four criteria the courts must consider the length of time that has elapsed since the parties ceased to live together, the length of time that has elapsed since the marriage/civil partnership was dissolved or annulled, the existence of any proceedings (relating to financial relief and property matters) between the parties (s 35(6)). It has been suggested that the shorter the marriage/partnership and the longer it is since the dissolution the harder it will be for a non-entitled spouse to obtain an order. The decisions in *Re Y* (2000) and *G v G* (2000) might also suggest that the last factor, the existence of outstanding proceedings, will work against an order being made; the courts are likely to prefer to wait until these matters are decided if they feel that there is a tolerable working solution for the interim. What is tolerable for the courts may however seem quite intolerable to the victim.

If the court decides to make an occupation rights order it must then go on to consider whether it is appropriate to make a regulatory order, for example excluding the respondent from the home. The criteria for deciding whether to make a regulatory order in favour of a non-entitled spouse are contained in s 35(7) according to which the court has a discretion to grant an order having regard to all the circumstances including the four basic criteria and the length of time that has elapsed since the parties ceased to live together. Under s 35(8) the court has a duty to make an order if the balance of harm test is satisfied, in other words, if the applicant or relevant child are likely to suffer significant harm if the order is not made, unless the respondent or relevant child would suffer harm as great or greater. Orders made in favour of non-entitled spouses can only be of six months' duration but can be extended for a further periods of six months (s 35(10)). Although the Act does not set a limit on the number of times that an order may be extended for former spouses it is clear that the underlying intention of the provision is that orders should be short-term and transitional.

The position of non entitled cohabitants and former cohabitants is dealt with in FLA, s 36. Again, as with former spouses there is a two-stage process; first the courts must decide whether to make an occupation rights order and then whether to make a regulatory order. When deciding whether to make an occupation rights order the courts shall have regard to all the circumstances including, the 'basic criteria' and the nature of the parties' relationship, the length of time during which they have lived together as husband and wife, whether there are or have been children who are the children of both parties or for whom both parties have or have had parental responsibility, the length of time that has elapsed since the parties ceased to live together and the existence of (specified) pending proceedings between the parties. Some of the additional criteria for cohabitants have proved controversial, not least the provision to consider the nature of the parties' relationship. Originally this was further defined in FLA, s 41 so that the courts were required to have regard to the fact that the parties had not given each other the commit-ment involved in marriage. It was generally felt that the provision was mean-ingless and only inserted to appease those who felt that the legislation should not be seen to be undermining marriage. The Domestic Violence, Crime and Victims Act 2004 repeals FLA, s 41 but adds to the provision on the nature of the relationship the words 'and in particular the level of commitment involved in it'.

Normally the respondent must be given notice of proceedings for non-molestation and occupation orders so that he has an opportunity to contest the making of an order. However in certain circumstances orders can be made without notice. Before the FLA came into force the courts emphasised that the power to make orders without notice should be used extremely rarely, only when an emergency required immediate intervention (*Ansah v Ansah* [1977] 2 All ER 638). The FLA imposes fairly strict requirements on the making of without notice orders as well (s 45). However if the applicant is likely to be deterred or prevented from proceeding unless the order is made immediately then it can be made without notice, likewise if there is risk to the applicant or relevant child attributable to the respondent's conduct or the respondent is evading service of notice and the applicant or children will be seriously prejudiced by delay. The empirical research, discussed more fully in the next chapter, suggests that it is difficult to obtain orders without notice even when these stringent conditions are met. It also suggests that the practice under the old law of accepting undertakings in lieu of court orders has not been sufficiently discouraged by provisions in the FLA. Under s 46 the courts have the power to accept undertakings instead of making orders but no powers of arrest can be attached to undertakings and s 47 states that the courts must not accept undertakings where a power of arrest is appropriate. In theory this should significantly limit the situations where the courts can accept an undertaking in lieu of making an order because the FLA strengthened the provisions for attaching powers of arrest to orders.

The Law Commission (1992) was concerned that powers of arrest were regarded as exceptional measures under the previous legislation and wanted to see much greater use. Under the FLA the courts are required to attach a power of arrest to an order where the respondent has used or threatened violence to the applicant or a relevant child, unless they are satisfied that the applicant and child will be adequately protected without such a power (s 47(2)). If the order is without notice the requirements for attaching powers of arrest are more demanding (s 47(3)) but since without notice orders are relatively exceptional, it might be expected that most orders would meet the requirements for a power of arrest to be attached. In fact it seems that judicial interpretation of this provision may have gone some way to undermining its effectiveness. In *Chechi v Bashier and others* [1999] Fam 528, following a bitter family dispute about property, the applicant applied for a non-molestation order against his brother and nephews. The court refused to grant a non-molestation order because it would have been required under the FLA to attach a power of arrest and it felt that would give the applicant unacceptable power over the respondents. Thus the provisions strengthening the enforcement procedure, through encouraging greater use of powers of arrest, were used to deny the applicant an order in the first place. The court could have granted the order but exercised the discretion afforded by the legislation to not attach a power in circumstances where the applicant is adequately protected without. If they did not think that the applicant would have been adequately protected without a power of arrest then the case for a non-molestation order was compelling and the courts were arguably wrong to refuse one. In another case the courts displayed similar ambivalence about attaching powers of arrest. The court granted a non-molestation order for an indefinite period due to ongoing hostility between the parties who had been separated for some time, but imposed a time-limited power of arrest. The Court of Appeal stated that an indefinite order could be justified in situations of long-standing hostility and that it was acceptable for powers of arrest to be shorter than an order (*Re BJ (A Child) (Non-Molestation Order: Power of Arrest)* [2000] 2 FCR 599. The potential difficulty with limited powers of arrest, that either don't cover the full duration of the order or all the terms of the order, are that it may generate confusion when it comes to enforcement. This was one of the arguments that was used to support criminalisation of breach of non-molestation orders by the DVCVA, s 1. The criminalisation provision will be examined more fully in Chapter 5, but it should be noted that whilst non-molestation orders no longer rely on powers of arrest for their enforcement the breach of occupation orders is not a criminal offence so they are still reliant to some extent on the attachment of powers of arrest for their enforcement. If no powers of arrest are not attached the court can issue a warrant for arrest if satisfied that the respondent has breached the order (s 47(8)), but this involves the applicant in additional legal proceedings with all the costs, financial and otherwise, that entails.

Breach of orders obtained under the FLA are punishable as a contempt of court, and this remains the case for non-molestation orders—despite criminalisation of breach. In relation to breach of non-molestation orders they can either be punished as a criminal offence or treated as a contempt of court, but not both (DVCVA 2004, s 1). In this section enforcement via proceedings for contempt of court will be considered, leaving aside the punishment of breach as a criminal offence for Chapter 5. The approach to sentencing perpetrators of domestic violence for contempt of civil orders has been the subject of repeated judicial guidance. The issue was extensively considered in *Hale v Tanner* [2000] 2 FLR 879, which led some commentators to conclude that the courts were taking an increasingly robust approach to those who breached protective orders made under the FLA (Kay, 2001). However in the particular case the courts allowed an appeal against a six-months' suspended sentence imposed for breach of a non-molestation order and imposed a 28-day suspended sentence instead.

The decision in *Hale v Tanner* has been criticised for unjustifiably blurring the functions of imprisonment in contempt proceedings with those of criminal law. In particular it was suggested that it was inappropriate to give the respondent a discount for admitting the breach (Kay, 2001). However, although the primary purpose of committal proceedings is to ensure the protection of the victim through future compliance with the court orders, it is at least in part designed to show the disapproval of the court with past conduct in flouting orders. In *H v H* [2001] 3 FCR 628 the Court of Appeal upheld a sentence of 10-months' imprisonment for repeated breaches of a non-molestation order. The most important factor in this decision appears to have been a desire to reprimand the respondent for his flagrant disregard of the authority of the court, but the impact upon children involved in this case was another factor underpinning what is an usually long sentence. The Court of Appeal had opportunity to revisit the guidelines for penalties for breach of protective orders in *Lomas v Parle* [2004] 1 FLR 812. The facts of this case revealed a long history of domestic violence subject to multiple interventions by both the civil and criminal justice systems. The first committal proceedings for breach of a non-molestation order resulting in 56-days' imprisonment, second proceedings and third proceedings, which were punctuated by criminal proceedings for related charges, both resulted in 4-months' imprisonment. The Court of Appeal lamented the difficulties of parallel proceedings in different courts and gave guidance on how the courts might approach the management of concurrent proceedings in different jurisdictions in the absence of an integrated domestic violence court (Burton, 2004). The court concluded that the 4-month sentence imposed in the third committal proceedings was unduly lenient. Although the Court of Appeal has repeatedly stated that it does not find it appropriate to set a tariff for the sentences to be imposed for different types of breaches, it is implicit in the case law that certain features, such as the presence of children, multiple breaches and the nature of the breaches (if 'sinister'), point towards prison sentences that are closer towards the 2-year maximum that can be imposed for contempt. The court in *Lomas* also indicated the view that the penalties for breaches of orders under the FLA should be consistent with those imposed for criminal offences of breach of restraining orders under the PHA. Whether this is practicable or desirable has been analysed elsewhere (Burton, 2004), but for these purposes it suffices to note that the decision in Lomas does signal that breaches of FLA should be treated seriously when dealt with as contempt. This remains important for those non-molestation orders which proceed down the civil enforcement route post-DVCVA, and crucially important for occupation orders which do not have the criminal enforcement route.

Child contact proceedings under the Children Act 1989

The issue of parental separation and contact with children has become one of the most controversial legal issues for women experiencing domestic violence. Traditionally they have faced significant obstacles in getting the courts to recognise that the abuse they have suffered and that it should be relevant to contact proceedings. Violence towards the child's mother has not always been seen as relevant in cases where there has been no direct physical harm to the child, despite empirical evidence revealing the strong links between domestic violence and child abuse. As will be seen in the next chapter there is also research suggesting that violent men use contact proceedings as a way of continuing to abuse their former partner and, either directly or indirectly, their children.

When the relationship between parents of a child breaks down and they become separated the absent parent can apply for a contact order under the Children Act 1989 (CA), s 8. Contact orders can take many forms, they may allow direct contact for example by visiting or staying, or indirect contact for example by letters or telephone. The court have discretion to either specify closely the degree and nature of the contact, or they can leave the arrangements to be more flexible by specifying that 'reasonable' contact take place. Sometimes an absent parent will seek a residence order under s 8, and the court has power to make shared residence orders but this is unpopular and a presumption of shared residence lobbied for by some father's groups has not been accepted by the government. It is normally assumed that the child's best interests are served by parents reaching their own agreements over contact and residence; a view embodied in the no order principle (CA, s 1(5)). Most people do in fact reach their own agreements but the no order principle may be particularly problematic in domestic violence cases, for example if victims of domestic violence feel coerced by their violent former partner into making contact arrangements which leave them and their children unsafe. Agreements over contact arrangements are partly, as research discussed in the next chapter highlights, bargains made in the shadow of the law. The legal framework for determining disputed contact arrangements is the welfare checklist in the CA, s 1(3).

Under the 'welfare checklist', as it will be referred to hereafter, the courts are required to take into account a range of factors including the physical, emotional and educational needs of the child, the capacity of each parent (or other person the court considers relevant) for meeting the child's needs, and the harm that the child has suffered or is at risk of suffering. The welfare checklist does not specifically list the harm that children may suffer indirectly as a result of domestic violence, but the CA, s 31, which relates to public law proceedings, does now have an expanded definition of 'harm' which includes 'impairment suffered from seeing or hearing the ill-treatment of another'. It was expected that this expanded definition of harm would be influential in private law contact proceedings and implementation was delayed whilst administrative action was taken to ensure court forms were amended to try to flag up details of domestic violence at an early stage in CA, s 8 applications. However, flagging up domestic violence is only helpful if the judiciary gives appropriate recognition to its significance.

The Children Act Sub-Committee has issued official guidance on how the courts should deal with contact applications involving allegations of domestic violence (Children Act Sub-Committee of the Lord Chancellor's Advisory Board on Family Law, 2002). The guidance has the backing of the Court of Appeal in the leading case of *Re L (Contact: Domestic Violence)* (2000) 2 FLR 334. The court acknowledged that domestic violence is harmful to children and can constitute 'a significant failure in parenting'. It endorsed the view that findings of fact need to be made, observing: 'There has, perhaps, been a tendency in the past for the courts not to tackle allegations of violence and to leave them in the background on the premise that they were matters affecting the adults and not relevant to issues regarding the children' (Butler Sloss, *Re L*). However it was cautioned that when making findings of fact the courts should remember that allegations 'may not always be true or may be grossly exaggerated'. Despite this caution against false allegations, *Re L* reaffirmed the need for the courts to make an assessment of the risks of contact in domestic violence cases and set expectations for violent men seeking to have contact that they acknowledge and take responsibility for their behaviour. When weighing up whether to allow contact the court should consider 'the ability of the offending parent to recognise his past conduct, be aware of the need for change and to make genuine efforts to do so' (Butler Sloss, *Re L*).

Re L was undoubtedly a landmark judgment in signalling domestic violence as an issue that the courts should take seriously in contact proceedings (Kaganas, 2000), but its real significance lies in how it has been subsequently applied. Empirical evidence, discussed in the next chapter, suggests that the spirit of *Re L* may not be reflected in the day-to-day practices of the courts which continue to allow dangerous contact arrangements in domestic violence cases. Even at the level of reported case law there is some cause for disquiet about whether judges are taking domestic violence seriously enough in contact proceedings. One case which highlights these concerns is *Re H (A Child) (Contact: Domestic Violence)* [2006] 1 FCR 102. In *Re H* the father sought contact with his three-year-old daughter but her mother objected on the basis of his alleged violence. The judge at first instance made an order for direct contact, albeit supervised, despite the fact that two expert witnesses had given evidence that it would not be in the child's best interests. The Court of Appeal examined how things went 'badly wrong' in the initial determination. The judge regarded the mother as manipulative, praying on the respondent's vulnerability and grossly exaggerating alleged incidents of violence towards herself and the child. Despite the applicant having to attend hospital on one occasion to receive treatment for multiple injuries sustained during a beating with a shoe, the judge was able to conclude that the assault was in part provoked by the fact that the respondent had been treated in an 'autocratic and domineering way'. The most common complaint of certain fathers' groups is that the family justice system is biased against men seeking contact with their children (Geldof, 2003), although it has been observed that both sexes tend to see the system as biased against them (Kaganas and Day Sclater, 2004). In so far as there was any individual, as opposed to systemic, bias—in this case it was clearly against the mother. In an understatement the Court of Appeal remarked; 'The judge clearly did not form a favourable impression of the mother, and was equally sympathetic to the father, whom he thought had been badly treated by the mother and members of her family' (Wall LJ). The father was viewed as a devout Muslim but the mother was said to have put her position above her religious duty by breaking her promise to her husband to conceal the abuse. The Court of Appeal were highly critical of the suggestion that the mother might in anyway be bound by her promise describing it as 'plainly wrong'. The judge's lack of cultural and religious sensitivity was also evident from a number of inappropriate comments made about the mother's appearance and dress, despite the attempts made by one of the expert witnesses to sensitise him to the particularly degrading nature of the assault perpetrated against the mother. The expert evidence was also presented with specific reference to the judgement in *Re L*, highlighting the fact that the father has made no acknowledgement of his violence or responsibility for it, either blaming others or completely denying any violence took place. When the judge suggested to the expert that the violence might have been provoked, for example by infidelity, she said 'I cannot accept as a professional that any amount of unhappiness and provocation justifies an assault on a woman' to which he replied it might not justify it but explain and perhaps excuse it. The difference between excuse and justify in this context looks like a matter of semantics and the judge was roundly criticised by the Court of Appeal for his partial view of the parties which became 'increasingly polarised'. In one sense the judgment in *Re H* is reassuring because the Court of Appeal did strongly criticise the trial judge and took the opportunity to reaffirm the guidance in *Re L* and praise the experts for their measured approach to the case. However, perhaps more disconcerting is the observation by Lord Justice Wall that 'there are very few cases that reach this court, and when one does, we have no means of knowing whether it is an aberration or the tip of a particularly nasty iceberg'. The empirical evidence examined in the next chapter will provide some insight into whether the judge in *Re H* is reflective of the day-to-day practice of the family courts or not.

Conclusion

The legal framework for the civil justice response to domestic violence has undergone considerable changes over the last 40 years. The early legislation embodied restrictive tests for protective orders and judicial interpretation at appellate level further diminished the scope of the legislation to offer meaningful protection to victims by emphasising the perpetrator's rights. The FLA was intended to refocus the law on the need for effective protection but it proved difficult for the judiciary to break away from traditional views that excluding a man from his home is a 'draconian' solution. The tension between victim's and defendant's rights is also manifest in the way the courts deal with child contact in domestic violence cases. Contact is not supposed to be about a father's rights but the welfare of the child, but in some cases the courts seem to lose sight of this principle. It seems that in terms of the civil justice response to domestic violence the law itself has constituted a significant part of the problem, although the improvements brought about by the FLA should not be underplayed. The legal framework is however only partly relevant to understanding how the civil justice system response has evolved in domestic violence cases. The implementation of the civil law remedies in everyday practice is just as, if not more, important. The next chapter will take up this theme of the civil law in action in domestic violence cases.

3 The civil justice response

Protection in practice?

Prior to the implementation of the Family Law Act 1996 there was a body of research showing the weak protection the civil justice system provided to victims of domestic violence. This research was based on both observations of the court process and interviews with victims and showed that the courts were quite reluctant to intervene, especially to exclude the perpetrator of abuse from 'his' home. The role of solicitors in undermining the effectiveness of the legal provisions designed to protect women and children from violence was also highlighted. This chapter will examine this research in more detail as it provides the baseline for evaluating to what extent the civil courts and the legal profession have progressed post-implementation of the Family Law Act 1996 in improving the civil justice response to domestic violence. There is a growing body of empirical work on the operation of the civil remedies under the Family Law Act 1996, including analysis of statistical trends and service providers views' of the effectiveness of the new regime.

The implementation of remedies before the Family Law Act 1996

Relationship with solicitor

The process of communication between solicitor and client can be a troubled one. Solicitors are far from uniform in their background and the type of work they undertake (Cownie et al, 2007, Ch 8), however the nature of the legal profession is strongly 'masculine' and both male and female solicitors may adopt approaches which are aggressive, assertive and lack the 'feminine' qualities of empathy. A lack of empathy may be critical to how victims of domestic violence experience their relationship with their solicitor. Membership of the legal profession makes solicitors part of a community with (to an extent) shared values and, within local settings, ongoing working relationships with each other. The maintenance of working relationships has in some contexts been found to be more important to solicitors than their relationship with their client. Victims of domestic violence seeking civil remedies in the courts have reported feeling excluded from the discussions taking place between solicitors about the resolution of their own claims.

The important role of solicitor as 'gatekeeper' to the civil remedies for domestic violence was emphasised by both Radford (1987) and Barron (1990). Radford (1987) observed that solicitors would often discourage victims from seeking legal remedies. This process of discouragement and insensitive treatment of victims effectively gave support for the violence to continue and contributed to what Radford (1987) described as the 'legalising' of abuse. Even in cases which were taken forward to the courts the concerns of solicitors and the needs of women were often ill-matched. Solicitors were criticised for not listening, for making up 'facts' and for changing the victim's own words. Women interviewed by Radford complained that solicitors emphasised aspects of their partner's behaviour which they considered to be either irrelevant or less important than some other aspects which were left out. Sometimes when women were manipulated by their solicitors into presenting a story which did not reflect their experiences they were left feeling upset despite achieving the outcome desired in court proceedings. If women were subjected to cross-examination on a story constructed by their solicitor then this could result in their losing credibility in the eyes of the court.

Radford considered possible explanations for the negative experiences some women had of their own solicitors and suggested, in accordance with earlier research, that some solicitors may be unsympathetic to victims of domestic violence and do not view certain types of behaviour, for example 'shoving', to be violent. Even amongst solicitors who were supposed to be representing the victim there was a strong presumption that victims precipitated the violence. An alternative explanation of the mismatch between solicitors' accounts and victims' experiences is that solicitors have to present an account which is relevant to the court; translate victims' accounts into legally relevant accounts which are required for legal remedies to be implemented. Constructing a 'good case' may therefore take precedence over describing the victim's experiences in her own words. This phenomenon of case de-construction has been observed in the criminal justice context (Cretney and Davis, 1995). It would be surprising if case construction were not a feature of the civil justice system and would be wrong to think that solicitors are motivated purely by a desire to undermine their clients due to not believing their accounts. In fact as Radford concluded: ' "Good" solicitors may be the ones especially vulnerable to this need to put women's complaints into acceptable legal language' (Radford, 1988, p 324).

Victims of domestic violence need supportive solicitors if they are going to take the first steps to securing civil remedies. Barron interviewed 31 women for her study of the civil remedies prior to implementation of the FLA. She found that even after years of abuse many women were reluctant to take steps which might appear to them to be irrevocable. Injunctions of course are not irrevocable but solicitors did not always inform their clients of this and some solicitors were reportedly reluctant to apply for injunctions unless clients took steps towards the more irrevocable solution of obtaining a divorce by initiating proceedings. Barron (1990) also noted that many victims of domestic violence find it difficult to talk about the details of their relationship with their violent partner and take in information about the options available to them. In this respect it is crucially important that women have a sympathetic solicitor who is prepared to explain all the options in language that the victim can understand. Whilst about a third of the women Barron interviewed were positive about their solicitor, an equal proportion were critical and several were ambivalent. Barron (1990) notes the women she interviewed often felt that they had little control over outcomes and it was a matter of lawyers conferring and reaching agreements amongst themselves, for example about the acceptability of undertakings.

The court process

In relation to the court process, Radford observed that in contested applications for injunctions the perpetrator's bare denial of allegations was often sufficient to offer a viable defence whereas the victim's claims had to be vigorously corroborated. In her analysis judges tended to give more weight to men's counter-allegations than women's corroborated claims and a 'presumption of disbelief' shifted the emphasis to the woman's role of precipitator of violence and away from her need for protection. Judges were partly hampered by the cases presented to them and the fact that solicitors could minimise the seriousness of the violence and overplay the victim's role, but judges added to the unsympathetic treatment that women already received from their own lawyers in some instances.

Barron (1990) found that in the County Court women were not usually called upon to give oral evidence unless the application was contested, but in the magistrates' court they nearly always were asked to testify. The process of giving evidence is often traumatic for victims of domestic violence and solicitors often used this as a justification for persuading their clients to accept undertakings. However undertakings were regarded as a greatly inferior outcome to an injunction because the issue of blame is sidestepped, and they were seen as a less effective remedy (see also Kewley, 1996). Like Radford, Barron found that women feel a lack of control over the court process and feel that they are not able to give 'their' account.

The reported case law, discussed in the previous chapter, showed judicial reluctance to exclude perpetrators of domestic violence from the family home. Perhaps unsurprisingly then, Barron found that women were unable to obtain exclusion orders because the courts were overly concerned about depriving a man of his home. Barron noted that consideration of the perpetrator's accommodation needs could result in him being given several weeks to leave the shared home. Where women had started relationships with other men then a decision about whether to grant an exclusion order was apparently influenced by allegations of 'infidelity'. Allegations of infidelity could be regarded as a form of provocation and result in the refusal of protection. Judges also refused to make orders whilst the custody of the children was in dispute. If a woman had left the family home to escape violence and left the children behind this worked to her disadvantage. Women were judged badly for leaving children, but similar negative evaluations did not attach to men who left children.

The enforcement of injunctions was viewed as highly problematic. Judges were often reluctant to attach powers of arrest and generally believed that the order itself, or an undertaking, should be sufficient to prevent further violence. This faith in the power of court orders or promises was misguided. Barron found that half the women who obtained orders or undertakings said that their partner disobeyed them at least once. Some breaches were serious and repeated but the police and courts seemed to do little about it. The poor enforcement of injunctions contributed to the conclusion that they are in most cases 'not worth the paper' they are written on. Committal proceedings rarely led to the imprisonment of perpetrators who had breached injunctions. Judges appeared willing to tolerate multiple breaches without imposing penalties of any significance.

Barron concluded that it was not so much the law that was problematic as its (non) implementation. If the main failings did in fact lie with solicitors and the judges then it is possible to speculate that little would change with the implementation of the Family Law Act 1996. Changing the legal rules does not necessarily mean a change in the court culture and values of the legal profession. Lockton and Ward (1997) carried out a study of domestic violence legislation over the period of transition from the old regime to the FLA. Their study found relatively low success rates in terms of the applications made for non-molestation, ouster and exclusion orders. There were high levels of undertakings or a mixture of undertakings and court orders with the consequent difficulties of enforcement, although in relation to orders where a power of arrest was applied for the success rate was quite high. Overall their assessment of the pre-FLA was that it was 'susceptible to failing' (p 48). Did the implementation of the FLA bring about significant improvements in the civil justice response to domestic violence?

Implementing the Family Law Act 1996

Edwards (2001a) considered whether the FLA brought about any change to the effectiveness of the civil law protection for victims of domestic violence by examining the annual trends in injunctive relief prior to and following implementation. She found that, looking at the first three years post-FLA, there was no change in the grant of non-molestation orders when compared to the number of personal protection orders made under the previous legislation just before the new laws came in. However there was a dramatic increase in the number of occupation orders granted; the roughly equivalent ouster orders available prior to the FLA stood at just 2,945 – this rose to over 9,000 occupation orders granted in 1998, dropping back slightly in 1999. Edwards sounded a note of caution regarding this increase by observing that only some of the orders would have contained a provision for exclusion, some would have been made regarding proprietory rights rather than for personal protection. Another dramatic increase was observed in relation to the use of powers of arrest; these were attached to 44 per cent of orders in 1996 (pre-implementation) but this rose to 80 per cent of all orders by 1999. However Edwards also found that undertakings continued to be used in a large proportion of cases, almost 7,000 undertakings were accepted (17 per cent of cases) over one 18-month period post-implementation of the FLA. These general trends masked some regional variations, for example undertakings were more likely to be used in some areas then others. In addition Edwards observed that there was significant regional variation in the attachment of powers of arrest to occupation orders, less so in relation to non-molestation orders.

In Edwards' (2001a) opinion the 'new Act may not be as effective as anticipated' (p 200). She notes that one of the key difficulties that victims have in accessing protection under the civil law is the financial cost of seeking an injunction. Revised criteria for public funding, coinciding with the introduction of the FLA, may have made it more difficult for victims of domestic violence to obtain public funding for an injunction application. This is one possible explanation for the fact that the numbers of non-molestation orders plateau around the introduction of the FLA, when otherwise one might expect an increase due to the more victim-focused criteria. Alternatively Edwards suggests that the introduction of the FLA might have coincided with a period where there was an improvement in the police response to domestic violence, making it less necessary for victims to seek a civil justice remedy. This might be regarded as an overly optimistic assessment of the improvements to police practice. Edwards notes another possible, 'more invidious', explanation is that judges became reluctant to grant non-molestation orders in situations where they did not want to attach a power of arrest but would have legislatively been required to do so. Despite these concerns Edwards concludes that 'bringing the remedies under one Act has produced a more effective remedy for dealing with domestic violence'. This view seems to be shared by voluntary sector support agencies providing services for victims of domestic violence.

Five years after the introduction of the FLA, the Women's Aid of England (WAFE) commissioned research to examine the views of workers in refuges, outreach projects and advice centres on how well the needs of women and children experiencing domestic violence were being met (Barron, 2002). The research found that 65 per cent of respondents felt that the FLA had improved the level of protection available to women and children, although approximately one-fifth (21 per cent) of respondents thought it had not. Respondents were asked about the different types of orders that can be obtained under the FLA and expressed more confidence in the ability of non-molestation orders to protect victims than occupation orders. Although respondents were slightly less confident in the ability of non-molestation orders to protect women in a refuge, than if they were rehoused, 55 per cent thought that they did offer protection even if the woman stayed or returned home. This compared with 43 per cent of respondents who felt that occupation orders protected women who stayed or returned home. Barron notes that almost a quarter of respondents did not answer the questions about whether non-molestation orders and occupation orders offer protection, or said they did not know. She speculates that this may be because they do not recommend the use of such orders to women they work with, possibly because they lack confidence in them. The qualitative evaluation of comments on the FLA orders reveals respondents felt the effectiveness of the orders varied greatly according to the victim's individual circumstances, for example whether the perpetrator had left home.

Barron (2002) observes that the ability to get orders quickly can be crucial in ensuring effective protection for victims of domestic violence. In general the respondents in her study felt that women were able to get orders as quickly as they needed; more than half said that an order could be obtained within one week without notice, but it was noted that occupation orders without notice can be difficult to obtain. Given the documented increase in the proportion of orders where powers of arrest were attached post-FLA (Edwards, 2001a), it might be expected that voluntary sector support agencies would be positive about the improvements in enforcement provisions. However Barron (2002) found that the same proportion of respondents said powers of arrest were 'sometimes' imposed on non-molestations as those who said they 'usually' were imposed. In relation to occupation orders more said they 'sometimes' were than 'usually' were imposed. There was a clear impression that powers of arrest were attached less frequently to occupation orders than non-molestation orders, which is borne out by the judicial statistics. Some respondents thought that orders were useless unless a power of arrest was attached to them, but others thought that even with the power of arrest a lot depended on the attitude of the perpetrator and the police. Barron concludes: 'Overall, despite the general feeling that the Family Law Act has improved the protection for abused women, it seems that court orders are only effective if the perpetrator has some respect for the law, and the police are prepared to enforce the order' (Barron, 2002, p 9). The effectiveness of the civil justice system in protecting women and children from domestic violence depends on strict enforcement of orders obtained under the FLA, which means breaches being 'treated severely by the police and the courts'.

Barron's research provided useful insights into the perspectives of voluntary sector support agencies helping women and children experiencing domestic violence. As the organisations most closely involved with some women seeking protection from domestic violence via the civil justice system, their views on the effectiveness of the FLA are undoubtedly important. However there are many other service providers involved in supporting victims of domestic violence and implementing the FLA. The views of a wide range of service providers were accessed in a study carried out by Burton et al (2002). The study was commissioned by the Lord Chancellor's Department, as it was then, to examine the effectiveness of the civil remedies for domestic violence under the FLA and to consider whether a provision in s 60 of the Act, for third party applications for protective orders, should be implemented. The findings on third party applications will be considered more fully in the next chapter; this section will concentrate on service provider's views on the effectiveness of the FLA regime without third party applications. The research comprised 60 interviews with a wide range of service providers including, judges, magistrates, solicitors, police officers, housing officers and representatives from agencies such as Victim Support, NSPCC and Refuge and Women's Aid. Respondents were asked to identify aspects of the FLA that they thought were working well to protect victims of domestic violence and comment on any perceived gaps in the protection offered by the FLA and the civil justice system, identifying further improvements that might be made.

Service providers interviewed by Burton et al (2002) thought that the FLA had improved the level of protection offered to victims of domestic violence but a number of obstacles to effective protection remained. One of the main ways that the FLA was thought to have improved the protection for victims of domestic violence was by opening up the categories of person eligible to apply for remedies. Nonetheless it was remarked that there were ongoing problems with people who fell outside the categories of associated person but nevertheless needed a remedy. The types of people mentioned by respondents, for example non-cohabiting girlfriend/boyfriends, are now covered by amendments made to the FLA by the DVCVA. A more pressing problem insofar as many respondents were concerned was the failure of the FLA to provide effective remedies for victims suffering non-physical abuse.

The definition of molestation, as discussed in the previous chapter, is potentially broad. Respondents stated however, although it was quite easy to obtain remedies for physical abuse, it was in their experience still very difficult to obtain remedies for non-physical abuse. Some respondents attributed the failure of the civil justice system to provide effective remedies for non-physical abuse to the difficulties that victims experienced in recognising their experiences as 'domestic violence'. They commented that agencies and individuals supporting and advising victims of domestic violence, particularly solicitors, needed to do more to help victims recognise the types of behaviour that amount to abuse and for which they could seek remedies. There was an impression that some solicitors were operating according to narrow definitions of domestic violence and advising their clients that there needed to be physical violence evidenced by physical injury before they could seek a remedy under the FLA. One respondent described a woman she helped as a 'victim of severe mental abuse'. She wanted to obtain protective orders under the FLA but met resistance from her legal advisers and the courts: 'All they were interested in was had he hit her. She was trying to tell them what she was suffering and they kept saying "has he hit you?". It was almost as if the other bits didn't really matter. You know the fact that he was torturing her in ways that were possibly even worse than hitting her'. Another respondent commented: 'the whole range of abusive behaviours is little understood by people who advise, but particularly judges and magistrates . . . the whole debate has been kaleidoscoped down to one view, did he/she/they hit you and what was the severity of the injury'. Even a County Court judge commented that the FLA was 'working well for those who have got bruises and broken bones' but not very well for those suffering non-physical abuse. Although some solicitors interviewed claimed to be aware of the significance of mental abuse they stated that they would find it difficult to justify an application for public funding for clients who had not experienced some physical violence and injury. This appeared to be reinforced by interviews with representatives from the Legal Services Commission who stated that public funding would not be considered urgent for non-physical abuse and that medical evidence would be required to document the fact that mental abuse was having a serious impact on the victim's health.

The importance of the victim's solicitor as 'gatekeeper' to civil protection remains as important post-FLA as it was under the old law. Many respondents commented that whether victims were able to access remedies under the FLA depended a great deal on the quality of legal advice they received, their solicitor's level of competence with the legislation and their skill when dealing with victims of domestic violence. The inaccessibility of legal language to lay persons can be a problem in all solicitor/client communication but respondents in this study noted again that approaching a solicitor who appears remote and uses inaccessible legal language can be particularly difficult for victims of domestic violence, whose confidence may already be sapped by years of abuse. The importance of getting a solicitor who specialises in making applications under the FLA was emphasised: 'Not all solicitors understand about the FLA. We have dealt with solicitors who are still working on the previous legislation and saying you cannot get an injunction.' It was observed that even solicitors who had expertise with the FLA could improve their practice by more flexible working arrangements, for example, seeing the victim at a venue where she feels more comfortable. This provides support for the argument that cultural change is needed as well as legal changes to make civil justice remedies more accessible.

Just under half of the 60 respondents interviewed by Burton et al (2002) stated that solicitors were still keen to deal with cases by undertakings if possible. The solicitors themselves claimed that it was more difficult to obtain undertakings since the FLA came into force, but the study provides some support for Edwards (2001a) analysis that this probably varies from area to area. A judge in one area commented that she had taken a strong line against accepting undertakings and this usually led to the defendant accepting the order rather than contesting the case. However in another area a judge commented: 'I would imagine there are less undertakings, but who cares? The purpose of the legislation is to provide protection and it you are providing protection then I don't care whether it is an undertaking or an order'. This comment seems to underestimate the difficulties in enforcing undertakings. Overall, few respondents seemed to think it was a good thing for cases to be dealt with by undertakings.

In relation to occupation orders, the majority of respondents noted the difficulties of obtaining them without notice. More than half of the solicitors interviewed stated that it was virtually impossible to get *ex parte* occupation orders. Even when proceedings for occupation orders were with notice there was a perception that they were difficult to obtain where the violence was not severe. Some respondents stated that the courts assumed, perhaps incorrectly, that victims of domestic violence would be more readily able to obtain alternative accommodation than respondents. This is consistent with the reported case law discussed in the previous chapter.

The issue of enforcement of court orders was foremost in service provider's assessments of the effectiveness of the FLA. The ability to obtain powers of arrest quite readily was one of the key significant improvements identified by all the solicitors interviewed. This is consistent with the statistics showing an increase in the proportion of orders with powers of arrest attached as discussed above. However one problem that was repeatedly highlighted was that powers of arrest are often only attached to part of the order and not the whole of the order: 'if there are four or five points, they will only attach it to the violence. Sometimes the harass and pester part hasn't got a power of arrest attached to it ... the police get really confused.' This is one of the arguments which was used to support criminalisation of breach of non-molestation orders, which will be discussed more fully in the next chapter. Respondents commented that it was not helpful for the police to be unclear about whether they had powers because it was not conducive to their taking effective action when victims called for help and could leave victims confused about when they should call for help. Of course having the power to arrest is only part of the picture insofar as the police response is concerned and comments were made about police officers adjudicating on the quality of the breach; dismissing some incidents as too trivial to warrant action even when they had powers. Less than a quarter of respondents in this study felt that powers of arrest were being acted upon properly by the police.

The response of the courts to breaches of orders also attracted considerable criticism, with many complaining that breaches were not treated seriously enough, particularly by magistrates. The use of fines was strongly criticised and several respondents commented that victims were put off reporting breaches because of inadequate penalties. It was stated that imprisonment was rarely considered except for repeated breaches and then the duration of the term was generally short. A significant number of respondents were in favour of a broader range of penalties for contempt of court, but there were more mixed views about the proposal, as it was then, to make breach of protective orders a criminal offence.

Other empirical evidence on the use of the FLA was provided by an overview of 27 projects aimed at finding effective approaches for responding to domestic violence (Hester and Westmarland, 2005). The focus of the projects and evaluations was mainly on criminal justice interventions, but some projects supported women through the civil justice system and therefore there was some limited discussion of the civil justice remedies. One project in Bradford found a reasonably high success rate amongst 136 women who applied for protective orders; 60 per cent got an order of some sort, almost half obtained a non-molestation order and slightly fewer (38 per cent) obtained a non-molestation and occupation order. There seemed to be quite a low level of reported breaches of orders (7 per cent; but it is not known whether this reflected the true level of breaches due to missing data. Much higher levels of reported breaches were found in other projects. One factor which the research identified as important in securing effective protection under the civil law was close links between the projects and good family law solicitors who are willing to work rapidly on cases referred to them. Again this reinforces all of the research, both before and after implementation of the FLA, which highlights the crucial role of solicitors in ensuring that legal remedies technically available under the civil law are effectively translated into practice. Having police officers located within projects was also noted, in some cases, to enhance the enforcement of civil orders through making action on breach more likely and bringing about a speedier response.

Child contact

Domestic violence is a significant feature of many child contact cases (Hester and Radford, 1996; Hester et al, 2007). There is now extensive evidence that witnessing domestic violence has a detrimental impact on the health and well-being of children (Abrahams, 1994; Mullender and Morley, 1994; McGee, 2000; Mullender et al, 2002; Humphreys and Stanley, 2006; Radford and Hester, 2006; Hester et al, 2007). There is an overlap between domestic violence and the physical and sexual abuse of children. Domestic violence is also the context for a number of child deaths, and contact arrangements have been implicated in some of these (Saunders, 2004: Wall, 2006). Concerns about domestic violence and child contact are evident in other jurisdictions (Cahn, 1991; Mahoney; 1991) and many of the issues highlighted resonate with experiences of abused women and children in contact proceedings in England and Wales.

One of the early studies of contact arrangements in domestic violence cases found that a high proportion of the women interviewed (21/53) reported that children had been sexually or physically abused by their fathers (Hester and Radford, 1996). Most of the children were also reported to have been suffering adverse effects as a result of witnessing violence against their mother. In six cases of direct child abuse no contact was formally ordered, but many mothers were still left in a position where court ordered contact left them fearing for their own safety and the safety of their children. In only 7 of the 53 cases was there no further abuse or harassment of the women involved as a result of the contact arrangements. Child contact arrangements are often used as a means for the perpetrator of domestic violence to continue to abuse the mother and children. Child abuse is frequently part of the abuse of the woman and children can sometimes become implicated in the violence against their mother by being forced to carry out their father's instructions (Hester and Radford, 1996). Women's fears for their own and their children's safety are not 'unreasonable'; they have accurate perceptions of the risk of harm involved (Radford et al, 1999). It has been generally agreed that professionals dealing with domestic violence need to be aware that children are affected by domestic violence, but there has been less agreement about the appropriate response (Mullender and Morley, 1994, Mullender, 2000, Humphreys et al, 2000; Humphreys and Stanley, 2006).

The issue of how seriously the courts take post-separation violence has become a predominant concern for campaigning organisations such as WAFE. Failure to adequately address the risks of contact and make app-ropriate arrangements for safety has led to serious criticism of the family justice system (Saunders, 2002; Saunders and Barron, 2003). This criticism is most strident in cases where contact arrangements have been implicated in child deaths (Saunders, 2004). Saunders (2004) examined the cases of 29 children killed in the decade ending in 2004. She found that in five cases residence or contact with the perpetrator of abuse was either ordered or endorsed by the court, in three instances without professional agreement. Her conclusion was that the cases raised 'serious questions about the account-ability of the family justice system' (Saunders, 2004). A subsequent examin-ation of these five cases, which involved the deaths of 11 children, concluded that eight of the deaths could not have been reasonably foreseen or prevented by the court (Wall, 2006). However Lord Justice Wall, the author of the report, concluded that in relation to three children who died 'it is arguable that the court should have taken a more proactive stance and refused to make the consent order for contact'.

There is a view that domestic violence does not necessarily make a man a bad father. This proposition has recently been reaffirmed by the President of the Family Law division (Sir Mark Potter P, oral evidence to the House of Commons, Children Act Committee, 2006). Sir Mark Potter observed; 'there is no doubt than a child may have a close and loving relationship with a parent, being ignorant of that violence and in a situation where there is no reason to think that it would ever be perpetrated vis-à-vis that child'. However to be confident of this the courts need to be in a strong position to make reliable risk assessments and, as Sir Mark conceded, the process of risk assessment is fraught with difficulties. The court is reliant on the expertise of the Children and Family Court Advisory and Support service (CAFCASS), which has itself been criticised for its lack of attention to safety planning and lack of formal risk assessment (HMICA, 2005). Her Majesty's Inspectorate of Court Administration (HMICA, 2005) found numerous examples of bad practice on the part of CAFCASS officers, for example officers who failed to take seriously the impact of violence upon children. CAFCASS were also criticised for assuming that contact should always take place irrespective of violence. HMICA (2005) concluded 'The presumption of contact drives and constrains practice' and risk assessment should be the priority.

It is arguably not only CAFCASS that needs to move away from a presumption of contact in domestic violence cases. Solicitors have also been found to assume that it is the father's right to contact with his children, irrespective of violence, and have seen their role as being to overcome the resistance of women to contact. Contact should be about welfare rather than father's rights, although it has been argued that it is misguided to argue that there is no right to contact (Bainham, 2003). McGee (2000) found that women were frequently told by their own solicitors that the child's father has a right to contact and it should not be opposed. She comments: 'Women felt that their perception of risk to their children from the violent man was completely overlooked by their solicitors and there was also no recognition of the danger to the woman in maintaining contact with the violent man' (McGee, 2000, p 176). Children themselves were ambivalent about contact with their fathers; torn between wanting to see him but not wanting to watch him continuing to abuse their mother, whilst many loved their fathers they detested the violence. Some were very frightened and did not want contact, but like their mothers believed that the application of law was biased against them.

Threatening to take children away can be one of the factors which works to keep women trapped in violent relationships (Glass, 1995), but clearly some do, despite fears of escalated violence post-separation facilitated by court mandated contact, make the break. Mothers can be denigrated as 'bad mothers' for refusing contact, whilst the image of 'good enough' fathering includes men who have harmed children through domestic violence. Women who refuse to comply with court ordered contact have experienced different approaches to enforcement (Kaganas and Day Sclater, 2004). The approach to non-compliance hardened in the 1990s, although Kaganas and Day Sclater observed some softening in recent years. The Children and Adoption Act 2006 extended the options for enforcing compliance with contact orders and provided that enforcement orders need not be made if the court is satisfied that the person failing to comply has 'reasonable excuse'. WAFE would have liked to have seen a much more robust approach to contact in domestic violence cases. In some other jurisdictions there are legislative presumptions against unsupervised access in domestic violence cases (Perry, 2006). One practical problem that can flow from such presumptions is the availability of adequate facilities for supervision, which has been a matter of concern in the UK (Aris, Harrison and Humphreys, 2002; Humphreys and Harrison, 2003). A presumption of no contact is not a panacea for all the problems, but without such a presumption it is clear that the civil justice system still has a considerable way to go in making it such that orders made under the Children Act 1989, s 8 do not place women and children in greater danger.

Conclusion

This chapter has shown that many of the problems identified with the civil remedies for domestic violence prior to the FLA continue to be significant post implementation. This reinforces the well-established view that changing the legal framework is not always adequate to change what happens in practice. Judicial attitudes and the approach of solicitors to domestic violence can be resistant to change. Solicitors' attitudes can be significant not only in relation to the remedies available under the FLA but also to the advice that they give to clients who wish to oppose contact with abusive partners post-separation. The empirical evidence on child contact in domestic violence cases does give cause for concern that the tip of the iceberg, seen by the courts in *Re H* and discussed in the previous chapter, concealed fairly widespread bad practice in the family courts.

Some authors, commenting upon the implementation of the Family Law Act 1996, doubted the potential of the legislation to provide the protection victims of domestic violence need, even if the new provisions were adequately utilised (Lockton and Ward, 1997). This scepticism stemmed in part from research in the US which suggests injunctions do little to provide long-term protection (see the studies reported in Buzawa and Buzawa (1996), cited in Lockton and Ward (1997) pp 80–85). There is little research in the UK examining the effect of civil orders on perpetrators of domestic violence (Paradine and Wilkinson, 2004, pp 20–21). However it may be that civil orders are most effective for victims who seek them early in the abusive relationship. This level of scepticism about the potential for the civil justice system to effectively respond to domestic violence, suggests that victims might be better to look outside the law or perhaps to the criminal justice system for protection. There are further options for trying to improve the civil justice response to domestic violence and, as will be seen in the next chapter, some of these are being currently being implemented. Whether they will take the civil justice system much further towards the goal of effective protection for victims of domestic remains to be seen.

4 Improving the civil justice response

The Government's strategy for improving the civil justice response to domestic violence primarily relates to enhancing the process for enforcing civil orders once breached. In the past there have clearly been some difficulties with the effective enforcement of injunctions. This chapter will examine whether the provisions for strengthening enforcement, in the Domestic Violence, Crime and Victims Act 2004, are well placed to remedy the previous deficiencies in enforcement. However the question of enforcement only becomes relevant once an order is in place and, as was seen in the previous chapter, obtaining a protective order in itself can be a significant challenge for victims of domestic violence. The remedies available under the Family Law Act 1996 rely on action taken by the victim to secure protection; an 'associated person' can apply but no-one can apply on her behalf. In some other jurisdictions, third parties such as social workers or police officers can apply for protective orders on behalf of victims of domestic violence. There is an unimplemented provision in the Family Law Act 1996 for designated third parties to apply for protection orders on behalf of victims of domestic violence in England and Wales. This chapter will consider whether this provision ought to be implemented and whether it has any potential to bring about significant improvements in the civil justice response to victims of domestic violence.

Obtaining an order—time for third party applications?

The Family Law Act 1996 was designed to provide victims of domestic violence with easy access to a single set of remedies in all courts with family law jurisdiction. It undoubtedly streamlined the complex patchwork of provisions that existed previously, but in one respect the legislation brought no change; the onus is still upon the victim of domestic violence to seek a remedy for herself. The victim of domestic violence must initiate the application for protective order, although in that respect she may be supported by outside agencies and have a solicitor acting on her behalf. Sometimes the solicitor will be paid for by public funds—but not always, and as has been seen the financial costs can amount to a significant barrier in seeking redress for domestic violence under the civil law. One possible solution to the difficulties, financial and otherwise, that victims of domestic violence encounter in obtaining a remedy under the Family Law Act is to allow someone else, perhaps a public service agency, to seek remedies on her behalf. The Family Law Act 1996, s 60 contains a provision that would allow, subject to further regulations, a third party to apply for a protection order on behalf of a victim of domestic violence.

The Family Law Act 1996, s 60 was not implemented at the time the rest of the Act came into force in October 1997 because it was envisaged that there would be a period of bedding down for the new non-molestation and occupation orders before reconsideration of the advantages of allowing third parties to apply for them (Law Commission, 1992). The Law Commission could see that there were strong arguments for third party applications for protection orders and noted that there was empirical evidence that such applications worked effectively in some other jurisdictions. The apparent successes of third party applications in Australia fuelled calls for s 60 to be implemented in England and Wales, despite concerns about some of the drawbacks with the third party procedure (Humphreys and Kaye, 1997). Five years after the Family Law Act 1996 came into force the Government decided to commission research to examine service provider's views on how the civil remedies under the Family Law Act were working and whether s 60 ought to be implemented (Burton et al, 2002; Burton, 2003a). Some of the views on the effectiveness of the remedies without the third party provision were examined in the previous chapter; this chapter will concentrate on perspectives on the potential value of third party applications in England and Wales.

The research examined the perspectives of a wide range of service providers in domestic violence cases, including the judiciary, solicitors, prosecutors, police officers, social workers, housing officers, and voluntary sector support agencies such as refuge workers and independent advocacy support workers for women and children. The majority of the 60 service providers interviewed supported the implementation of s 60 to allow for third party applications to be made for non-molestation and occupation orders. There were a variety of different reasons for supporting implementation but the main reason was to remove the burden of seeking the order from the victim, with a consequent removal of the fear of intimidation and feelings of guilt associated with seeking an order.

In some ways it can be argued that the rationale for implementing third party application is paternalistic; it assumes that the victim of domestic violence is incapable of trying to protect herself from harm and needs someone else to do it for her. Echoes of this paternalistic perspective were evident in some of the statements made by service providers who supported implementation of third party applications. Service providers spoke of victims whose self-esteem was so eroded by years of domestic violence that they were incapable of seeing that they were in need of a remedy, let alone applying for one on their own behalf. The disempowerment of women who had experienced years of systematic abuse was non-cyclical on this view; it was a gradual process of erosion whereby the victim would never regain the resources required to seek a remedy and escape a violent relationship without the help of a third party. The assistance of the third party itself was not viewed as further disempowering because the victim was effectively regarded as in a situation where she had no power left to lose; implicit in this however is no acknowledgement of the transfer of power from the perpetrator to the third party. Some service providers were conscious that third party applications could be simply replacing one form of control, that exerted by the perpetrator, with another, that wielded by the third party applicant for a protective order. The process of successfully obtaining an order on one's own behalf was regarded by some as an empowering experience, which could potentially go some way to restoring the self-confidence lost through years of domestic abuse. Others pointed out that if victims of domestic violence successfully overcome all the obstacles that they face in seeking civil remedies themselves then this is something that they are proud of, but on the other hand if it leaves them sapped of energy and disillusioned with the legal process they may be reluctant to return to court for enforcement if the order is breached.

The process of seeking a protective order can be either punishing or rewarding, the experiences of victims of domestic violence are not uniform in this respect, as they are not in many others. Some victims of domestic violence, for example those who have independent advocacy support, tend to get more support through the legal process than those who do not (Kelly and Humphreys, 2001). One of the key differences that independent advocacy support can make to a victim of domestic violence is having someone who believes in her experience and can empathise with her situation. Some service providers felt an advantage of third party applications would be having a person, the third party, who believed them and could help to rebuild their confidence not only through the outcome (the obtaining of the order) but through the process. However, perhaps it should be noted that this perceived benefit does not automatically flow from third party applications—the extent to which victims feel that they have someone who believes them would probably depend greatly on who the third party was. Taking action on someone's behalf does not, of itself, imply acceptance and understanding of their situation.

One of the most commonly expressed reasons for removing the burden of seeking civil protection orders from the victim was to create a 'smokescreen' for the perpetrator of the abuse. Many victims of domestic violence certainly fear reprisals if they seek legal remedies against their abuser. Service providers interviewed for the s 60 evaluation commonly expressed the view that the fear of reprisals would diminish if a third party were responsible for seeking the civil order. This reasoning partly turns on how the perpetrator perceives the third party intervention. If the third party intervention is perceived by the perpetrator to be under the real control of the victim then perhaps much or all of this perceived benefit is lost. Perpetrators may feel that the third party intervention is always under the control of the victim because if the victim had concealed the abuse more effectively from all outside scrutiny then no third party could intervene. Thus, in the perpetrator's analysis, the third party can only intervene if the victim has alerted them to behaviour which would justify the making of a protective order. Furthermore, the role of the victim in relation to the third party application may place some of the burden and responsibility for obtaining the order back in her hands, opening her up directly to the danger of reprisals and intimidation that third party applications are designed in part to overcome.

Whilst a third party could, if s 60 were implemented, formally make the application for an order on behalf of a victim of domestic violence, some of the evidential burden would seem likely to fall back upon the victim. Unless there were independent witnesses who were willing to testify to the abuse, or other evidence that could discharge the civil test of balance of probabilities, the victim would need to provide evidence to support the application. If the victim needs to provide evidence to support the application, the matter is not completely out of her hands and she may be vulnerable to intimidation to withdraw her evidence, or reprisals if she goes ahead and gives evidence in a civil case. Roughly one-quarter of the service providers interviewed by Burton (2003a) commented that third party applications would probably not reduce the victim's fear of reprisals because the perpetrator would still feel that the victim had some role in the application being made, either an evidential role, or simply alerting the third party to the existence of the violence.

Third party applications involve a number of tradeoffs in terms of the scope of the powers and the perceived detriments and benefits. If the scope of the power is limited to the extent that the third party can only apply with the consent of the victim, the potential benefit of removing the burden from the victim is diminished. However if the consent of the victim is not required then this may reinforce the lack of power and control the victim has experienced as a result of the abuse. The majority of the service providers who were interviewed about their views on implementing s 60 stated that the victim's consent should be an absolute requirement of the application: less than a quarter felt there were circumstances in which the victim's consent could be dispensed with. There is some overlap here with the discussion about the merits of mandatory prosecution, which will be taken up in a subsequent chapter, but even amongst respondents who could see the arguments in favour of mandatory prosecution there was some reluctance to support obtaining civil orders without the victim's consent. Partly the arguments against seeking protective orders without the consent of the victim are pragmatic; if the victim does not consent then the order may be of limited value because its enforcement relies, in many situations, on her cooperation in reporting breaches.

The reforms discussed in this chapter involve an actual, or at least potential, blurring of the boundaries between the civil and criminal justice responses to domestic violence. The potential blurring of the boundaries with third party applications comes with the issue of the identity of the third party applicant. When the Law Commission (2002) considered the issue of third party applications in the run up to the Family Law Act 1996, it envisaged that it would be the police who would be granted powers to apply for civil protective orders as a third party because they are already involved in enforcing the criminal law in situations of domestic violence and have a clear role in protecting individuals from violence. That the Commission had confidence that the police would act with proper motives and the victim's interests would be foremost seems implicit in their statement that; 'It would be difficult to ensure that other categories of representation were always acting from proper motives and with the interests of the victim at heart'. Although service providers interviewed by Burton (2003a) saw some advantages in authorising the police as third party applicants, they did not display the same confidence as the Law Commission, particularly in relation to the perceived benefit of the order carrying greater authority because it is obtained by an agency whom perpetrators might be 'scared' of or 'respect'. Respondents were concerned that police officers might be tempted to use their third party powers to apply for civil orders as an alternative to criminal prosecution in situations where a prosecution might be a better alternative. There was therefore a fear that the introduction of new third party powers in the hands of the police would reinforce the traditional public/private dichotomy whereby domestic violence is seen primarily as a civil/private matter rather and a public/criminal matter. In addition to this the 'service' victims received from the police might be greatly diminished by their lack of competence in the civil arena when compared with criminal proceedings. Alternatively, obtaining an order was thought by some to give a greater sense of ownership of that order, the implication being that the police would be keener to enforce orders that they had obtained via third party powers than orders obtained by the victim herself.

The Government decided not to go ahead with implementing the Family Law Act 1996, s 60, despite the fact that many service providers were in favour of the provision being brought into force, especially if voluntary sector support agencies were granted the powers to act as third party applicants. Whether women's voluntary support agencies would have welcomed the role is uncertain. In the eyes of other service providers, they are the agencies most likely to inspire trust and feelings of safety amongst victims. It should be noted however that very few women access refuge services and there are resource issues with the existing level of service provision (Dobash and Dobash, 1992). Expanding into a third party role could therefore put further strain on resources and perhaps upset the balance of the relationship between the victim and refuge (Burton, 2003a). Nonetheless, a significant proportion of victims interviewed for one study (Humphreys and Thiara, 2002) said that they would have preferred someone to be able to make an application for a civil order on their behalf. These women were apparently not asked their views on who that third party should be, however it would not be surprising, given their evaluations of services provided by various agencies (Humphreys and Thiara, 2002), if refuge workers and advocacy services came out top of victims' preferred third party applicants. The financial costs for voluntary sector support agencies would probably be a significant obstacle to them acting as third party to seek civil orders. Given that one of the key reasons for a quarter of respondents supporting the implementation of third party applications was to reduce the financial burden on the victim of applying for the order herself, it might be more appropriate to go for a direct solution of improving public funding of applications for domestic violence remedies. To view third party applications as a solution to a 'financial problem' of seeking protection is simply to move the problem around the system; someone is going to end up paying for the obtaining of the order somewhere down the line. If it is the police then the buck ultimately stops with the state, but the danger is that seeking civil remedies would not be very high priority in terms of allocation of the police resources. It is difficult, given all the pros and cons outlined above, to come to a firm conclusion on whether the decision not to implement s 60 is to be regretted. On balance, bearing in mind the benefits of a similar provisions in Australia (Alexander, 2002), perhaps a pilot of third party applications in England and Wales should have been tried. A pilot would have enabled a fuller assessment of the implications of implementing the provision and could have monitored any adverse effects of authorising agencies such as the police as third party applicants. No mention was made of s 60 in *Safety and Justice* (Home Office, 2003), so it must be concluded that implementation will not be part of the Government strategy for dealing with domestic violence in England and Wales for the foreseeable future. Instead the emphasis is upon strengthening the regime for imposing protective orders in criminal proceedings and improving the enforcement of protective orders once imposed

Enforcing orders—criminalisation of breach

The Government's White Paper, *Justice for All* (2002), first signalled that consideration was being given to making breach of a non-molestation order obtained under the Family Law Act 1996 a criminal offence. Shortly afterwards the Government announced that it proposed to criminalise breach of non-molestation and occupation orders so that the police always had powers of arrest (Home Office, 2003). The Government expressed concern that the enforcement of orders was dependent on whether the court attached a power of arrest and even in instances where a power was attached it was felt police officers were unclear about the scope of their powers because the power might only relate to part of the order and information about the power might not effectively filter through to the police. The Government referred to a provision in Northern Ireland, where breach of protective orders in domestic violence cases already constituted an arrestable offence, and noted that this appeared to be working well to effectively protect victims of domestic violence. The reservations of some commentators, for example that criminalising breach would put victims under increased pressure to accept undertakings instead of court orders, were thought to be outweighed by the potential benefits of criminalisation. Thus, the Domestic Violence, Crimes and Victims Act 2004 (DVCVA), s 1 (which was brought into force in July 2007) made breach of non-molestation orders obtained under Part IV the Family Law Act 1996 a criminal offence.

It is still early days for evaluating whether criminalising breaches of non-molestation orders will enhance the enforcement of these orders in the way the Government envisaged. By making breach a criminal offence the Government signalled that domestic violence is a serious matter and reaffirmed their political commitment to improving the legal response to the problem. However it could be argued that the reform has simply blurred the already unclear boundaries between the civil and criminal justice response to domestic violence, and in some respects may prove counter-productive in-so-sfar as victims of domestic violence are concerned (Burton, 2003b).

There can be little doubt that there were genuine concerns about the poor enforcement of civil orders prior to criminalisation of breach. As was highlighted in the previous chapter, the procedure of enforcement via committal proceedings for contempt provided the courts with limited options for dealing with the offender. Few offenders were imprisoned and fines can actually be detrimental for victims of domestic violence. By making breach of protective orders a criminal offence the courts have opened up the range of penalties that may be imposed, including the possibility of the offender being sentenced to attend a perpetrator programme.

Recent guidance on appropriate sentencing for domestic violence cases will be considered in detail in the next chapter, but it is appropriate here to look at what this guidance says about sentencing for breach of protective orders. The Sentencing Guidelines Council (SGC) has issued guidance which states the purpose of sentencing breach of a protective order is to ensure that the victim is protected from harm; the primary aim should be to ensure that the order is complied with and achieves the protection that was intended (SGC, 2006b). This reflects the position in relation to sentencing for contempt; that the primary purpose should be to protect the victim, although in some cases the courts seem to have confused the functions of imprisonment in the context of criminal and civil proceedings (*Hale v Tanner* [2000] 1 WLR 2377; Kay, 2001). In fact it seems that protection of the victim was only one, possibly subsidiary, function of imprisoning the defendant for contempt. It appeared an important objective was also to mark the disapproval of the court; punishing the defendant for flouting a court order, rather than to ensure future compliance (*Thorpe v Thorpe* [1988] 2 FLR 127). Some commentators suggested that committal proceedings placed too little emphasis on protection (Burton, 2003b). In this sense the SGC emphasis on trying to ensure that the protective order is complied with may be welcomed. The availability of community based penalties may provide the courts with more effective means of trying to meet this primary objective. The guidance indicates that for many breaches the starting point will be a custodial sentence. However in appropriate cases, if the court is satisfied that the defendant genuinely intends to reform his behaviour and there is a real prospect of rehabilitation, the court may impose a community sentence with requirement to attend an accredited perpetrator programme as an alternative to a short custodial sentence that might otherwise have been imposed.

It has been argued that the benefits of criminalising breach of protective orders, at least in terms of extending the sentencing options, could have been achieved by simply amending sanctions for civil contempt (Burton, 2003b). This option would have had the benefit of preserving some of the distinctions between civil and criminal proceedings which can, in some cases, work in favour of the victim. In criminal proceedings, in theory, the victim lacks decision-making capacity once the matter comes to attention of the police. The civil process is much more under the control of the victim who can choose to initiate proceedings for contempt and also withdraw from those proceedings if she wishes. The differences between the criminal and civil routes for enforcement are in fact not so clear. In practice the victim may effectively control the outcome of criminal proceedings by withdrawing her complaint, although the prospect always exists for her to be compelled to support a prosecution against her wishes (see Chapter 6). Nonetheless, the role of the victim is more prominent in civil proceedings, so criminalising breach can be said to have curtailed her choices to the extent that the police and prosecutors may choose to take action against her wishes.

It may be that the prospect of the criminal justice agencies taking action for breaches against the victim's wishes is more a theoretical concern than a practical problem. The alternative concern is that the police and prosecutors will fail to act on breaches as a criminal matter and the victim will be left to seek enforcement via the contempt route which is preserved by the DVCVA. In one sense it could be argued that a victim left to enforce the order herself via contempt proceedings is no worse off than she was before the provision for criminalisation came into force, however this view is arguably flawed. The victim may be left with a period of uncertainty about whether the criminal justice agencies intend to take action in relation to the breach. The police and CPS may take several weeks to decide whether they are going to initiate a prosecution, if they do they can always subsequently decide not to go ahead. Experience with other civil orders, such as Anti-Social Behaviour Orders, where the police have powers to respond to breaches as a criminal matter, suggests that the police do not always regard enforcement as a high priority (Campbell, 2002). Police officers and prosecutors may perhaps regard the nature of the breach as too trivial to warrant prosecution in some cases. Another potential problem is that the CPS may drop prosecutions for breach in favour of prosecuting a substantive linked offence.

The SGC (2006b) notes that where breach of a protective order constitutes a substantive offence it is desirable that both the breach and the substantive offence should be charged as separate counts, and where necessary consecutive sentences should be imposed to reflect the seriousness and totality of the offending. However it notes that on some occasions only the substantive offence, or only the breach, will be charged, and gives the courts guidance on how to sentence to reflect the totality of the offending. Basically, if the substantive offence only is charged, breach of a protective order should be regarded as an aggravating feature. If only the breach is charged, the sentence should reflect the nature of the breach (the conduct amounting to a substantive offence) aggravated by the breach. In either scenario the result should be the same as if both the breach and substantive offence had been charged. If this guidance is implemented successfully it should mean that appropriate weight is given to the seriousness of breaches in cases where the CPS prosecutes either for the breach or a substantive linked offence, or both. In most cases there will be a relevant substantive linked offence which can be charged, not least because of the provisions in the Protection from Harassment Act 1997 that considerably extended the scope of the criminal law in responding to domestic violence (see next chapter). There will probably be very few cases where criminalisation of breaches of protective order extends the scope of the previously existing criminal law to respond to domestic violence (Burton, 2003), however one danger envisaged was a reduction in the availability of the civil law remedies.

The difficulty envisaged related to the evidential requirements for obtaining civil orders. The standard of proof in civil proceedings is normally lower than in criminal proceedings and the rules on admissibility of evidence are generally more generous (Redmayne, 1999). However in relation to ASBOs the courts imposed a higher standard on the making of the civil order taking into account the fact that breach was punishable as a criminal offence (McCann [2002] 3 WLR 1313; MacDonald, 2003). It was speculated that the criminalisation of breaches of protective orders under the Family Law Act 1996 might result in a higher standard of proof being applied to the making of the original order, thus making it more difficult for victims of domestic violence to obtain protective orders. Subsequent case law gave reason to think that this anticipated detriment would not in fact arise. In *Hipgrave v Jones* [2005] 2 FLR 174 the Court of Appeal considered the standard of proof to be applied in making restraining orders under the Protection from Harassment Act 1997 (PHA), which have potential criminal sanctions for breach. The court draws a distinction between ASBOs sought by public authorities and aimed at preventing crime and disorder, and injunctions under the PHA which are concerned with the protection of the rights of an individual. In relation to injunctions under the PHA it was asserted that the civil standard of proof applied, despite the fact that breach could be treated as a criminal offence. By analogy, the provisions for criminalising breach of protective orders under the DVCVA should not lead to a higher standard of proof being applied to the making of non-molestation orders (Hitchings, 2005). Protective orders under Part IV of the Family Law Act

1996 are arguably more akin to injunctions under the PHA than ASBOs. Because one objection to criminalising breaches of protective orders has apparently gone, this does not mean that no difficulties will be encountered. It is still plausible to argue that the wider consequences of conviction for a criminal offence will result in more respondents contesting applications for protective orders in the first place and more contested proceedings for breach (Burton, 2003b).

It is important to acknowledge the potential that criminalising of breaches of protective orders has for enhancing the legal protection offered to victims of domestic violence. The Australian experience, as with third party applications, shows some of the benefits of taking the onus of the victim by making the police responsible for enforcing protection orders (Alexander, 2002; Burton, 2003). However it too highlights the pitfalls, in particular the potential that victims themselves may be prosecuted for aiding and abetting the criminal offence of breach. In England and Wales such a prosecution is highly unlikely, but it is very plausible that defence lawyers will seek to rely on the victim's alleged collusion in mitigation of breach. As will be seen in the next chapter, the current sentencing guidelines currently note victim-initiated contact as a mitigating factor in sentencing. This is arguably a flawed approach, and if followed by the courts, suggests that criminalising breaches of protective orders will do little to ensure that the civil law response to domestic violence is given some 'teeth'.

Civil protective orders in criminal proceedings

In addition to criminalising breaches of protective orders the Government strategy for enhancing the legal protection offered to victims of domestic violence included extending restraining orders to make them available when the courts sentence for any offence of violence (Home Office, 2003). Controversially the Government also proposed making restraining orders available to criminal courts when there is insufficient evidence to convict but the court considers it necessary to make an order to protect the victim. This proposal demonstrates most clearly the blurring of the boundaries between the civil and the criminal law. The idea of imposing restraining orders on acquittal provoked objections on grounds of anticipated miscarriages of justice and violations of the defendant's rights (Collinson, 2004). Whilst advocates of the proposal thought it was a waste of time and money to require a victim of domestic violence to go to another court to obtain protection when the criminal court was already in a position to deal with the matter, others thought that the evidential and procedural issues might be too challenging: 'The problem could be most acute in the magistrates' court where a bench of magistrates will come to the conclusion that the evidence is insufficient for guilt on the criminal standard, but will then be required to consider whether an restraining order should be made on the civil standard of proof. There may be a temptation for the bench to 'fudge' the issue on this and to make some sort of order against the defendant, perhaps thinking that the CPS would not have brought proceedings in the first place without good reason. Things may be worse in the Crown Court where the judge may regard the jury's acquittal of the defendant on the criminal charge as perverse and may decide to make a restraining order to redress the balance' (Collinson, 2004, p 69).

At the time of writing the provisions in DVCVA, s 12 for extending the powers of the court to make restraining orders upon conviction and acquittal have not been brought into force. The reforms, if implemented, have potential to afford much greater access to civil remedies to victims of domestic violence. Victims would not have to go to the civil courts to secure the restraining orders if they were involved in an incident resulting in a criminal prosecution. However the effectiveness of the new remedies would depend a great deal upon how the courts and prosecuting authorities responded. Restraining orders have not always been imposed in cases where defendants have been convicted of offences under the PHA (Harris, 2000). Collinson (2004) might therefore be over-anticipating the willingness of the courts to make orders where the defendant is acquitted in criminal proceedings.

Conclusion

There can be little doubt that the civil justice response to domestic violence is in need of significant improvement. The DVCVA presented the ideal opportunity for the Government to implement reforms, supplemented by non-legislative action, to ensure a more effective civil justice response to domestic violence. Yet, although it was haled as 'the biggest overhaul of the law on domestic violence since the 1970's' (Blunkett, Home Office Press Release, 26 November 2003), the changes introduced by the DVCVA were in the main quite minor compared with, for example, the Family Law Act 1996 and the Protection from Harassment Act 1997. Some of the key provisions in the DVCVA, which have the potential to help victims of domestic violence, such as extending restraining orders, are yet to be implemented. The criminalisation of breaches of protective orders has now been implemented but it has been argued in this chapter that the consequences of this may be detrimental to victims of domestic violence and will not necessarily enhance the protection offered to them by the legal system. The DVCVA does represent a departure from the traditional approach of compartmentalising the criminal and civil justice responses to domestic violence, but overall it looks like a missed opportunity. The courts may struggle with the fusing of the criminal and civil responses to domestic violence in the absence of an integrated court that can deal with domestic violence in a truly holistic way (Burton, 2004). Chapter 8 will revisit the question of the development of an integrated domestic violence court, capable of dealing with all domestic violence related matters. This chapter has already shifted the focus of legal responses to domestic violence from the realms of civil law and the civil justice system to the criminal law and criminal justice system, the next two chapters will bring these to the fore.

5   The criminal law

Slow or no recognition

There is no specific offence of domestic violence in English criminal law. Police and prosecutors have to rely on the same non-fatal and fatal offences against the person that may be prosecuted in relation to interpersonal violence perpetrated against a stranger. Many existing criminal law offences apply to domestic violence, such as assault, false imprisonment, harassment, rape, criminal damage, attempted murder, and in cases of fatal violence, murder and manslaughter. In some instances the general criminal law has evolved specifically to take into account the position of victims of domestic violence. The abolition of the marital rape exemption in 1991 is one example of how the substantive criminal law has evolved to take into account the position of spouses subjected to serious domestic violence. The law for the first time, in theory at least, gave wives access to a criminal prosecution when raped by their husbands. Another notable example of a change to the criminal law which had significant implications for victims of domestic violence and was, in part at least, specifically directed at improving their position, is the development of the defence of provocation on a charge of murder. These examples of the criminal law being adapted to accommodate the experiences of victims of domestic violence can be usefully examined for what they tell us about evolving judicial attitudes towards domestic violence. However it should be remembered that it is the attitudes of the senior judiciary that are being examined and that these may not necessarily be reflected in the day-to-day practices of the courts lower down the hierarchy. It is not necessarily the scope of substantive criminal offences which have proved problematic in the criminal law response to domestic violence, although in some instances they have. In general however, it is the responses of criminal justice agencies such as the police and CPS and the courts of first instance that have posed the most significant obstacles to achieving effective protection from domestic violence under the criminal law. This tension has already been noted in other contexts and serves as a reminder that the law in action does not always reflect the law in books. This theme will be re-examined in the next chapter; this chapter concentrates on the substantive criminal law and its application to domestic violence. Reference will also be made to the sentencing guidelines for relevant crimes and the insights these provide into the grading of offences in the domestic context compared with those perpetrated against strangers.

Non-fatal offences against the person

The main statute that applies in cases of interpersonal violence is the Offences Against the Person Act 1861 (OAPA). There are a range of offences that can be prosecuted under the OAPA, including assault occasioning actual bodily harm (ABH) (s 47), threats to kill (s 16), malicious wounding and inflicting grievous bodily harm (s 20) and wounding and causing grievous bodily harm with intent (s 18). Most of these offences, except s 18, are triable either way and can be dealt with in either the magistrates' or Crown Court. On the bottom rung of the hierarchy of assaults is the offence of common assault (Criminal Justice Act 1988, s 39), which is triable in the magistrates' court only. Assault can be by words or actual force; it is sufficient for the victim to apprehend imminent force, or in the case of force being applied the merest touching of another in anger is adequate. If there is no injury, provided the defendant had *mens rea*, common assault is the most relevant offence. If there is injury, depending on nature and degree of severity of the injury and the defendant's *mens rea*, one of the aggravated offences under the OAPA might be charged. There is no space here for a full account of the requirements of the various offences (see Ashworth, 2006; Clarkson et al, 2007); the purpose is to highlight particular features of the offences which make them more or less suitable in their application to domestic violence. In addition, the Protection from Harassment Act 1997 (PHA) will be considered in some detail as the two new criminal offences created by the PHA have particular relevance for domestic violence.

The different manifestations of domestic violence have not always been readily accommodated within the general criminal law of non-fatal offences against the person (Edwards, 1996, pp 180–189). The definition of domestic violence discussed in Chapter 1 shows that there is now broad acceptance, including amongst the criminal justice agencies, that domestic violence is not limited to physical violence but includes emotional or psychological abuse. Psychological or emotional abuse has been one area in which, traditionally, there has been limited redress under the criminal law. Historically the criminal law has focused on physical injury and neglected psychiatric injury as a form of harm. This changed to some extent with the landmark judgment in *R v Ireland and R v Burstow* [1997] 4 All ER 225.

Ireland and Burstow was not a domestic violence case, the appeal concerned one defendant, Ireland, charged with s 47 ABH as a result of making silent phone calls (occasionally heavy breathing) to three different women, and another, Burstow, charged with s 20 maliciously inflicting grievous bodily harm as result of an 8-month campaign of stalking which resulted in his victim suffering a severe depressive illness. One of the main questions that the courts had to consider was whether phone calls could amount to an assault because the defendant was not present in the same room as the victim, therefore arguably she could not apprehend immediate force. The House of Lords stretched the definition of immediacy, perhaps further than was really necessary (Wells, 1997). This flexibility has potential to assist in domestic violence cases where the victim apprehends imminent force but the defendant is not in her physical presence. Of greater potential significance for cases of domestic violence, is the extension of the meaning of bodily harm.

In Ireland and Burstow the House of Lords extended the concept of bodily harm to include harm to the mind in cases where there is recognisable psychiatric injury. Lord Steyn observed: 'The appeals under consideration do not involve structural injuries to the brain . . . [nor] . . . psychotic illnesses or personality disorders . . . [they involve] . . . mental disturbances of a lesser order, namely neurotic disorders.' He stated that neurotic disorders such as anxiety disorders or depressive disorders 'must be distinguished from simple states of fear, or problems in copying with everyday life', however neuroses are recognisable psychiatric injuries and, as such, under the authority of *Chan-Fook* [1994] 1 WLR 689 can amount to bodily harm. He concluded: 'I would hold that "bodily harm" in ss 18, 20 and 47 must be interpreted so as to include recognisable psychiatric illness.' By extending the definition of bodily harm to include anxiety disorders and depressive disorders, the House of Lords paved the way for the psychological effects of domestic violence on victims to be covered by the criminal law of assault. It is important to note however, states of mind which are not supported by medical evidence of psychiatric injury are still not covered by the criminal law of assault.

The insistence upon a clinically recognised condition may perhaps be unduly restrictive in domestic violence cases. The unfortunate consequences of this restriction were evident in the case of *R v D* (2006) 2 Cr App R 24. In this case the victim of domestic abuse committed suicide and her husband was prosecuted for unlawful act manslaughter. In order to succeed the prosecution had to show that there was an unlawful and dangerous act. The victim had kept a diary of the abuse in the five months preceding her death which recorded two incidents of physical assault. There was also medical evidence and statements from close relatives. There was an incident of physical abuse on the evening the victim took her life; the defendant had struck her on the forehead, but the prosecution did not feel able to establish a causal connection between the physical assaults and the victim's death. Instead the CPS constructed the manslaughter charge upon an offence contrary to OAPA, s 20. The essence of the allegation was that the defendant had, by repeated psychological abuse and some physical abuse, inflicted serious psychological injury on the victim. The prosecution sought evidence from three psychiatric experts; two of the three could not make a definitive diagnosis of psychiatric illness. Unsurprisingly, they were hampered by the fact that the victim was dead. Reviewing the available evidence one expert concluded that the victim was 'experiencing psychological systems consequent upon her protracted experience of domestic violence' but despite 'some features of depression' recorded in the victim's diary she did not believe the victim was suffering clinical depression. The other expert could not make a diagnosis of identifiable psychiatric illness but did believe that the victim's experiences would have impacted on her psychological functioning and that psychological impact of the assault on the day of her death would have been greatly magnified by her previous experiences of domestic violence. The prosecution failed because the court applied the authority of *Chan-Fook* and *Ireland and Burstow*, adhering to the view that bodily harm requires recognisable psychiatric injury. Whilst come commentators argue that there was a route to conviction in the case (Horder and McGowan, 2006), the reaffirmation of the limitations of psychiatric injury may nevertheless continue to be problematic for victims of domestic violence who lack a definitive medical diagnosis of the serious psychiatric harm they have suffered as a result of years of domestic violence.

The creation of two new criminal offences by the PHA did open up new possibilities for criminal prosecutions in domestic violence cases. Although the legislation was introduced to tackle stalkers, research suggests that it has been used far more to deal with domestic violence than the stalking of strangers scenario that the legislators had in mind (Harris, 2000). The PHA creates both civil remedies and criminal offences and creates a link between the two by making a breach of a protective order, which may be made in either civil or criminal proceedings, a criminal offence. Although the civil aspects of the legislation are rarely used when compared with the criminal (Harris, 2000), it is one of the early examples of breach of a civil order being made a criminal offence, and as such has proved a useful comparison for the provision in the DVCVA 2004 examined in the previous chapter. In this chapter the focus is upon the two criminal offences of harassment created by the PHA, but of course the breach offences are criminal offences that can be prosecuted in the context of domestic violence and their importance is worth remembering here.

The PHA creates a criminal offence of harassment which is defined as pursuing a course of conduct which amounts to harassment of another and which the defendant knows or ought to know amounts to harassment (s 1). This offence is summary only and carries a maximum penalty of six-months' imprisonment. Section 4 of the PHA creates the more serious offence of pursuing a course of conduct which causes another to fear, on at least two occasions, that violence will be used against him. This is a triable either way offence, which is punishable by up to five-years' imprisonment in the Crown Court. To be convicted the defendant must either know or ought to know that his course of conduct will cause another to fear violence on each of the occasions If convicted of either of these offences, as mentioned above, a restraining order can be made by the court prohibiting the offender from further similar conduct.

The PHA has been welcomed by groups who offer support and campaign on behalf of victims of domestic violence, for example the Women's Aid Federation of England (WAFE). The director of WAFE and a WAFE researcher have argued that 'For women who have never lived or no longer live with their abuser, the introduction of new criminal offences for "stalking" under the Protection from Harassment Act 1997, may provide more effective protection in these cases than there has been available heretofore' (Harwin and Barron, 2000, p 212). WAFE also applauds the fact that the focus is upon the defendant's conduct and that this is judged objectively. The term defendant 'ought to know' means that the defendant can be convicted if any 'reasonable person' in possession of the same information would have known that such conduct would amount to harassment or put a person in fear of violence. WAFE sees the PHA plugging some of the gaps left by the offences against the person which require psychological injury: 'it will allow the courts to deal with serious stalking without having to wait until psychological or bodily harm is caused' (WAFE). Although the Public Order Act 1986 has a range of overlapping criminal offences, the distinct advantage of the PHA is the power to impose a restraining order on conviction. The victim then gets the equivalent of an injunction that she might have pursued under the Family Law Act 1996, but without the expense of pursuing it herself. Of course criminal proceedings are not 'cost free' for victims, but they do not bear the same financial burden that they might otherwise incur in pursing a civil remedy, especially if they are eligible for legal aid. The enforcement provisions for restraining orders are now the equivalent to those for an injunction under the Family Law Act so there is no advantage, or disadvantage, for victims in that respect.

Sentencing domestic violence

The Sentencing Guidelines Council (SGC) has now issued definitive guidance on the sentencing of domestic violence (SGC, 2006a). The guideline states 'offences committed in the domestic context should be regarded as being no less serious than offences committed in a non-domestic context'. In fact, it is stated, the domestic context may result in aggravating factors that make an offence more serious. The guideline provides a non-exhaustive list of aggravating and mitigating factors in the context of domestic violence. An abuse of trust or power is said to be an aggravating feature of some offences. It could be argued that all offences of domestic violence involve an abuse of trust or power and the SGC recognises this argument and notes that many offences of domestic violence will display this feature. Nevertheless it maintains that there may be some instances of domestic violence, for example involving former partners who have been separated for a long time, where abuse of trust and power is not such a significant feature. A second aggravating feature is said to be the vulnerability of the victim. There are a range of factors highlighted which potentially make the victim more vulnerable, for example cultural and language barriers. The SGC does not say these factors should aggravate the offence per se, but where the defendant has exploited the vulnerability, for example to prevent the victim seeking help, then this may be regarded as an aggravating feature. The exposure of children, either directly or indirectly, to domestic violence is noted as an aggravating feature. This factor is based on substantial empirical research demonstrating the adverse impact of domestic violence upon children. In addition the SGC lists, as a separate aggravating feature, the exploitation of contact arrangements to commit domestic violence. Again empirical research suggests that child contact arrangements can prove a significant danger for women and children trying to escape domestic violence. It has been noted in a previous chapter that the family courts have not always been robust in preventing contact being used as a means of ongoing abuse. One of the key limitations of the criminal law is its inability to recognise a history of domestic violence and its cumulative impact on the victim due to the fact that it tends to focus on single incidents, with the exception of the PHA. This has been one of the arguments for a separate offence of domestic violence (see below). The guidelines indicate that, if possible, the cumulative effect of a series of incidents or threats over a long period should be taken into account as an aggravating feature, however this can only be done where the conduct has been proved or accepted. In cases where the defendant has a previous conviction for a domestic violence related incident then this will be an aggravating feature under the Criminal Justice Act 2003, s 143(2). An offence committed in breach of a protective order or conditional discharge is noted as an aggravating feature, although separate guidance is given on sentencing breaches of protective orders. Finally, if the victim is forced to leave home as a consequence of the offence this is to be regarded as an aggravating feature.

The factors which it is stated may mitigate the seriousness of the offence can include the defendant's good character. The inclusion of this factor is controversial since, as the Women's National Commission pointed out in their response to the Sentencing Advisory Panel consultation, 'Perpetrators regularly appear charming and in control and often "win over" officials in the system when compared with women' (WNC, 2004). The SGC acknowledges that the defendant may display a different persona in public and recommend that no account be taken of good character where there is a proven pattern of behaviour. Nevertheless it is asserted that good character is relevant mitigation in cases where the court is satisfied that the offence was an isolated incident. The SGC includes 'provocation' as a potential mitigating factor. Again this is controversial given the historical claim that the criminal justice agencies have regularly taken into account departures from traditional stereotypical notions of appropriate wifely behaviour, in many cases of an extremely trivial nature, as 'provocation' (Edwards, 1987). The SGC qualifies the inclusion of provocation as mitigation by asserting that great care should be taken with this factor and normally it should relate to actual or anticipated violence. However the inclusion of 'psychological bullying' as potential provocation means that the courts will need to be very sensitive in their handling of this criterion if they are to free themselves from criticism that alleged 'nagging' of a low-level nature is regarded as provocation for serious domestic violence.

The SGC outlines other factors which may be relevant to the sentencing of domestic violence and these include the wishes of the victim. In general the wishes of the victim are not a significant factor in sentencing decisions, and this is defended on the basis that it would result in sentencing disparity; some victims may be particularly vengeful, others particularly forgiving. Taking into account the victim's views as to appropriate sentence would distort the proportionality principle that the seriousness of the offence should be the primary determinant of sentence (Ashworth, 2005). In the context of domestic violence the victim's wishes have the added complexity that they may not be freely expressed. The SGC notes that in the domestic violence context it may be particularly important to observe the general principle that offence seriousness, and not the victim's wishes, is the key determinant of sentence for three reasons; first it is undesirable for victims of domestic violence to feel responsibility for the sentence imposed, second, the victim's wishes may be induced by fear or threats made by the defendant and third, the risk of such threats would increase if the victim's wishes were taken into account. Yet the SGC was keen to accommodate the situation where the victim might be in a continuing relationship with the defendant which, in its view, might be relevant to the type of sentence given. Thus the guidance states that the expressed wish of the victim for the relationship to continue may be a relevant factor in sentencing provided the court is satisfied the wish 'is genuine, and that giving effect to it will not expose the victim to a real risk of further violence'. These conditions may be difficult to establish but the guidance makes reference to the importance of the court having access to a victim's personal statement. The interests of any children may also be taken into account in reducing the sentence but this has to be offset against the likely effect of further incidents of domestic violence upon them.

Little mention is made of the type of penalties that may be most effective in domestic violence cases. It is stated that offences of serious violence will warrant a custodial sentence in most cases. Nonetheless, where a custodial sentence is likely to be short, the guidance notes that the court should consider whether a suspended sentence order or a community order, including a requirement to attend an accredited perpetrator programme, might be a better alternative. The record of perpetrator programmes in reforming violent men is subject to ongoing debate and evaluation. The WNC expressed strong support for perpetrator programmes working to the RESPECT guidelines, arguing that 're-education programmes are the most efficient form of sentencing. . . rehabilitation and re-education is essential whether the relationship is continuing or ceasing' (WNC, 2004). 'Changing violent men' is however a difficult process, and perpetrator programmes seem to work better for certain types of perpetrator, and in certain contexts, than they do for others (Dobash et al, 2000). The SGC observes that perpetrator programmes will 'only be appropriate where the court is satisfied that the offender genuinely intends to reform his behaviour and that there is a real prospect of rehabilitation being successful' (SGC, 2006).

The SGC separate guidance on breach of protective orders (SGC, 2006b) includes starting points for different types of activity and highlights aggravating and mitigating features. The starting point for a breach involving significant violence and significant physical or psychological harm to the victim is a custodial sentence of more than 12 months. The guidance states it is likely that all breaches will pass the custody threshold, but this does not preclude the courts from imposing other types of sentences where appropriate—for example, as an alternative to a short custodial sentence, a non-custodial sentence that will allow the defendant to attend an accredited perpetrator programme. The aggravating and mitigating factors highlighted are in many respects similar to those in the general guidance on sentencing domestic violence discussed above, but additional aggravating features include a breach that takes place close in time to the order being made or following earlier breach proceedings. Conversely, the guidance states that a long period of compliance with an order may be viewed as mitigation. In addition if the breach is initiated by the victim this can be taken into account as mitigation. Implicit in this criterion is the idea that the victim bears some responsibility for compliance with the order and therefore carries some blame for the breach if she initiates contact with the defendant, despite the explicit (and seemingly contradictory statement) that compliance with the order is the defendant's responsibility. If the courts are going to take into account suggestions that the victim initiated the breach, then arguably these allegations need to be scrutinised very carefully. Even if the victim is willing to back up the defendant's claim that the she initiated the breach, establishing that support as genuine and voluntary may prove as problematic as ensuring the autonomous nature of victim retractions in general.

In the next chapter empirical evidence on the sentencing practices of the courts in domestic violence cases will be examined. Although this evidence predates the SGC guidance it provides a useful benchmark for assessing the impact of the guidance once it has had time to bed down. In symbolic terms the main thrust of the guidance does send out a message that domestic violence is to be viewed seriously by the courts when it comes to sentencing, nevertheless there are aspects of the guidance, highlighted above, which may perpetuate negative stereotypes about victim behaviour.

Is a special offence of domestic violence needed?

The issue of whether the criminal law should seek to distinguish between different forms of violence according to the context in which it is perpetrated is a thorny one. As noted above the law does distinguish between different degrees of violence and has a ladder of offences starting at the bottom with common assault and rising to the most serious offence of wounding or causing grievous bodily harm with intent. The current ranking of offences is done by reference to both the degree of harm caused and the degree of fault in the person causing it, although the current scheme has been described as 'a somewhat shakily constructed ladder' (Ashworth, 2006, p 332). In general the status of the victim is not reflected in separate offences, however it may be argued that the context in which violence occurs should be reflected in the label given to the offence and its ranking in terms of offence seriousness. The way in which violence is perpetrated, the presence of provocation, premeditation, and the status of the victim are all factors which a revised scheme could take into account (Horder, 1994; Genders, 1999). If it is accepted that the status of the victim, for example the fact that they are a child, should be considered a distinctive feature in the ranking of the substantive offence due to their vulnerability, then it is difficult to know where to draw the line. It would be easy to argue the vulnerability of the victim in an intimate relationship is sufficient justification for a separate substantive offence. The multiplicity of distinctions that can be made has persuaded many that distinctions between the seriousness of assaults dependent upon the nature of the victim and their relationship to the perpetrator should be left to the sentencing stage rather than reflected in the offence label. Others have argued that the context in which violence occurs, in particular a 'domestic' relationship, should be reflected in the label given to the offence and its ranking in terms of offence seriousness.

Tadros (2005) has lamented the fact that there is no specific offence of 'domestic violence' in the criminal law. He argues that a special offence should be created to identify the particular, distinctive kind of wrong (Tadros, 2005). Tadros argues that the intimacy of the relationship and the systematicity of domestic abuse diminish the freedom of the victim by limiting the range of options she has and her capacity in relation to available options: 'the wrong done through domestic violence is not just that the defendant denies the victim's options, but also that he denies her the freedom to recognize and exploit the options that she has' (p 128). Another argument he cites for the creation of a separate distinct offence of domestic violence is that traditionally the criminal justice system has failed to recognise and effectively police this type of conduct. He argues that a specific offence might encourage the more effective investigation and prosecution of domestic violence and send out a clear message to abusers and victims that domestic violence is taken seriously and that the state no longer tolerates domestic violence. However this argument presumes that the elements of the new offence would be easier to prove than existing offences under the criminal law. Tadros does not discuss the components of the proposed separate offence in any detail, but it is implicit in his conclusions that he believes that it should be based upon a course of conduct. He asserts one of the practical implications of the new offence might be to reduce some of the evidential difficulties encountered where single offences of assault are prosecuted because there might be sufficient evidence to convict for a course of conduct where there is insufficient to convict of any single assault. This evidence could come from persons other than the victim, further enhancing the possibility of prosecutions without victims. The separate offence would be an addition, not a replacement, to existing offences that can be prosecuted—thus adding 'another string to the bow of the criminal justice system' (p 141). Some other jurisdictions do have specific domestic violence offences, for example Sweden has an offence of 'gross violation of a woman's integrity' which supplements other offences and allows for prosecutions for a pattern of behaviour (Kelly, 2002).

It seems highly unlikely that a separate offence of domestic violence will become part of English criminal law in the foreseeable future. In its consultation paper, *Safety and Justice* (Home Office, 2003), the Government rejected the argument that creating a separate offence of domestic violence would improve the protection offered under the criminal law to victims of domestic violence. The consultation paper concluded that a specific offence would reduce the range of options and diminish the offence. This conclusion does seem to be premised on the view that the separate offence would be an alternative rather than supplementary to the existing crimes. Even if that was not the case there might be the tendency to prosecute for the separate offence where other, potentially more serious offences, could be prosecuted. This could be particularly so if, as Tadros envisages, the separate offence were easier to prove. Depending on how it was formulated, a separate offence would not necessarily be easier to prove than the existing offences and, if this is so, the practical arguments for a separate offence remain unconvincing. Symbolically the marking out of domestic violence as a distinctive wrong is defensible, but the educative value of the criminal law may be overstated if it is assumed that the separation of the offence can effectively communicate a message that domestic violence is a serious form of misconduct which the state will not tolerate.

Rape

For centuries the common law of England accepted that a husband could not be guilty of raping his wife. The basis of that immunity could be traced by to an extra-judicial statement by Hale CJ, endorsed by the courts in *R v Clarence* [1889] QBD 23, to the effect that by marriage a wife gives non-retractable consent to sexual intercourse with her husband. Following Clarence there were a line of cases in which the courts considered situations where specific exceptions to the general consent might be invoked, for example where a separation order was in place (*R v Clarke* [1949] 2 All ER 448), or where a degree *nisi* had been obtained (*R v O'Brien* [1974] 3 All ER 663). In the early 1990s the courts radically reconsidered the status of the marital rape immunity in *R v R*. Lord Lane in the Court of Appeal (*R v R* [1991] 2 All ER 257) considered the option of retaining the exemption and developing further exceptions to it but concluded that the exemption was based on a fiction inconsistent with the proper relationship between a husband and wife in modern times and ought to be removed entirely. Although the courts had been eroding the exemption for some time to meet changing social attitudes, Lord Lane stated; 'there comes a time when the changes are so great that it is no longer enough to create further exceptions restricting the effect of the proposition; a time when the proposition itself requires examination to see whether its terms are in accordance with what is generally regarded today as acceptable behaviour'. Lord Lane concluded; 'The idea that a wife by marriage consents in advance to her husband having sexual intercourse with her whatever her state of health or however proper her objections . . . is no longer acceptable . . . a rapist remains a rapist subject o the criminal law irrespective of his relationship with his victim'. The House of Lords upheld this decision (*R v R* [1991] 4 All ER 481). Lord Keith stated that Hale's proposition of non-retractable consent reflected a state of affairs at the time it was enunciated: 'since then the status of women, and particularly married women, has changed beyond all recognition'. He continued 'Marriage is in modern times to be regarded as a partnership of equals, and no longer one in which the wife must be the subservient chattel of the husband'. Thus the marital rape exemption was formerly swept out of English law, an outcome welcomed by the Law Commission (Law Commission, 1992b) and subsequently confirmed by a statutory amendment to the Sexual Offences Act by the Criminal Justice and Public Order Act 1994, s 142. The whole legislative framework for sexual offences has now been overhauled (Clarkson et al 2007) but rape in marriage remains a crime and arguments that it should be defined as a separate category of 'relationship rape' were rejected (Home Office, 2002b, para 2.8.8). Embodying a hierarchy of rapes, in which relationship rape ranked as less serious than stranger rape, into the definition of rape would have been a retrograde step. It would have reinforced traditional views, such as those expressed by Williams (1991) that the harm is not serious when the parties are married. Indeed in Williams' view the label common assault would be adequate to reflect the nature of the harm in non-consensual intercourse between spouses.

However, the proposition that 'rape is rape' whatever the rapist's relationship to the victim has never fully been accepted by the judiciary. Distinctions between different categories of forced or 'unwelcome' sexual intercourse remain evident in the nature of rape trials and the sentencing practices of the courts (Rumney, 1999; Warner, 2000). Rumney (1999) has observed that 'in the context of sentencing, it becomes apparent that a rapist most certainly does not remain a rapist "irrespective of his relationship with his victim'. [the courts] . . . continue to discriminate against married women by passing lower sentences than for other types of rape'. By doing so Rumney (1999) argued that the courts were departing from the sentencing guidelines which were then in place and 'betraying the spirit' of the decision in *R v R*. It is difficult to disagree with these conclusions when cases such as *R v M* (1995) 16 Cr App R (S) 770 and *R v W* (1993) 14 Cr App R (S) 256 are considered. In *R v M* the Court of Appeal reduced a sentence of a man convicted of raping his wife from 3 years to just 18 months. The court treated the absence of aggravating factors, such as violence, as mitigation. This approach is surely flawed, as it would, as Rumney (2003) suggests, allow for mitigation in all cases, since it is unlikely any single case will contain every aggravating feature. In *R v W*

(1993) the defendant was given a sentence of five-years' imprisonment for raping his wife, but given the presence of five aggravating features, it has been convincingly suggested that this should have been higher (Rumney, 1999).

The sociological literature on rape in marriage is at odds with the judicial perception of the harm involved. There is little empirical research examining rape in marriage in the UK (Painter, 1991), but research in other countries shows that rape in marriage is rarely an isolated experience, it is traumatic, and not necessarily less emotionally or psychologically disturbing than rape by a stranger (Russell, 1990; Finkelhor and Yllo, 1985). The breach of trust and the ongoing abuse that can be features of marital rape may make it more traumatic than stranger rape. The motives of rapists may also be misunderstood by the judiciary, for example the perception that the rapist is simply unable to control his sexual desires, rather than rape being an expression of power and control in a situation where the defendant is sexually possessive and jealous (Groth, 1979). Many of these points are made by Rumney in his analysis of the decisions leading up to and beyond the Court of Appeal decision in *R v Millberry* [2003] 1 WLR 546 (Rumney, 2003).

In *R v Millberry* the Court of Appeal issued new guidelines on the sentencing of rape taking into account the advice of the Sentencing Advisory Panel (SAP, 2002), which had commissioned research on public attitudes to relationship and date rape (Clarke et al, 2002). The SAP was of the opinion that the courts had traditionally underestimated the seriousness of non-stranger rape and commented that rape by a husband or other sexual partner could 'be as serious as stranger rape' in terms of its impact on the victim. The Court of Appeal accepted the Panel's recommendation that the starting point for the sentencing of 'relationship' and 'acquaintance' rape should be the same as for 'stranger rape', with the sentence then being increased or reduced according to the particular aggravating or mitigating features. However there are elements of the *Millberry* judgment which can be regarded as troublesome because they create the potential for negative and outmoded attitudes to continue to play a significant role in judicial responses to marital and relationship rape. The Court of Appeal noted for example that:

> Where, for example, the offender is the husband of the victim there can, but not necessarily, be mitigating features that clearly cannot apply to a rape by a stranger. On the other hand . . . because of the existence of the relationship the victim can feel particularly bitter about an offence of rape, regarding it as a breach of trust. This may, in a particular case, mean that looking at the offence from the victim's point of view, the offence is as bad as a 'stranger rape'. The court has the task of balancing any circumstances of mitigation against the aggravating circumstances.

Although these comments appear to accept that the victim's experience may be worse and more traumatic due to the fact of her relationship with the defendant, it is very unclear what mitigation may arise from the existence of a marriage. The passage continues:

> In drawing the balance it is not to be overlooked, when considering 'stranger rape', that the victim's fear can be increased because her offender is an unknown quantity. Is he a murderer as well as a rapist? In addition, there is the fact . . . that when a rape is committed by a stranger in a public place, not only is the offence horrific to the victim it can also frighten other members of the public. This element is less likely to be a factor that is particularly important in a case of marital rape.

These comments reveal a continuing lack of understanding about the dynamics of relationship rape. For example, Rumney (2003) has commented that highlighting the fear of an 'unknown quantity' as distinctive to stranger rape is inconsistent with the research on marital rape which suggests that victims are equally fearful because they do not know where their husband or partner will stop.

The danger that the courts will continue to minimise the seriousness of relationship rape were evident in the description the Court of Appeal gave in *Millberry* of circumstances that might amount to mitigation. It was stated:

> It may be the case where, while the offender's conduct cannot be excused, the continuing close nature of the relationship can explain how a particular offender came to commit what is always a serious offence that is out of character. There can be situations where the offender and victim are sharing the same bed on a regular basis and prior to retiring to bed both had been drinking and because of the drink the offender consumed he failed to show the restraint he should have. It would be contrary to common sense to treat such a category of rape as equivalent to stranger rape.

Rumney (2003) criticises this passage as sanitising the relationship rape and affording mitigation for intoxication in relationship rape cases without explaining why it should not also be relevant for stranger rape, and also for implicitly endorsing a view that rapists are simply unable to control sexual urges (due to intoxication). To what extent have these criticisms been justified by subsequent case law?

In *R v Price* [2003]2 Cr App R (S) 73 the Court of Appeal upheld a sentence of five-years' imprisonment for rape and three years consecutive for indecent assault committed against a former girlfriend. The rape took place whilst the couple were still cohabiting and resulted in the complainant leaving her own home for a while. The indecent assault took place after the complainant had ended the relationship and the defendant let himself, uninvited, into the complainant's home. The defendant used considerable force and repeatedly told the complainant he wanted to rape and humiliate her. The court took as its baseline the case of *M*, and noted that the court in *Millberry* opined that a sentence of three years in that case would not have been regarded as excessive by them. May LJ continued: 'If three years was not excessive for *M*, we have additional features in the present case, firstly, the appellant used quite considerable violence on his victim, and secondly, that he was to be sentenced following a contested trial'. Thus a sentence of five years for rape was not considered excessive. However this suggests that the court were approving a starting point of three years for rape rather than the five years that should flow from the statement in *Millberry* that the starting point for the sentencing of marital rape should be the same as stranger rape. The Court of Appeal did appear to view the indecent assault in a more serious light because the relationship between the complainant and defendant had ended: 'although the rape may have taken place while the appellant was living with the victim. The indecent assault occurred rather later when he was not living in the same house, when he had been asked to leave when, nevertheless, he took himself back to the victim's house, against her explicit wishes and when, additionally, he committed the offence of quite some seriousness within its class'. If the offence had been rape then the fact that the defendant had gained access to the victim's home would have justified a higher starting point. Implicit in this is the notion that a sexual assault that takes place in what should be the safety of one's own home is more serious because there is a violation of the home and feelings of security in addition to the violation of the person. Although it is arguably flawed to think that the safety and security of the home is not violated by the commission of offences by someone who resides there, the courts are nevertheless following the *Millberry* guidelines in this respect.

In *R v E (Keith)* [2005] 1 Cr App R (S) 59 the Court of Appeal upheld a sentence of three-years' imprisonment for rape which took place whilst the victim and defendant were cohabiting and both had been drinking. The court observed the defendant was, it seems, drunk, the complainant 'claims to have been somewhat less so'. The defendant used violence to carry out the rape and the victim sustained bruising to her upper arms, shoulders and inner thighs. Commenting on photographs of these injuries the court remarked; 'compared with many other regrettable cases in this case the bruising is relatively slight'. The complainant went through a distressing cross-examination which centred on her lifestyle, including her medical history, drinking habits and psychiatric state. However the court remarked; 'although there is clearly evidence that the impact on this victim was of significance, it may be, as was put to her in cross-examination, that there is some degree of exaggeration in the victim impact statement'. Referring to the *Millberry* guidelines LJ Kennedy asserted that the fact a relationship existed between the victim and defendant 'cannot, of itself, be regarded as a mitigating factor . . . But having said that, any case of this kind does have to be approached with a degree of common sense'. He referred with approval to the passage in *Millberry*, cited above, where Woolf LCJ referred to situations were the victim and defendant shared the same bed and defendants failed to show restraint due to intoxication. The court concluded four years might have been appropriate but three was not unduly lenient. How this conclusion is appropriate when the starting point is five years and there was apparently no mitigation, aside from the dubious comments about intoxication, is unclear. Again the absence of aggravation; the absence of sufficient violence (with attendant injuries) to satisfy the court, and the doubt cast on the veracity of the complainant's account of her long-term suffering, seems to have been treated as mitigation.

It is very common in rape cases to attack the credibility of the complainant as a way of avoiding liability altogether (Lees, 1996) or mitigating the seriousness of proven offences. Usually the complainant has some opportunity to present her account, although this may be severely distorted through the process of cross-examination. In *R v F (Davis Nigel)* [2006] EWCA Crim 2305 the complainant had no opportunity to present her account because she died before the case was finalised. In any event she had indicated she would not be able to attend court because of poor physical and emotional health. However in this case the prosecution had a 999 tape of the defendant raping his wife, an event which she claimed had occurred about once a week since the parties separated two years previously. The first instance judge who passed a sentence of two and a half years imprisonment referred to the tape as 'troubling' listening, describing how the victim was crying out in pain and begging the defendant to stop. Yet he remarked 'in your case it was not pure lust because you did have a genuine affection for your wife and even when this sexual act was over you asked her to give you a cuddle and then you told her that you loved her'. This statement clearly reveals a misunderstanding of the nature of the crime and the motives of rapists. The victim in this case was physically disabled, suffering severe arthritis in her knees, asthma, and was effectively imprisoned in her own home by agoraphobia. The defendant let himself in to her home on numerous occasions and perpetrated assaults which, in her description to the police, left her feeling 'powerless . . . isolated and not in control'. To view the events as 'sex' motivated by love, belies the real exploitation of power and control evident in this case. The judge concluded that the complainant was vulnerable, but not so vulnerable as to justify an eight-year starting point for the offence; instead he started with five years and gave credit for the defendant's guilty plea, also taking into account his previous good character and remorse. The flawed approach of allowing absence of aggravating features, in this case the absence of any audible violence, was seemingly also allowed as mitigation. Given the complainant in this case was unable to put up much physical resistance to the attack it should be no surprise that significant violence was not required. To treat a lack of violence as mitigation minimises the vulnerability of the complainant. The Court of Appeal rejected the argument that the sentence imposed was unduly lenient given the vulnerability of the victim and the fact that the defendant repeatedly visited the complainant in her own home and engaged in 'unwelcome' sexual activity. The court asserted it could not sentence on the basis of alleged previous rapes, and it had before it evidence which cast doubt upon the level of the victim's vulnerability. The primary source of that evidence was the complainant's daughters who did not wish to see their father imprisoned, but the court claimed it was not necessary to deal with it in any detail, focusing instead on credit for guilty plea. The court concluded that the judge was entitled to find that the defendant had pleaded guilty at the first reasonable opportunity, and despite the absence of admissions and remorse in interview, his plea after her death might well indicate remorse at that stage. Even if the defendant was given a maximum credit of one-third discount for a guilty plea that should still have meant a longer sentence than the one imposed, but the Court of Appeal nevertheless concluded it was not unduly lenient.

There are other cases where the courts seem to have taken fuller account of the five-year starting point for relationship rape and given weight to aggravating features (*R v Julkowski* [2006] EWCA 3077) but the cases discussed above suggest that the *Millberry* guidelines give too much scope for discretion to be exercised in a way that undermines the serious harm that can result from relationship rape, the culpability of the offender and the level of risk that the offender poses to society, particularly to women who may get involved in a relationship with him in the future.

Homicide

So far this chapter has concentrated on non-fatal offences against the person but, as was noted in the introduction to this book, every week in the UK two women are killed by their current or former partner. A much smaller, but nevertheless significant number of men, are killed by female partners—between 10 and 15 each year. Domestic homicide is therefore a significant problem for society and the law. The evolution of the law has taken into account to some extent the unique circumstances of domestic killings. The partial defences of provocation and diminished responsibility available to a charge of murder have been developed, some would argue unsuccessfully, to take into account the position of 'battered women' who kill their violent partners. In this section the development of the defence of provocation will be analysed. In the context of homicide it is also important to note the introduction in the Domestic Violence Crime and Victims Act 2004 of a new offence of causing death of a child or vulnerable adult. This offence was primarily designed to deal with a perceived problem of obtaining convictions for child killing when it is unclear which parent did it (Hayes, 2005). The potential for this offence to be prosecuted in cases where the mother of the child is a victim of serious domestic violence and was unable to protect herself or her children has however caused some disquiet (Herring, 2007). Although the offence is only committed by those who fail to take 'reasonable steps' to protect children, a lot will depend on judicial interpretations of what steps it is reasonable for an abused woman to take to protect her children from violence. The measure of reasonableness is one that has proved problematic for victims of domestic violence who wish to argue provocation as a defence to killing.

The provocation defence

The provocation defence developed at common law. Its roots are medieval but significant developments came in the seventeenth century when four categories of provoking conduct were established, including seeing a man in the act of adultery with one's wife (Horder, 1992). To seventeenth century judicial minds the affront to a man's honour was obvious in the case of adultery; there was no greater affront than to find himself cuckolded. The provocation defence was originally based on a justificatory rationale. On this early view a man who shot his wife and her lover dead on catching them in the act of sexual intercourse was regarded as fully morally justified. By the middle of the nineteenth century judges were looking at provocation as more an excuse than justification, and the defence was also broadening out from the four specific categories of conduct (Horder, 1992). Nevertheless, despite considerable reworking of the defence which was eventually placed on a statutory footing by the Homicide Act 1957, s 3, elements of judicial tolerance to fatal violence in the context of alleged sexual infidelity remain even in modern times.

The statutory definition of provocation, which supplements and amends but does not replace the common law, has both subjective and objective components. The subjective component requires a jury to consider whether the defendant was provoked to lose his self control. The objective component requires the jury to consider whether the reasonable man would have been provoked to lose his self-control and to do as the defendant did. Both the subjective and objective components have proved difficult to satisfy for abused women who kill their violent partners (Burton, 2001).

Insofar as the subjective component of the defence is concerned it was said in the case of *R v Duffy* [1949] 1 All ER 932 that the loss of self-control must be 'sudden and temporary'. The defendant in that case had been subjected to brutal treatment by her husband over a number of years. On the night of the killing they quarrelled and blows were struck by the husband. The defendant left the room for a while and changed her clothes. When her husband was in bed she returned with a hatchet and a hammer and killed him. The time lapse between when her husband last hit her and when she struck the fatal blow was problematic. The Court of Appeal approved a direction that a long course of conduct causing suffering and anxiety is not itself sufficient for the defence of provocation to succeed. The further removed an incident is from the crime, the less it counts, and a desire for revenge is inconsistent with provocation because it indicates time to think and reflect, which negatives a sudden temporary loss of self-control. The trial judge concluded that in considering whether provocation is made out it is important to consider whether there was a time for passion to cool and for reason to regain dominion over the mind. The Court of Appeal, approving the trial judge's direction, accepted that a time lapse might represent a 'cooling off' period.

The *Duffy* interpretation of the loss of self-control requirement made it difficult for female victims of domestic violence who kill their abusive partners to rely on the defence. When abused women kill violent men there will often be a lapse of time between the final act of violence by the man and the killing. The differences in the physical capacities of men and women may make it difficult for women to respond immediately, particularly if there is no weapon at hand. Despite this, any delay may be interpreted as a 'cooling down' period. Since *Duffy* the appellate courts have re-examined the application of the subjective provocation test to battered women and incorporated a notion of cumulative provocation and accepted the possibility of a 'slow burn effect'.

In *Ahluwalia* [1992] 4 All ER 889 the Court of Appeal recognised that a history of violence might progressively weaken self-control so that a final relatively minor act of provocation may result in a sudden and temporary loss of self-control. The defendant in this case was an Asian woman who entered into an arranged marriage which from the start was characterised by violence. On the night she killed her husband he had threatened to beat her up the next morning unless she provided money for him. He had also indicated his desire to end the marriage which would have resulted in her being ostracised in her community. The defendant waited until her husband went to sleep, went up to his bedroom, poured petrol on his bed and set it alight. On the issue of loss of self-control LCJ Taylor said:

> Time for reflection may show that after the provocative conduct made its impact on the defendant, he or she regained self-control. The passage of time following the provocation may also show that the subsequent attack was planned or based on motives, such as revenge or punishment, inconsistent with the loss of self-control and therefore with the defence of provocation; that, however, depends entirely on the facts of the individual case and is not a principle of law.

Counsel for the defendant submitted that violent treatment over a number of years might have a 'slow burn' effect. To which Lord Taylor replied:

> We accept that the subjective element in the defence of provocation would not as a matter of law be negatived simply because of the delayed reaction in such cases, provided at the time of the killing there is a sudden and temporary loss of self-control caused by the alleged provocation. However, the longer the delay and the stronger the evidence of deliberation on the part of the defendant, the more likely it will be that the prosecution will negative provocation.

Thus following *Ahluwalia* it was clear that whilst delay may negative the requirement of sudden and temporary loss of self-control, it does not necessarily do so and the response of women who have experienced domestic violence needs to be looked at in the context of their history of being abused. Such a history may make it inappropriate to view any delay between the final act of violence by the man and the fatal response by the woman as a cooling-off period. Thus, although it is still difficult, it is not impossible for abused women to satisfy the subjective test for a successful provocation defence.

However, even if the defendant satisfies the subjective test the jury must also consider whether the objective element of the defence is satisfied. The objective element has also posed difficulties for abused women who kill their partners. In considering whether the provocation was enough to make the reasonable man lose self-control and do as the defendant did (the objective test), the question arose which, if any, of the defendant's characteristics should be attributed to the reasonable man. Before the Homicide Act 1957 it was clear that the reasonable man did not share the characteristics of the defendant for the purposes of determining the standard of self-control (*R v Bedder* [1954] 1 WLR 1119). If abused women who kill have none of their characteristics or history attributed to the reasonable man then it is difficult to conclude that he would have lost his self-control and do as they did.

After the provocation defence was placed on a statutory footing the relevance of the accused's characteristics was reconsidered in a series of cases which created considerable confusion about the scope of the objective component of the defence. Much of this confusion stemmed from varying interpretations of the House of Lords decision in *R v Camplin* [1978] AC 705. In that case Lord Diplock held that some of the harshness of the common law in ignoring the defendant's characteristics had been mitigated by the Homicide Act 1957 so that a reasonable person is: 'a person having the power of self-control to be expected of an ordinary person of the sex and age of the accused, but in other respects sharing such of the accused's characteristics as they think would affect the gravity of the provocation against him'.

After *Camplin* it was unclear which of the defendant's characteristics were relevant to the gravity of the provocation, the 'provocativeness', and which could modify the standard of self-control, 'provocability', although some commentators have doubted whether a meaningful distinction between the two can be maintained (Norrie, 2001). The early cases suggested that taunts relating to a particular characteristic could affect the gravity of the provocation (*R v Newall* (1980) 71 Cr App R 331; *R v Morhall* [1996] 1 AC 90). If the cases had stopped here then it would have arguably been extremely difficult for battered women to satisfy the objective component of the provocation defence since their status as an abused woman would only be relevant if the provocation was directed at that particular characteristic. However, in a series of decisions in the 1990s the Court of Appeal suggested that the standard of self-control could be modified by the defendant's mental infirmities. Three significant cases involved women who killed their violent partners.

The first case was *Ahluwalia* (1992) in which the trial judge had directed the jury that some of the defendant's characteristics; the fact that she was an Asian woman and university educated, might be relevant. On appeal it was argued that the judge should have directed the jury that 'battered woman syndrome' was a relevant characteristic to consider. Lord Taylor said that no medical or other evidence had been put before the trial judge and jury to suggest that the defendant was suffering from post-traumatic stress disorder or battered woman syndrome. However the Court of Appeal did hear evidence that the defendant had experienced such a history of abuse that it had affected her personality and had produced a state of learned helplessness or battered woman syndrome. Lord Taylor held: 'Had the evidence which has now been put before this court been adduced before the trial judge different considerations may have applied'. It was implicit in his comments that in cases where evidence of battered woman syndrome is put before a jury it might be appropriate for them to be directed to consider it as a relevant characteristic for the purposes of judging the standard of self-control. It seemed following *Ahluwalia* that battered woman syndrome might be attributed to the reasonable (wo)man. Not all commentators saw this as an entirely welcome development (Nicolson and Sanghvi, 1993) due to the shift in emphasis towards a medical explanation for why battered women kill. However in practical terms it did open up a defence that otherwise was unlikely to succeed. Lord Taylor did not say that the provocation had to be directed at the characteristic in order for it to be relevant. This is underlined by the fact that he did not criticise the trial judge's direction that the defendant's ethnicity and education could be relevant characteristics, even though the provocation was not directed at these. However Lord Taylor's comments on provocation in *Ahluwalia* are technically obiter because the appeal was allowed on grounds of diminished responsibility.

The next case, *R v Humphreys* [1995] 4 All ER 1008, was decided on the basis of provocation, but the relevance of 'battered woman syndrome' to the objective provocation test remained somewhat unclear. The defendant was aged 17, she had a history of self-harming and was cohabiting with an older abusive man who lived in part on her earnings from prostitution. On the night of the offence she feared that she was going to be beaten and forced to have sex with her cohabitee and other men. She cut her wrists and when she was taunted about not making a very good job of it she stabbed her cohabitee in the back with a knife killing him.

The Court of Appeal stated that attention seeking by wrist slashing, is closely comparable to anorexia and as such can be regarded as a psychological illness or disorder which is in no way repugnant to or wholly inconsistent with the concept of the reasonable person. Thus it was open to the jury to conclude that the provocative taunt relied upon as a trigger hit directly at this very abnormality and was calculated to hit a very raw nerve. Lord Hirst also stated immaturity is also in no way repugnant; indeed it suggests that the appellant was unduly young for her comparatively young age and thus brings the case, on this ground, close in comparison with *Camplin*. Thus, the Court of Appeal concluded, the trial judge should have left these two characteristics, immaturity and attention seeking, as eligible for attribution to the reasonable woman, it being for the jury to decide what weight should be given to them in all the circumstances.

The case of *Humphreys* could be read in two ways. It can be read as compliant with the case of *Camplin* which recognises that immaturity (age) is one of two characteristics that can modify the standard of self-control. Attention seeking and other psychological illnesses may affect the gravity of the provocation (provocativeness) if the provocation is directed at the characteristic, as it was in this case. However a broader interpretation can be contended; that mental conditions are relevant to modify the standard of self-control regardless of whether the provocation is directed at them. Depending on which interpretation is made of the case, the provocation defence at this point was either not especially adaptable to the circumstances of abused women who kill, or was evolving so as to modify the standard of self-control in a way that would make it much easier for abused women to successfully argue that they satisfied the objective component of the defence. The third case in the trilogy, *R v Thornton (No 2)* [1996] 2 All ER 1023, seemed to signal most clearly that battered woman syndrome could be a relevant characteristic for the purposes of modifying the standard of self control (provocability).

The defendant, Sara Thornton, suffered from personality disorder before she met and married her husband who was a former police officer. He was an alcoholic and assaulted the defendant on numerous occasions after drinking. Following a violent argument during which her husband threatened to kill her, she went into the kitchen and obtained a knife. When she returned he threatened again to kill her and called her a whore, whereupon she stabbed him to death. The trial judge directed the jury to consider provocation, but told them that they had to consider whether a reasonable sober woman in Mrs Thornton's position would have done as she did. He added: 'There are many unhappy, indeed miserable husbands and wives. It is a fact of life . . . But on the whole it is hardly reasonable, you may think, to stab them fatally when there are other alternatives available, like walking out or going upstairs'. The trial judge showed no appreciation of the difficulties that women have in leaving violent men and made no reference to battered women's syndrome. On appeal Lord Taylor said that battered women's syndrome may be relevant to the defence of provocation depending on the medical evidence. The syndrome may have affected the defendant's personality so as to constitute a significant characteristic relevant to the question of whether the reasonable woman would have lost her self-control. In this case the defendant had two characteristics, her personality disorder and the effect of the deceased's abuse on her mental make-up; the jury ought to have been directed to consider both in deciding whether the reasonable woman would have lost self-control as the defendant did.

The expansion of the provocation defence to cover female victims of domestic violence, through a dual attack on the subjective and objective components, was thus gathering momentum by the time that the House of Lords came to decide the case of *R v Smith* [2000] 3 WLR 645. Although *R v Smith* is not a domestic violence case its implications for women who kill were explicitly acknowledged, not least in the fact that two women's groups obtained leave to intervene in the appeal to argue in favour of an interpretation of the defence that, in their eyes, favoured abused women. They were arguing against the Privy Council decision in *Luc Thiet Thuan* [1997] AC 131 that mental characteristics were not relevant to the objective provocation test.

The House of Lords decision in *Smith* was split. Lord Hoffman, in the majority, concluded that the Homicide Act 1957 modified the common law so that the question of whether the objective component was satisfied was entirely a matter for the jury: 'the judge is not entitled to tell them that for this purpose the law requires them to exclude from consideration any of the circumstances or characteristics of the accused'. He argued that this conclusion was consistent with the decision in *Camplin* because, in his view, age and sex were mentioned in that case only as illustrations not exclusive itemisation of relevant characteristics. However, Lord Hoffman was aware that imposing no limitations on the characteristics of the accused that can be taken into account for the standard of self-control would be criticised. In particular he anticipated that it might be that violent sexually possessive men should be able to rely on their obsession with their victim as a relevant characteristic to modify the standard of self-control (Allen, 1999). He said that juries should be directed in a way that minimised the risk of them considering characteristics like obsession as an acceptable reason for loss of self-control by instructions to ignore characteristics like obsession and jealously in considering the objective component of the provocation defence. Hoffman asserted: 'Male possessiveness and jealously should not today be an acceptable reason for loss of self-control leading to homicide, whether inflicted upon the woman herself or her new lover'.

In saying that (nearly) all characteristics must be left to the jury Lord Hoffman was clearly including battered women's syndrome. Indeed he explicitly endorses an interpretation of *Ahluwalia* that PTSD suffered by some abused women could be relevant to the standard of self-control. The other judges in majority, Lord Slynn and Lord Clyde agreed that mental infirmities were relevant to the standard of self-control. Lord Clyde observed justice would not be done if no regard were paid to the infirmities of individuals who, through no fault of their own, were unable to meet the standard of self-control of others not suffering such infirmities. Although Lord Clyde does not mention 'battered woman syndrome' specifically nor does he exclude abused women from the category of those who might on occasion suffer mental infirmities. He states that where an abused woman's condition falls short of mental abnormality: 'The reasonable person in such a case should be one who is exercising a reasonable level of self-control for someone with her history, her experience and her state of mind'.

In one sense the decision of the majority in *R v Smith* could be seen as a victory for women who kill their violent partners, however it was not an unqualified victory. To an extent it continues to medicalise 'battered women' to fit them into a mould of battered women's syndrome or PTSD; recognised psychiatric disorders which can then be ascribed to the 'reasonable man'. Although Lord Clyde in the majority and Lord Millett in the minority suggested that it was possible to accommodate the experiences of abused women who kill without medicalising their situation. The desire to accommodate abused women within the defence of provocation was no doubt well motivated. Nevertheless, seeking to reverse the traditional gender bias of the defence by including abused women, whilst at the same time trying to exclude jealous men, was arguably doomed to failure.

It has been argued elsewhere that the way that the objective component of the provocation defence was expanded in *R v Smith* was dangerous for abused women (Burton, 2001a). Although it had the potential to help women who killed their violent partners, it also exposed women killed by sexually possessive men to greater danger. Lord Hoffman's comments relating to jealous men were technically obiter. It was argued that juries might ignore the advice of progressive judges such as Lord Hoffman, and that the majority decision in *Smith* left women who knew violent men intimately 'at the mercy of judges and juries who think that fatal violence is an understandable response to women's assertions of independence' (Burton, 2001a). The passage of years since the decision in *Smith* has given little reason to think that such an assessment was wrong.

In December 2002 the Court of Appeal heard three combined appeals against unduly lenient sentences for domestic homicide (*R v Suratan, R v Humes and R v Wilkinson* [2003] 2 Cr App R (S) 42). In two of the three cases a central element of the mitigation was alleged infidelity on the part of the victim. The Court of Appeal acknowledged that juries would not always share Lord Hoffman's view that the defence of provocation should fail because it was based on allegations of sexual infidelity. Mantell LJ stated that the defendant's possessiveness and jealously should not be used to argue for a heavier sentence. According to Mantell LJ the comments in *R v Smith* went 'to the availability of the defence rather than the consequences of a verdict arrived at by a jury that does not share Lord Hoffman's view'. It has therefore been argued that the decision of the Court of Appeal implicitly approved the mitigation afforded to jealous men who kill and that any gains made in *R v Smith* were outweighed by a retreat on the sentencing front (Burton, 2003). The decision of the Court of Appeal in *R v Weller* [2004] 1 Cr App R 1 confirmed that Lord Hoffman had been unsuccessful in his attempts to prevent the defence of provocation being used by sexually possessive men who kill.

Weller strangled his girlfriend following an argument about her conduct with other men. She had wanted to end their relationship because he was unduly possessive and jealous. Lord Mantell stated: 'it is plain from the majority speeches in Smith that characteristics such as jealousy remain with the jury as matters which fall for consideration with the second, objective element of provocation and section 3. Plainly the jury must not be directed that they should take no account of them and it is essential that it is made clear that such matters may form part of their deliberations.'

The expansion of the objective component of the provocation defence was criticised for a host of reasons (Macklem and Gardner, 2001), not simply because of the implications for domestic homicide. However the implications for domestic homicide particularly worried the Government. *Safety and Justice*, the Government's consultation on a strategy for domestic violence, flagged up the need to look at the way the law of homicide works in domestic violence cases (Home Office, 2003). It noted concern that the partial defence of provocation was used in circumstances where the provocation is minimal and in relation to domestic homicide where the provocation relied upon is sexual jealousy or infidelity. Furthermore it highlighted concerns that the current sentencing practices for domestic homicide upon provocation do not adequately reflect the seriousness of the cases or the loss of life. The Government therefore referred the sentencing of cases involving provocation to the Sentencing Advisory Panel and referred the operation of the partial defences to the Law Commission.

The Law Commission produced a consultation paper on the partial defences to murder (Law Commission, 2003) making proposals for the reform of provocation. Before the Government had the opportunity to take reform process any further, the senior judiciary, in *AG of Jersey v Holley* [2005] 2 AC 580, decided to yet again redefine the scope the objective component of the provocation defence.

Holley was another domestic homicide. The defendant and victim were cohabitants and both were alcoholics. The defendant had been drinking at home all day when the victim returned from a public house and allegedly told him she had just had sex with another man. He picked up an axe and killed her by striking her with it several times. The Privy Council had to consider whether the defendant's alcoholism was a relevant characteristic for the jury to consider in determining whether a reasonable person would have lost his self-control. By a 6–3 majority they decided that it was not relevant and favoured a return to the more objective standard of self-control. Lord Nicholls said: 'the powers of self-control possessed by ordinary people vary according to their age and, more doubtfully, their sex. These features are to be contrasted with abnormalities, that is, features not found in a person having ordinary powers of self control'. So the reasonable man is of the same age and sex as the defendant but other characteristics are relevant only to the gravity of the provocation; the standard of self-control does not vary 'from defendant to defendant' and does not 'leave each jury free to set whatever standard they consider appropriate in the circumstances'.

Despite being a Privy Council decision, *Holley* is to be treated as authoritative for the purposes of English law (*R v James* [2006] EWCA Crim 14). As such it is useful to examine the implications of the decision for domestic homicides. Those who welcomed the decision in *R v Smith*, as affording greater opportunity for abused women who kill to have their characteristics taken into account for the purposes of assessing the standard of self-control, will no doubt think that the return to a more objective standard is to be regretted (Rights Of Women, 2005). The decision in *Holley* essentially redraws the boundaries between the defences of provocation and diminished responsibility; mental infirmities are relevant to the latter but not the former insofar as the standard of self-control is concerned. Some commentators have pushed for some time for the boundaries of the defences to be redrawn in this way (Horder, 1999). In respect of abused women who kill this means that they will be much more likely to succeed with a defence of diminished responsibility than provocation where there is evidence of battered women's syndrome. Lord Nicholls considered the position of 'battered women' in *Holley* and remarked:

> the evidence of the woman's condition may be relevant on two issues: whether she lost her self-control, and the gravity of the provocation for her. The jury will then decide whether in their opinion, having regard to the actual provocation and their view of its gravity for the defendant, a woman of her age having ordinary power of self-control might have done what the defendant did. More importantly . . . the defendant will in principle have available to her the defence of diminished responsibility.

One potentially beneficial effect of the return to a more inflexible objective standard of self-control is that it should, theoretically, also act as a hindrance to violent men who wish to rely on sexual jealously as the basis for a provocation defence. Whether this follows in practice remains to be seen. If the provoking words are directed at the characteristic of sexual jealously, for example it is alleged that the victim taunted the defendant about him being jealous of her relationship with another man, it seems that could still be relevant to the gravity of the provocation. However, it is to be hoped that juries will conclude that the ordinary man, who is not sexually possessive and jealous, would not respond to such taunts by killing. This will in part depend on their ability and willingness to perform the 'mental gymnastics' required to distinguish between provocativeness and provocability.

In *Holley* their Lordships endorsed the long-standing view of many that the wholesale review of the law of murder should be undertaken. That review is well underway and the Law Commission has published proposals on a revised three-tier structure for homicide (Law Commission, 2005; Law Commission, 2006). Under this structure provocation would be a defence to first degree murder, reducing the offence to second degree murder. Partial defence killings will therefore attract a more serious label than the current one of 'manslaughter'. The defence of provocation will not apply to cases where the defendant killed in circumstances which under the new scheme would amount to manslaughter, although some have argued that perhaps the defence ought to be available to lesser degrees of homicide and that in general the revised scheme is insufficiently nuanced to distinguish the different levels of culpability in killings (Tadros, 2006; Quick and Wells, 2006). Insofar as the elements of the provocation defence are concerned the Law Commission endorses its proposals in its earlier paper. In that paper (Law Commission, 2003) the Commission noted the widespread criticism of the defence and 'agreement that the concept of provocation has become far too loose'. It recommended that the defence should be reshaped to be available when the defendant acted in response to gross provocation and/or fear of serious violence towards himself or another. It proposed that 'gross provocation' means words or conduct, or a combination of both, which caused the defendant to have a justifiable sense of being seriously wronged. The proposals were criticised for the lack of reference to the defendant's state of mind at the time of killing (Mackay and Mitchell, 2005). Loss of self-control would not be an essential element of a successful plea under the proposals. However the jury must be satisfied that 'a person of the defendant's age and of ordinary temperament, i.e. ordinary tolerance and self-restraint, in the circumstances of the defendant might have reacted in the same or a similar way'. In deciding this the court can take into account 'the defendant's age and all the circumstances of the defendant other than matters whose only relevance to the defendant's conduct is that they bear simply on his or her general capacity for self-control'. It has been observed that, broadly speaking, this would take the law back to *Camplin* (Mackay and Mitchell, 2005), which according to the interpretation given to that case in *Holley*, is effectively where the law is now; age would be the only characteristic relevant to the standard of self-control, all other characteristics would be relevant only to the gravity of the provocation so mental infirmities, unless they were the objects of the provocation, would not be relevant (Mackay and Mitchell, 2005).

How the Law Commission's proposals might work in practice is of course a matter of pure speculation at this stage. If the proposals are implemented, arguably a lot would turn on how the courts interpret the requirement that the defendant have a 'justifiable sense of being seriously wronged'. There is at least potential for the reformulated defence to accommodate jealous and possessive men who kill. Interestingly the Law Commission cites the empirical work of Mitchell and Cunningham (2006) in working through its proposals. Two of the cases that Mitchell and Cunningham describe involve men killing their partners who were allegedly having affairs. Mitchell and Cunningham suggest that the cultural/anthropological background of these cases might support an argument that the victim's conduct was 'gross provocation' such that the defendant had a 'justifiable sense of being seriously wronged'. Presumably such a defendant would be expected to fail with the defence because of the 'ordinary tolerance' requirement, but the potential for the judicial Pandora's box to be opened up yet again should not be underestimated.

The flaws of the provocation defence have led some to call for its abolition

(Wells, 2000). In relation to domestic homicide it has been suggested that it would be better to develop a specific defence of 'warranted excuse' which recognises battering is a crime but infidelity is not (Nourse, 1997). There are other existing defences which could be developed to accommodate battered women who kill, the prime candidate being self-defence, which is restrictive for both men and women but particularly 'skewed to the detriment of women' (Edwards, 2004). Abused women traditionally fall foul of both the imminence and proportionality requirements, although it has been argued that the judiciary could be more understanding of the situation of battered women when interpreting these (McColgan, 1993).

Sentencing domestic homicide

It was noted above that the sentencing of domestic homicide has been as controversial as the substantive components of the defence. The decision in *Suratan, Humes* and *Wilkinson* persuaded the Government to refer the matter to the Sentencing Advisory Panel (SAP). The SAP was unconvinced that there is gender bias in the sentencing of domestic homicide, citing research by Mackay (Law Commission, 2005) which it says 'appears to disprove this theory'. The fact that two of the female defendants in Mackay's study received non-custodial sentences whereas none of the men who killed their female partners did, arguably conceals as much as it reveals. Out of 16 female victims, 11 resulted in murder convictions, with 'only' four defendant's successfully pleading provocation. However if we look at the circumstances of these four cases it can be seen that one defendant claimed that the victim had goaded him about his appearance and alleged incompetence in shopping, another killed his wife because she had begun a relationship with another man and they had an argument about the children, another alleged his victim refused to end her affair and laughed at him, and the fourth killed his girlfriend when he saw her behaving affectionately towards a man she had claimed raped her. The sentence of eight years for the first two examples and four years for the second two, do not seem to suggest that the courts are unsympathetic to the argument that alleged infidelity is highly provocative. In Mackay's sample there were three cases where alleged infidelity was involved but the courts convicted of murder, rejecting provocation as a defence. However as can be seen from above there were an equal number of cases where infidelity was accepted as provocation and two cases where it was regarded as sufficiently provocative to justify a sentence of four-years' imprisonment. Mackay's study seems to provide limited grounds for complacency about the gender bias of the provocation defence. The idea that the courts are not biased against female defendants when compared to men needs to be set in the context of the above descriptions of provocative conduct and the fact that seven of the female defendants in Mackay's sample were victims of domestic violence and more than half of these did receive custodial sentences—three of which were four-years' imprisonment. On the basis of that it is just as plausible to argue that the courts regard a history of domestic violence as, roughly, as provocative as seeing your girlfriend flirting with another man.

There was an obvious need for the SAP to give clearer guidance to the courts on the appropriate weight to be given to domestic violence and allegations of infidelity when sentencing domestic homicide. The panel recommended three sentencing ranges for provoked manslaughter defined by reference to the degree of provocation; high (0–4 years imprisonment), substantial (4–9 years) and low (10–life). The SGC accepted the recommendation (SGC, 2005) and its guidance states that an assessment of the degree of provocation should be made by reference to, amongst other things, its nature and duration. It states; 'discovery or knowledge of the fact of infidelity on the part of a partner does not necessarily amount to high provocation' but it might depending on the circumstances. Provocation can be 'cumulative' as in cases of domestic violence, and actual and anticipated violence 'will *generally* be regarded as involving a higher degree of provocation than provocation arising from abuse, infidelity or offensive words'. In relation to the timing of the retaliation the SGC notes that in general the shorter the delay the less culpable an offender is likely to be, but notes this may not be so where there is domestic violence. Use of weapons is also highlighted as an aggravating feature but it is noted that the gender of the offender and whether the weapon was brought to the scene could be more significant. The guidelines were hailed as bringing a tougher approach to men who kill partners in a jealous rage (Guardian, 29 November 2005). However it should be remembered that the guidelines do not rule out infidelity counting as high provocation; if there are allegations of persistent taunting then this could amount to 'psychological bullying' which overrides the statement that violence is generally more provocative than words.

Allegations of sexual infidelity, whether made during the course of a trial or at the sentencing stage, put the victim 'on trial' and neither she (because she is dead), nor her family and friends have traditionally been able to contest these allegations or defend the victim's reputation (Radford, 1992; Lees, 1992). The CPS now has greater responsibility to consult the victim's family about the acceptability of pleas and to challenge defamatory mitigation (Attorney General, 2005). Victims' families are also being given more of a direct voice in murder and manslaughter trials. How far these reforms will go to ensuring dead women have no more 'tales told about them' (Morgan, 1997) remains to be seen.

Conclusion

The substantive criminal law sometimes appears to be context blind when it comes to domestic violence; judges are either unable or unwilling to adapt the law to accommodate the experiences of victims of domestic violence. On occasions where the law has evolved to accommodate domestic violence, it has sometimes done so unwittingly; seeking to provide redress for other types of phenomena but incidentally bringing significant improvements to the potential capacity of the criminal justice system to respond to domestic violence. There are nevertheless significant examples of the judiciary making deliberate attempts to take into account domestic violence when developing the criminal law. Although these developments, in the law of rape and provocation, were undoubtedly well intentioned, nevertheless it seems easy for these good intentions to be undermined by a retreat on the sentencing front, where less progressive attitudes to what constitutes serious domestic violence continue to be demonstrated. Overall the criminal law is in a better place than it was two decades ago to accommodate the experiences of victims of domestic violence. However the effectiveness of the criminal law is not simply about its substantive components but the practices of those charged with implementing it on a day-to-day level—a matter to which we must now turn.

6 The criminal justice system
Justice for victims?

Although the criminal law provides a range of offences that can be prosecuted in the domestic violence context, the willingness of the criminal justice agencies to effectively utilise these offences has long been questioned. Early research into the experiences of women trying to access the protection of the criminal law suggested that the police and the courts were reluctant to engage with them and take their complaints seriously. The bulk of the early research was on the police response to domestic violence. This is unsurprising given that they are the gatekeepers to the criminal justice system and thus a key point in the attrition process. If the case does not make it past the police decision-making filter then it never enters the domain of the courts where there is the potential for greater public scrutiny of the decision making. The early studies of police decision-making in domestic violence cases therefore provide a benchmark for assessing how far the criminal justice agencies have come in improving their response to domestic violence. New players such as the Crown Prosecution Service, which entered onto the scene in the mid-1980s, have been subjected to critical scrutiny against a backdrop that suggested that the system was failing to meet the need of victims of domestic violence and hold perpetrators to account. This chapter will trace the evolution of the criminal justice response to domestic violence from the days when it was regarded as essentially a non-criminal matter to recent years when the imperative has been to communicate that domestic violence is taken seriously by the criminal justice system and is not a purely private or civil matter.

Police response

Early failings: policing domestic violence in the 1970s and 1980s

Dobash and Dobash (1979) were amongst the first to document the poor police response to domestic violence in the UK. They found that the police showed little empathy with victims of domestic violence and little commitment to tackling the problem. Police practices were characterised by 'animosity or at best indifference' (Dobash and Dobash, 1979, p 191). The police generally received no training on domestic violence and when they did the emphasis was upon mediation and preserving the family unit. In the early 1980s there were a number of empirical studies examining the police response to domestic violence (Faragher, 1985; Chatterton, 1983), one of the most notable of these was the study carried out by Edwards (1989). Edwards (1989) found that there was a great reluctance to record domestic violence as a crime and a high proportion of domestic violence incidents were in fact 'no crimed' by the police. She attributed some of this reluctance to police stereotypes about domestic violence, commenting that the under-enforcement of the criminal law is influenced by 'private attitudes regarding appropriate sex roles, appropriate conduct and family ideologies' (p 91). Thus the legal victim does not always turn out, in the eyes of the police, to be the moral victim and the decision to arrest is affected by the moral perspective: 'that is to say by the extent to which "she" deserved it and whether "his" behaviour was justified' (p 95). Thus poor housekeeping could be regarded as provocation for assault (Edwards, 1987). Edwards (1989) found that police officers would attempt to mediate between the parties or encourage the victim to use civil remedies, even when the victim wanted the perpetrator to be arrested and the police had the powers to do so. Complainant withdrawal was a major reason given by the police for refusing to take action against domestic violence offenders. Police officers displayed little understanding of why women might withdraw their complaints; 'Police explanations for withdrawal emphasized the women's fickleness, rather than her fear of further violence, homelessness or poverty, all of which frequently follow if she takes legal steps to protect herself' (p 104).

Another study carried out in the 1980s, by an assistant chief constable, found that 'most officers had a negative attitude towards marital violence, often feeling that they should not become involved' (Bourlet, 1990, p 74). Domestic violence work was not popular, the majority of officers felt inadequately trained and were reluctant to make arrests because, in their experience, women withdrew their complaints. Many police officers felt that domestic violence should be dealt with by agencies other than the police and became frustrated at being called to the same house again and again, only to have their advice ignored (p 82). It seemed to Edwards (1989) and some others that the police treated 'private violence' as much less serious than public violence. Sanders (1988) for example found that non-domestic assaults were twice as likely to be prosecuted by the police as domestic assaults. Victim withdrawal and unreliability were the main reasons given for not prosecuting but this did not necessarily prevent the police prosecuting non-domestic assaults, particularly where there was a public order element. Edwards situated these findings within the classic public/private dichotomy asserting that the police preference for diverting women to the civil remedies and refusal to enforce the criminal law reinforced the traditional dichotomy whereby violence in the home was not regarded as a public matter. Indeed the very existence of different remedies under the civil and criminal law could be regarded as reinforcing the dichotomy as the two systems 'deal out a different order of justice' (Edwards, 1989, p 51).

Policy changes: policing domestic violence in the 1990s

The research carried out by Edwards (1989) had a significant impact on the development of policy for the policing of domestic violence. The Home Office issued a circular to all police forces in England and Wales which was designed to encourage a more proactive police response to domestic violence. Home Office Circular 60/1990 (Home Office, 1990) stated that all police officers involved in cases of domestic violence should regard their overriding priority to be the protection of victims and the apprehension of perpetrators. The emphasis was on making sure that officers were aware of their powers of arrest and used them appropriately. It was recommended that domestic violence was recorded and investigated in the same way as any other crime. A more sympathetic and understanding attitude to victims of domestic violence was encouraged. The establishment of specialist domestic violence units was also recommended.

As a symbolic statement of the commitment to taking domestic violence more seriously the 1990 circular was important, however its practical impact was much more limited. A study by Grace in the mid-1990s found that there were significant deficiencies in the implementation of the policy (Grace, 1995). Grace found that most officers in her study felt that the policing of domestic violence had improved and that domestic violence incidents were taken more seriously, but over a third of operational police officers had not even heard of the circular and few officers had received any training on domestic violence. Even though most officers were aware that arrest should be a priority in domestic violence cases, almost half put it below other priorities and three-quarters said that they would attempt mediation if the perpetrator was still at the scene or if there had only been a verbal dispute. Only nine officers said that they would not attempt mediation. These findings do not seem to reflect the recommendation in the Circular that priority should be given the safety of the victim over attempting reconciliation between the parties. As with earlier studies, Grace found that an officer's decision to arrest was often affected by his judgement about whether the complainant would support an action, although less than a quarter thought that most victims withdraw their complaints.

Home Office Circular 60/1990 was to start a trend towards specialisation in domestic violence cases, however it was slow to take off and has been marked by concerns about the possible marginalisation of domestic violence work, with possible detrimental consequences. Grace (1995) found that whilst just over half of the forces had a specialist unit with some responsibility for domestic violence, only five forces had a unit that was solely dedicated to domestic violence. Specialist domestic violence officers were extremely committed to their work but they had little impact on generalist policing and they felt their work was low priority and that they were overworked. Many of the women who had contact with domestic violence officers commented positively on their input and the specialist officer's attitude towards them, but even amongst the women the view emerged that specialist units could marginalise the problem. One respondent commented that the heavy reliance on female police officers to run these units undermined the impact of police involvement on the perpetrator and 'made domestic violence "a woman's problem" ' (p 42). Grace concluded that more effort needed to be put into translating policy into practice and more emphasis needed to be placed upon making arrests and prosecuting perpetrators of domestic violence.

The Home Office followed up Grace's study with another evaluation by Plotnikoff and Woolfson (1998). Their study focused on the organisational and managerial issues in effectively policing domestic violence. Plotnikoff and Woolfson found that variable definitions of domestic violence and what constitutes 'repeat victimisation' made it difficult to make comparisons between different forces. However they did find that there was also a great deal of variation over the provision of specialist support in domestic violence units. Where domestic violence officers were in existence there was no uniform approach to the tasks and responsibilities undertaken by the officer. Overall they found a lack of managerial commitment to domestic violence work, which marginalised its significance and confirmed the traditional perception that it is low-status work. Despite the rhetoric at policy level to improving the police response to domestic violence, most police forces lacked a clear training strategy or effective lines of accountability to try to implement that policy in practice. The mechanisms for identifying domestic violence and communicating information to the officer attending the scene remained crudely developed and unreliable. Key recommendations made by Plotnikoff and Woolfson included the establishment of clear priorities for domestic violence officers and that their role should 'be more clearly integrated into the force structure by clarifying its interface with other police functions involved in responding to domestic violence' (p 48). They also recommended improved procedures for managing information and the development of a comprehensive training strategy on domestic violence for all officers.

Whilst much of the empirical evidence on policing of domestic violence in the 1990s suggested that the process of change was slow and patchy, a study by Hoyle (1998) challenged traditional interpretations of police failings. Hoyle found that police decisions were not affected by negative stereotypes that victims of domestic violence were 'undeserving' but rather by working rules which prioritised order maintenance and deferred to the victim's wishes with regard to arrest and prosecution. Looking at what women wanted from the police, Hoyle found that often they did not want to break up the family and believed that their partners were 'good fathers' despite being violent towards them. Thus women called the police in order to diffuse an immediate problem and to warn the perpetrator about his behaviour, not necessarily seeking an arrest. Consequently a disparity arose between what the women wanted and what the police thought that they wanted. Hoyle criticises writers who assume that not fully implementing the criminal law is a failure. She observes that it is often assumed that women will be dissatisfied with the police response if they do not make an arrest, but this is not always the case. In a follow-up study of her earlier work on the policing of domestic violence in the Thames Valley area, Hoyle and Sanders (2000) interviewed domestic violence victims and discussed with them what they wanted when they called the police to a domestic dispute. They found that just over half wanted an arrest to be made, but that the majority of these did not want a prosecution: 'They wanted an arrest without any further criminal justice intervention to "teach him a lesson" or to resolve the immediate situation temporarily' (p 22). Arrest is seen as useful tool for achieving the goal or separation, either temporarily or permanently. Thus Hoyle and Sanders are supportive of a pro-arrest policy, but question the mandatory prosecution model that has been adopted in some other jurisdictions.

Alongside the general policy initiative described above several policing initiatives were introduced in particular localities (Hanmer and Griffiths, 2001). Two projects; one in Merseyside (Lloyd et al, 1994) and the other in Killingbeck (Hanmer et al, 1999) had the specific objective of reducing repeat victimisation (Hanmer and Griffiths, 1998). A third project in Islington provided civilian support to women after police contact (Kelly, 1999). The Merseyside project introduced pendant alarms for women, set up a database on police attendance at domestic violence incidents and raised awareness of domestic violence amongst officers. The installation of alarms was positively received but the limitations of the research design meant that the researchers were unable to establish whether it reduced police attendance or increased separation as a means of achieving safety (Lloyd et al, 1994; Hanmer and Griffiths, 2001). The Killingbeck initiative aimed to reduce repeat victimisation through a three-tiered graded response, the higher tiers involving a 'cocoon' watch by neighbours with the consent of the victim. The initiative did reduce repeat attendances by the police and increased the time intervals between attendances (Hanmer et al, 1999). Improvements were made in the consistency of the police response, the identification of chronic offenders and factors which reduce or increase offenders (Hanmer and Griffith, 2001). The model of civilian intervention adopted in Islington aimed to contact victims within 24 hours of the police being called and offer support services including advocacy. The civilian follow-ups were effective and women welcomed the opportunity to talk through their options. However there were significant problems in the implementation of the initiative and Kelly (1999) concluded that force policy on domestic violence was not being properly implemented and women did not always get the respectful and assertive response they wanted from the police.

An overview of these three projects, and some other unevaluated initiatives, concluded that there were a number of issues relevant to assessment of effective policing of domestic violence (Hanmer and Griffiths, 2001), including training, information management and the continuing need to overcome the low status of domestic violence as police work. At the end of the twentieth century it was clear that much work still needed to be done on improving the police response to domestic violence.

Policing domestic violence in the twenty-first century

Since the studies of policing in the 1990s discussed above were carried out, there has been yet another attempt to change police practice with the introduction of revised policy (Home Office Circular 19/2000). The revised Circular reiterates and strengthens the pro-arrest policy. It is stated:

> Where a power of arrest exists, the alleged offender should normally be arrested. An officer should be prepared to justify a decision not to arrest in the above circumstances ... If the evidence is present, whether or not including evidence from the victim, then a charge or summons should be preferred, unless there are exceptional reasons. Such reasons should be recorded.
>
> (HOC 19/2000)

The revised statement highlights the need for police officers to gather all available evidence and not rely solely on the victim's statement. However recent empirical research shows that the policy of 'effective evidence gathering', as it has come to be known, has not yet been fully implemented in all forces and there continues to be other difficulties in the police response to domestic violence.

A study of attrition in a sample of cases taken from three police forces in Northumbria (Hester et al 2003; Hester, 2005) found that of 869 incidents recorded by the police 26 per cent resulted in arrest, 27 per cent of those were charged and just over half of those were convicted. It emerged that less than 1 per cent of incidents, just four cases, resulted in a conviction and custodial sentence. The researchers found that the police tended to regard the victims as key to attrition. Many police officers expressed frustration at victims being unwilling to provide a statement, nevertheless in 14 cases they proceeded despite a statement being refused and only one of these cases was subsequently discontinued. The research did find however very little effort by the police to gather other evidence to support the prosecution. Photographic evidence was rarely collected despite digital cameras being available for the purpose. Only three instances of photographic evidence being taken were recorded and in none of the cases resulting in arrest did photographic evidence appear to be used or made available to the court. The researchers also found that the police were not proactive in gathering other evidence such as witness statements from neighbours or CCTV footage, relying instead on requests from the CPS.

The most recent major review of the policing of domestic violence was carried out by Her Majesty's Inspectorate of Constabulary, in conjunction with Her Majesty's Crown Prosecution Service Inspectorate (HMCPSI and HMIC, 2004). The joint inspectorate report charts the investigation and prosecution of domestic violence and highlights the high level of attrition and possible explanations for it. The overall assessment of the police is that 'tremendous efforts have been made' to overturn the stereotype that violence in the home is 'just another domestic' and to 'ensure that domestic violence is treated as a serious incident, requiring a high standard of professional investigation . . . But all too often, policies and rhetoric are not matched on the ground by effective responses and solid investigative practice (HMCPSI and HMIC, 2004, p 6). The quality of the guidance given by individual forces in the wake of Circular 19/2000 was found to vary significantly and it is stated: 'Whilst all officers spoken to were clear about the fact that domestic violence was a priority within their force . . . with the exception of specialist officers, few had any real understanding of the dynamics of domestic violence' (p 33). The gap between specialist and generalist policing is therefore confirmed by the inspectorates' report.

The inspectorates' report assesses the performance of the police in implementing positive arrest and effective evidence gathering policies. It highlights the importance of call handlers effectively grading domestic violence incidents; where there is a disturbance ongoing at the time of the call, the main priority should be to dispatch officers to attend as soon as possible. This has always been a significant issue, for example Edwards (1989) found that call controllers often screened out domestic violence or accorded it low priority, although a decade later Hoyle (1998) noted it was rare for the police not to attend a domestic violence call. The inspectorates found that not all police forces are grading domestic violence calls appropriately, with almost half of calls being under-graded in two of the six forces examined, and on occasions victims having to phone again or wait several hours for an officer to attend. The quality of information on the incident log was also found to be variable. In general the inspectorates found that forces were relying too heavily on the commitment and experience of call handlers with insufficient emphasis on appropriate training. Whilst all the forces visited had systems in place for flagging domestic violence, the extent to which flags were being accurately applied could not be established. Some specialist domestic violence officers highlighted the unreliability of the systems and having to double-check that incidents had not been missed by non specialists.

Across the six forces examined the inspectorates found wide variations in the proportions of incidents resulting in arrest and crime reports being completed. The arrest rate varied from 63 per cent to 13 per cent. It was found to be the highest in the force where arrest policy was clearly articulated, officers were clear about their powers of arrest and the reasons for making an arrest. The inspectorates found that effective understanding and understanding of the policy of enhanced evidence gathering was not widespread. Although cameras were available in the majority of forces visited they were rarely used to take photos of the scene or victim's injuries. The quality of medical evidence was not high and there were few examples of CCTV evidence, statements from neighbours or 999 tapes being used. The inspectorates were clear in their view that the CPS were missing out on potentially valuable evidence due to the inadequate implementation by the police of the policy of effective evidence gathering.

In 2006 a campaign was run to try to improve the police response to domestic violence in three key areas; investigation at call receipt/in the control room, evidence gathering at the scene and targeting of prolific offenders (Home Office, 2006). Campaign participants ensured that call handlers received training to recognise and undertake first line investigation during their conversations with victims of domestic violence. They also used a call taker checklist so that call handlers were prompted about appropriate questions to ensure victim safety and obtain evidential information. Recordings of 999 calls were also made to assist the investigation and evidence gathering. During the campaign dedicated domestic violence response vehicles were deployed to assist with effective evidence gathering and the majority of participants used digital images to record evidence at the scene. Some participants used body-worn cameras and others left hidden cameras in the homes of prolific offenders. The percentage of arrests for offenders not at the scene when officers attended rose significantly during the campaign and participants were encouraged to identify their top offenders and offending locations and to take a proactive stance. All these initiatives can be viewed as positive responses to persistent criticisms about the police response to domestic violence. The campaign did not have national coverage, but it highlights good practice that can be disseminated. There is also a national training package designed to improve the investigation of domestic violence (ACPO and CENTREX, 2004).

Any catalyst for the improvement in the police response to domestic violence should be welcomed given the historically poor performance of the police in tackling domestic violence effectively. One-off initiatives or projects have potential for wider impact if good practice is effectively disseminated. However the process of change is likely to be slow in an organisation such as the police; changing working rules and police culture is not as easy as changing the formal policy and guidance. Some have argued that the masculine culture of the police accounts for the poor approach of the police to domestic violence cases (Gregory and Lees, 1999). Changing police culture is a difficult process, although it is perhaps useful to remember that the way that police behave in practice may not be a complete reflection of the attitudes demonstrated in the canteen (Waddington, 1999). In parts of the US the drive to improve police responses to domestic violence has resulted in the adoption of mandatory arrest policies; however the research from the US does not provide clear support for this approach. One study by Sherman and Berk (1984) suggested a significant deterrent effect for arrest, but others have failed to replicate the alleged successes of arrest in reducing future violence (Sherman, 1993). As Paradine and Wilkinson (2004) observe, measuring the causal link between arrest and violence is complex and instead of looking to the value of arrest as a long-term deterrent, perhaps it should be better viewed as giving the victim immediate respite and an opportunity to leave if she wishes.

Crown Prosecution Service

Prosecution of domestic violence in context

The CPS was set up in 1985 as a prosecuting authority formally independent of the police to address some of the perceived failings of the police being responsible for both investigation and prosecution. As a newcomer to the criminal justice system it was keen to establish a reputation for taking domestic violence seriously. In the early years of the CPS it was possible to attribute some of the problems with successfully prosecuting domestic violence cases to their relationship with the police. The CPS were in a structurally weak position as the police retained the decision as to whether or not to charge the suspect, and the CPS was heavily reliant on the police for information (Sanders, 1986). It was assumed that the CPS would not normally see cases that the police did not wish to be prosecuted (Sanders, 1986), thus the vast majority of domestic violence would be filtered out of the criminal justice process before the point of CPS involvement. However the process of attrition is complicated; not all cases that are forwarded to the CPS are forwarded with a view to prosecution. Whilst many cases forwarded to the CPS probably are constructed for prosecution (McConville et al, 1991) researchers found that certain kinds of cases, including assaults with victims where the police have misgivings about the status or commitment of the victim, are constructed with a view to discontinuance (Cretney and Davis, 1995). This is consistent with US research which suggests that prosecutors are aware that the police forward cases which they expect or even want to be dropped (Emerson and Paley, 1992). They do this for a variety of reasons including to seek 'cover' for rejecting potentially controversial cases (Emerson, 1991). Thus as the pressure was increased on the police to convey the message that they are taking domestic violence seriously, one strategy may have been to pass the buck to the CPS and let them take the criticism for dropping difficult cases (Baldwin, 1987). Although it is equally plausible to argue that, once the CPS became established, the police became aware of their failure to robustly prosecute domestic violence cases and thus put little effort into investigating them. In the US it has been argued that a poor response by the prosecuting authorities acted as a disincentive for the police to make arrests and put the resources into the kind of investigation that might sustain a successful prosecution (Lerman, 1992).

In the early years of the CPS many agencies supporting women experiencing domestic violence complained about a lack of coordination between the police and CPS and a reluctance to prosecute. For example the Women's Aid Federation of England (WAFE) argued that prosecutors were just as likely as police to believe that prosecution was inappropriate or to adhere to a myth that women always withdraw their complaints. Some organisations, such as Southall Black Sisters, complained that the CPS was less progressive than the police (House of Commons, 1993, Memoranda of Evidence to the

Home Affairs Committee on Domestic Violence). The strength of the criticism prompted the CPS in 1993 to make publicly available its policy statement for prosecuting cases of domestic violence. The policy asserted a commitment to prosecuting cases where the evidence is available and noted it would be rare that the public interest does not require a prosecution.

Prosecution policy

Since it was first issued in 1993, the CPS Policy Statement for the Prosecution of Domestic Violence Cases has undergone a number of revisions. Like its predecessors the latest version (CPS, 2005) deals with the application of the evidential and public interest tests in the Code for Crown Prosecutors (CPS, 2004) and in particular elaborates upon the role of the victim. The statement notes:

> The victim is often the only witness. This means that unless the defendant pleads guilty, or there is strong supporting evidence, it will usually be necessary for the victim to give evidence in court. We know that some victims will find this very difficult and may need practical and emotional support which agencies such as Women's Aid, Refuge, Victim Support or the Witness Service can give.
>
> (CPS 2005, para 4.1)

The reference to support available from other agencies clearly delineates the role of the CPS; it is not there to provide practical and emotional support to the victim, although within the framework of the legal process it commits itself to considering all options available to enable victims of domestic violence to give their best evidence. These options now include a range of special measures under the Youth Justice and Criminal Evidence Act 1999 (Ellison, 2001), although victims of domestic violence are not automatically entitled to use them (Burton et al, 2006). The policy statement asserts the CPS 'will not automatically assume that calling the victim is the only way to prove a case. We will actively consider what other evidence may be available, either to support the victim's evidence or as an alternative to the victim's evidence' (CPS, 2005, para 4.2). This statement is designed to underpin the policy of effective evidence gathering now being promoted for the police response to domestic violence. Using alternative evidence such as photographs of the scene and the victim's injuries, evidence of police officers and other witnesses, is seen as preferable to compelling the victim or seeking to get her written statement admitted. The option of compelling a victim to testify is mentioned in the policy statement, but the difficulties of proceeding this way are highlighted. The provisions for admission of written evidence are said to be of limited application, because 'If the victim is the only witness to the offence, it is very difficult to satisfy the court that justice is being served when the defence cannot cross-examine the only witness against them' (CPS, 2005, para 40.20).

The public interest determination is also predicated to a large extent on the involvement of the victim. It is stated that: 'if the evidential test is passed and the victim is willing to give evidence, we will almost always prosecute' (CPS, 2005, para 5.3). However if the victim withdraws a number of factors will be considered when deciding whether or not to continue on public interest grounds, including the seriousness of the offence, the victim's injuries (physical or psychological), whether the defendant used a weapon/planned the attack/has made any threats since the attack, the effect (including psychological) on any children living in the household, the chances of the defendant offending again, the continuing threat to the health and safety of the victim or anyone else who is, or may become, involved, the current state of the victim's relationship with the defendant, the effect on that relationship of continuing with the prosecution against the victim's wishes, the history of the relationship, particularly if there has been any other violence in the past and the defendant's criminal history, particularly any previous violence. It should be noted that many of the public interest criteria relate to risk assessment, however until relatively recently there has been little work in England and Wales on risk assessment in domestic violence cases and little progress towards implementing multi-agency arrangements for assessing risk (Walby and Myhill, 2001; Paradine and Wilkinson, 2004). However progress is now being made in these respects with the dissemination of Multi-Agency Risk Assessment Conferences (successfully utilised in Cardiff, see Robinson, 2004). The CPS may soon be in a better position than it has been to access the information it needs on the level and nature of threat to the health and safety of victims in domestic violence cases. The Policy Statement notes that generally 'the more serious the offence or the greater the risk of further offences, the more likely we are to prosecute in the public interest—even if victims say they do not wish us to do so' (CPS, 2005, para 5.8).

CPS practice

Since its inception it has struggled against the claim that it too readily discontinues domestic violence cases and fails to fully consider the options available when the victim is unwilling or unable to support the prosecution. One of the most notable early empirical studies of CPS decision-making in domestic violence cases (Cretney and Davis, 1996) found a significantly higher rate of victim withdrawal in domestic violence cases than in non-domestic assaults (30 per cent compared with 7 per cent). The researchers found that victim withdrawal was the main reason why prosecutors discontinued domestic violence cases. They monitored a sample of 79 cases referred to the CPS to examine how the CPS managed the process of victim withdrawal and found that prosecutors did not always follow their own guidance for the process. The policy statement in place at the time, like the existing one, required that the prosecutor delay any decision to discontinue a case until the police obtain a statement from the victim including her reasons for

withdrawing. The prosecutor was then supposed to consider all other possibilities for continuing the prosecution before discontinuing on evidential
grounds. However Cretney and Davis (1996) found in some cases where the
victim attended court to withdraw the CPS did not seek an adjournment for
the police to take a withdrawal statement, but instead required the victim to
go into the witness box and retract under oath. The researchers noted that
this approach appeared to be motivated more by a desire to protect prosecutors or the court, or even to punish the victim, rather than to protect the
victim against intimidation and ensure that the withdrawal was voluntary.

Cretney and Davis (1997a) found that prosecutors did not consider their
options for continuing a prosecution in absence of the complainant's support
(where there is no other evidence) to be viable. Prosecutors would not seek to
rely on the complainant's written statement because of the difficulties of
proving that the reason she refused to testify were fear, and the defendant's
due process rights. Compulsion was almost always rejected because prag-
matically prosecutors felt the chances of a conviction were low given that a
hostile witness was very likely to be a 'worthless' witness. They found that
prosecutors also took into account humanitarian considerations for not
compelling reluctant victims, such as not exposing the victim to risk of further
violence. However the assumption that prosecutors often made—that victims
who withdrew their complaints were 'reconciled' with their partners—may
often be inaccurate. Cretney and Davis (1997a) observe in many instances
'withdrawal need not betoken reconciliation in any real sense; there was quite
commonly no "family" for the prosecution to preserve'.

The notion of preserving a 'family' suggests that the CPS look to the
interests of any children that may exist and be affected by the domestic
violence. It is well documented that children suffer as both direct and indirect
victims of domestic violence (see the research cited in Chapter 3). Research
examining 105 domestic violence CPS case files found that almost half
included details of children under the ages of 16, many of whom had witnessed
the violence and were described as 'frightened' and 'extremely upset' (Burton,
2000). In these cases the police often adopted a 'child centred' approach;
marginalising the violence to the woman in their efforts to secure some form
of protection for the children. The police would advocate prosecution in cases
where the women did not support that action, particularly where the children
were young (under the age of 10), irrespective of whether the children were
hurt 'accidentally' or as a result of directly intervening to try and help their
mother. This 'child centred' approach was not followed by the CPS. Prosecutors appeared unconvinced that children derived any benefit from prosecution
and would blame both the victim and defendant for any adverse consequences
of the violence and prosecution. This research, like the earlier studies cited
above, found that prosecutors ordinarily acceded to the victim's wish for the
prosecution to be discontinued. In one case where an eight-year-old child
witnessed the defendant throw a TV set at the victim's head, resulting in
severe injuries and surgery to reconstruct the victim's jaw, the CPS decided to

discontinue the case because the complainant 'wanted to make a go of her marriage'. This decision was taken despite the prosecutor's assessment that there was sufficient evidence to proceed without the complainant. Whilst this may suggest family unity is an important consideration for prosecutors, in fact the research suggested that prosecutors were not generally interested in keeping families marred by violence together but felt that in situations where the parties were reconciled there was little benefit to be achieved for the woman or children by continuing a prosecution.

The emphasis on victim involvement is clearly not simply a matter of evidential imperative. Hoyle (1998) also appears to conclude that it is not so much a matter of anticipated evidential difficulties in prosecuting without the victim, as a working rule relating the perceived usefulness of a prosecution without the victim's cooperation and consent that is decisive. This conclusion has considerable implications for the view that initiatives aimed at circumventing the evidential difficulties of prosecuting without the victim can impact on the rate of attrition in domestic violence cases. It may be possible to circumvent the evidential difficulties of heavy reliance on victim testimony, although it should not be assumed that the evidential approaches evident in the US can be easily transferred to England and Wales (Ellison, 2002; 2003). However, even if the approaches can be successfully replicated, this does not necessarily mean that more prosecutions without the support of the victim are likely. The rules on the admission of hearsay evidence have been relaxed by ss 114–121 of the Criminal Justice Act 2003. Hearsay evidence can be admitted where the victim is unable to attend for physical or psychological reasons, where there is a previous inconsistent statement and where the incident has been reported to a third party. As with the earlier hearsay evidence provisions, decisions as to whether the court is likely to admit evidence under these provisions will remain a matter of discretion for the prosecutor. Whether prosecutors will be more willing to consider these provisions as offering a viable route to proceeding with a prosecution in absence of the victim's support remains to be empirically investigated. Although on the face of it the provisions look promising for cases of domestic violence, in practice it may be that they are no more utilised than their predecessors.

The CPS inspectorate has twice examined the performance of the CPS in domestic violence cases. Its first report in 1998 found that prosecution policy was not being complied with in a significant proportion of cases (HMCPSI, 1998). The inspectorate concluded 'our evidence and analysis suggest that the decision of the complainant to withdraw her evidence is often seen as a decisive factor, without obvious regard being paid to other ways of proceeding (HMCPSI, 1998, para 8.41). In 11 per cent of cases where the CPS terminated the prosecution due to victim withdrawal the inspectorate disagreed with the decision, noting the private wishes of the complainant seemed to take precedence over the public interest. The lack of any specific weighting to the public interest criteria make this an area of large discretion for prosecutors (Ashworth and Fionda, 1994) and it would be virtually impossible for anyone to challenge a decision not to prosecute on the basis that the public interest criteria have been incorrectly applied (Burton, 2001a). However, the CPS policy documents make it clear that it is the victim's interests rather than the victim's wishes that are a factor to be weighed in the public interest determination. In this respect it is important to note the inspectorate's conclusion that it was the victim's wishes, rather than necessarily their interests, which appeared determinative. The inspectorate noted that it was particularly disappointed to see the low proportion of cases where hearsay evidence was considered.

Several years later the joint inspectorates' findings (HMCPSI and HMIC, 2004) echoed many of the concerns of the earlier inspection. It was noted: 'Lawyers at initial review need to focus on evidence apart from that of the victim, either as an alternative to, or to support, the victim. Too frequently reviews in the file sample focused on the evidence provided by the victim' (HMCPSI and HMIC, 2004, p 80). The inspectorates found flaws in the flagging of domestic violence cases and also in the application of the Code for Crown Prosecutors. The Code sets out the priority of the evidential and public interest tests; if the case does not pass the evidential test then it must not go ahead no matter how important or serious it may be (CPS, 2004). However, the inspectorates found that occasionally prosecutors proceeded with cases where the evidence was weak, an approach it considered 'unlikely to assist the victim' (HMCPSI and HMIC, 2004, p 85). The reasons for this approach are unclear, perhaps it is part of a strategy for deflecting criticism, in this instance from the CPS to the courts (Baldwin, 1987)—although when a case fails it tends to be the CPS rather than the courts that are criticised, so this explanation appears somewhat unlikely.

In just under half (44 per cent) of the 418 cases examined by the joint inspectorate the victim sought to withdraw her complaint. Although the CPS has a clear policy for managing victim retraction, the inspectorates found that it complied with it in only 63.4 per cent of cases. Prosecutors are required by their policy to find out why the victim has retracted by asking the police to take a written statement from the victim explaining her reasons for withdrawing and stating whether the original statement was true. The decision as to what to do is then to be supervised by a senior prosecutor who should have access to a full risk assessment carried out by the police. The main deficiency that the inspectorates found was that the withdrawal statement did not address whether the original complaint was true or whether the withdrawal was under duress. Thus prosecutors were making their decisions on the basis of inadequate information and in some cases were not adjourning to request withdrawal statements but continuing with the old, much maligned practice, of asking victims to explain their decision to retract to the court under oath. The inspectorates found that there was scope for considerable improvement in the decision making of prosecutors when it came to considering options for continuing the prosecution upon victim withdrawal; alternatives were considered in only 60.8 per cent of cases and in only about half of the cases were the inspectorates able to establish that the decision whether or not to compel a victim to give evidence was made with the input of an experienced prosecutor. It was also concluded that prosecutors could have been more proactive in seeking material to support applications for the victim's original written statement to be admitted.

The performance of the CPS in domestic violence cases tends to be primarily assessed in relation to the decision whether or not to prosecute. However there are a number of process decisions whilst the case is proceeding in which the CPS has a significant role and which can be crucial to the victim's safety; one of the most significant of these process decisions is bail. Bail has the potential, if dealt with appropriately, to offer the victim of domestic violence a measure of protection whilst a criminal case is ongoing. The initial decision as to whether to release the defendant on bail will be taken by the police, but once the defendant first appears at court the CPS can influence the bail decision-making by appropriate representations to the magistrates. If the defendant is at very high risk of committing further offences or interfering with the victim or other witnesses then there are arguably strong grounds for seeking a remand in custody under the Bail Act 1976. Alternatively it may be possible to address such concerns by releasing the defendant on bail but subject to conditions, which may be imposed under s.3(6) of the Act, for example that the defendant does not contact the victim or go within a specified distance of where she lives and works (Hucklesby, 1994). There is very little empirical evidence available to assess the performance of the CPS in relation to bail decision-making in domestic violence cases. The joint inspectorates' assessment of CPS performance in this respect was hampered by the poor quality of file endorsement in their sample. The inspectorates were unable to ascertain whether appropriate representations were made in more than a quarter of their sample, but did ascertain in 5 per cent of cases the CPS did not make appropriate recommendations; this is compared with 68 per cent cases where they did. One troublesome issue is where the defendant is bailed with a condition not to contact the victim and the victim wishes to retract her complaint and comes to court to support removal of the bail condition. As with retraction, it is important to establish that the support of the victim for the condition to be removed is genuine and the inspectorates recommended that an adjournment be sought and that bail conditions should not be automatically relaxed. Technically the defendant is in breach of his bail by arriving at the court with the victim. As the CPS policy statement asserts it does not matter that the victim may have agreed to contact as abiding by bail conditions is the defendant's responsibility (CPS, 2005). However the robustness of the police and CPS response to breaches of bail continues to come under question. The inspectorates found that there were many cases where no action was taken in relation to breaches and no consideration was given to whether the breaches amounted to further offences. The protection offered to victims of domestic violence through bail conditions must therefore be questioned. Effective enforcement of conditions imposed by the courts is needed and the CPS has to play its part in this.

The CPS role in the criminal justice process has been enhanced considerably in recent years (Brownlee, 2004). The police no longer retain complete discretion regarding the decision to caution, prosecute or take no further action against an offender. The statutory charging scheme introduced by the Criminal Justice Act 2003 transfers the charging decision to the CPS and also introduces a scheme of conditional cautions for prosecutors. How these changes will impact on the prosecution of domestic violence cases has yet to be empirically evaluated. The CPS has begun to establish a reputation for itself as one of the more progressive government departments insofar as work on violence against women is concerned (Women's National Commission, 2006). It is claimed to be the only department 'able to give a coherent account of its strategic approach to violence against women, in terms of planning, targets, training, budgets or evaluation' (WNC, 2006, p 10).

As with arrest, there is little empirical evidence to back up the effectiveness of prosecution as a deterrent to future violence; the research in the US is ambivalent about the deterrent effect of prosecution (Ford and Regoli, 1993). There has been little support for mandatory prosecution policies in England and Wales; even in the US their validity has been questioned as a matter of principle (Hanna, 1996) and practical efficacy (Ford, 1991). The practice of 'soft no drop' policies has however received some support (Paradine and Wilkinson, 2004), and might play a role in reducing attrition.

Reducing the rate of attrition for domestic violence remains an important target for the criminal justice agencies. Thus the CPS continues to measure its success in terms of reducing discontinuances and improving the conviction rate. The CPS has carried out snapshot surveys of its performance in domestic violence cases every year since 2002. The surveys show that the conviction rate rose 20 per cent from 46 per cent in 2003 to 66 per cent in 2006; there has been a reduction in discontinuances from 17 per cent to 11 per cent and a fall in the number of victim retractions (CPS, 2006). These findings cannot all be solely attributed to the efforts of the CPS; part of the shifting landscape has been the development of specialist domestic violence courts.

Criminal courts

Empirical evidence on how the criminal courts in England and Wales respond to domestic violence is limited, but since the introduction of specialist domestic violence courts in England and Wales there is significantly more information available. The specialist domestic violence courts research will be discussed in the next chapter as it represents an innovative strategy for dealing with domestic violence. In this chapter the research on non-specialist courts will be examined.

The majority of all criminal offences that make it to court in England and Wales are dealt with by magistrates' courts (Darbyshire, 1997). As

Darbyshire (1997) points out, it would be wrong to regard the business of the magistrates as 'trivial'; they make significant decisions about where cases are heard, what happens to defendants pending trial and ultimately, if the case proceeds to summary trial, they will determine the guilt or innocence of defendants and if the defendant is convicted, the sentence to be imposed. There are a number of decisions taken by the magistrates that can be used to gauge how seriously they view particular categories of crime; two of the most significant of these are the decisions as to mode of trial and sentencing.

Decisions as to mode of trial are influenced by a range of factors, some of which are outside the control of the magistrates. One of the main factors is the level of charge, which is in the hands of the CPS. In the past the CPS has been criticised for charging the summary only offence of common assault in domestic violence cases when a more serious charge of an Offences Against the Person Act 1861, s 47 assault could have been sustained (Cretney and Davis, 1997b). The preference for the lesser charge was explained by a desire to keep domestic violence cases in the magistrates' court due to speed and a reduction of uncertainty. Prosecutors interviewed by Cretney and Davis (1997b) claimed that magistrates have adequate sentencing powers and are more likely than judges and juries to see domestic violence through to conviction. Cretney and Davis point out however that complainants may not always see the reduction of charges to keep the case in the magistrates' courts as reflecting the level of harm they have suffered (see also Fenwick, 1997). A more recent study of mode of trial decision-making has also found that domestic violence cases are more likely to be disposed of in the magistrates' court than the Crown Court (Cammiss, 2006). From a sample of 100 cases which included 17 examples of domestic violence, Cammiss found that domestic violence cases were deemed suitable for summary trial in 76 per cent of cases, compared to 43 per cent overall. As the profile of offences does not explain the differential treatment, one interpretation of these findings could be that the magistrates view domestic violence as less serious than other offences against the person and are too ready to retain jurisdiction in triable either way cases which should be sent to the Crown Court for trial. The decision as to venue in triable-either-way cases requires the magistrates to take into account the seriousness of the offence and whether their powers of punishment are adequate (Magistrates' Court Act 1980, ss 19–23). However the magistrates do not make this determination in an information vacuum. Researchers have long queried the strong correlation between prosecutors' representations and magistrates' mode of trial decision-making; asking whether magistrates are 'too prosecution minded' or whether prosecutors are anticipating and responding to local court cultures (Herbert, 2003; 2004). Cammiss maintains that the explanation for his findings lies in the partial accounts of prosecutors. He cites for example prosecutors minimising the manner of the assault by focusing on the outcome (lack of injury) rather than the manner in which violence was inflicted. Cammiss (2006) concludes that the victim's voice is often lost in mode of trial hearings. Prosecutors are more willing to recommend Crown Court trial when the relationship between the victim and the defendant has been ended and the complainant has demonstrated a clear commitment to the legal process. This study provides us with yet another example of the importance of appreciating prospective and retrospective decision-making horizons (Emerson and Paley, 1992) when analysing the criminal justice response to domestic violence. What on the face of it might be interpreted as 'courts failing victims' (Cretney and Davis, 1997b) might also be reinterpreted as the failure of the CPS to convey the full picture of domestic violence to the magistrates.

Whilst there is little research specifically examining the trial process in domestic violence cases, the general literature suggests that attacks on the victim's credibility are a key part of defence strategies (Rock, 1993). The nature of adversarial trial is not markedly different in assault cases than in other type of offences. Research in Australia for example has shown that there are a limited number of discrediting techniques which are common to both sexual and non-sexual assault (Brereton, 1997). One of the key discrediting techniques is to suggest false motives for making a complaint, for example to secure an advantage in residence or contact proceedings. However, as was noted in Chapter 3, the victim is unlikely to find that the presence of criminal proceedings, or even a conviction for domestic violence, is given much weight by the family courts when it comes to determining contact.

The empirical evidence on magistrates' approaches to the sentencing of domestic should be viewed through the lens of serial decision-making (Hawkins, 1992), as the practices of agencies earlier on in the process may affect the information and options available to the magistrates when it comes to sentencing. It has traditionally been asserted that the sentences imposed for domestic violence trivialise the violence and are a totally inadequate response (Edwards, 1989). Cretney and Davis (1997b) found that magistrates commonly bound over a defendant to keep the peace, and of those which proceeded to conviction and sentence the most common disposal was a conditional discharge (36 per cent), followed by a fine (20 per cent). The disparity in the treatment of domestic violence and non domestic violence was evident in their study; conditional discharges and probation were much more likely to be used for domestic (54 per cent) than non domestic assaults (21 per cent). A custodial sentence was imposed in only 11 per cent of domestic assaults. It was found that prison or community service was more likely when the court understood that the relationship had ended. Although magistrates tried to justify their penalties on the grounds that they did not wish to penalise victims in ongoing relationships, Cretney and Davis concluded 'the penalties imposed for domestic violence do not reflect the seriousness of these assaults and the complainants feel strongly this is so' (Cretney and Davis, 1997b, p 153). Although magistrates may be partly hampered by the nature of the legal framework; its focus on single incidents and inability to reflect a history of domestic violence (as discussed in Chapter 5), the attitudes of magistrates to domestic violence may also comprise part of the problem.

A study of magistrates' attitudes to domestic violence carried out by Gilchrist and Blissett (2002) used six vignettes to compare the effects of children being present, the effect of alcohol, the effect of need for medical treatment, and the effect location of the assault (in public/private) on sentencing recommendations. The researchers also compared an alcohol fuelled assault upon a stranger in public with an alcohol fuelled domestic assault in public. No statistically significant differences were found except for the magistrates' recommending more severe sentences when alcohol was involved and also when medical treatment was required. In addition domestic assault at home without alcohol or children present was less severely sentenced than any other vignette. Nevertheless qualitative analysis of the data showed that magistrates' decisions were influenced by victim blaming and 'magistrates discussed domestic violence very differently from stranger violence' (Gilchrist and Blisset, 2002, p 358). Although magistrates tended to see the presence of children as an aggravating feature, some felt that this made the matter more appropriate for the family courts. The researchers note that their findings have significant implications for those promoting a coordinated community justice response to domestic violence in England and Wales because such innovative intervention programmes rely critically for their success on the understanding and commitment of magistrates. This is a theme that will be taken up in the next chapter when innovative approaches to domestic violence in the criminal justice system are examined.

The criminal justice response to rape

The conviction rate for rape has long been a cause for concern (Lees, 1996; Harris and Grace, 1999; Gregory and Lees, 1999). At the same time as the judiciary was expanding the definition of rape to include marital rape the conviction rate for rape was falling. In 2002 the conviction rate for rape stood at just 5.6 per cent (Kelly et al, 2005). The majority of reported rapes are committed by acquaintances or intimates, although Gregory and Lees (1999) advise caution on the use of the term 'acquaintance' which may refer to stranger rapes barely concealed by the fact that the rapist introduced himself to the victim shortly before the attack to make his defence of consent more viable. In intimate rape cases identification is not the difficult issue it can be often be in stranger rape cases, although 'detection' is a different matter, given the narrow meaning of that term in the criminal justice context (HMCPSI, 2007). The process of attrition has therefore been the subject of a number of evaluations (Harris and Grace, 1999; Kelly et al, 2005; HMCPSI, 2007). The research shows that the majority of cases are lost in the early stages of the criminal justice process, with up to two-thirds lost during the investigation, often due to the victim withdrawing her complaint (Kelly et al, 2005). The decision to withdraw may be linked to the complainant's treatment by the police. Bad publicity in the early 1980s resulted in policy commitments to treat rape complainants sensitively but as Gregory and Lees (1999) observe, 'old attitudes die hard' (p 60).

CPS decision-making is another key point in the attrition process; Harris and Grace (1999) found 8 per cent of cases were discontinued by the CPS, and although Kelly et al found that discontinuance was a relatively small element in the attrition of cases that reach the CPS, they observe that the CPS were involved in many cases at an earlier stage and may have contributed to attrition during the investigation. More recently HMCPSI (2007) highlighted the need for both the police and CPS to revisit the processes in rape cases to ensure that defences of consent can be challenged rigorously. Whilst the CPS has introduced specialist prosecutors for rape cases the inspectorate found that there are no minimum standards of competence and the levels of knowledge and competence of the specialist varied enormously.

The trial itself represents another important point in attrition and many rape victims are rightly concerned about the nature of the trial and styles of cross-examination (Lees, 1996; Temkin, 2000). In the traditional adversarial system the opportunities for prosecutors to allay victim's concerns are limited, although modified approaches have been suggested (Ellison, 2007). Rape trials have been traditionally characterised by stereotypical views of the offence and the victim. The 'ideal' rape victim is a stranger to the rapist, sexually inexperienced, has a 'respectable' lifestyle, fights hard, is seriously injured and reports the attack immediately (Estrich, 1987; Adler, 1987). The legal system has in the past worked on the assumption that sexual experience indicates indiscriminate consent and a history of consensual sexual relations with the defendant made it difficult to establish rape. Despite new restrictions on the admissibility of sexual history evidence (Youth Justice and Criminal Evidence Act 1999, s 41), the trial process continues to be harsh for the victim and the protection offered by the new legislation may be weak (Kelly et al, 2006).

Conclusion

All the criminal justice agencies now have a policy imperative to treat domestic violence seriously, but understanding and translating this policy into practice at an operational level continues, it seems, to be difficult. It is clear that the criminal justice agencies rely heavily on victims to achieve their own goals and as such there is an ongoing dialogue between what the agencies want and what the victim needs. In this dialogue it often seems that the victim's voice is drowned out as the police, CPS and courts pursue their own performance targets and find new ways of marginalising the victim from the process. The research evidence discussed above focuses on accounts of how the criminal justice agencies perform in domestic violence cases, but has hardly touched on the victim's perspectives as to how they are treated by the criminal justice agencies. Arguably it is the victim's experience of the process that really matters and this will be taken up in the final chapter. Before that however, innovative approaches to tackling domestic violence in the criminal justice system will be examined.

7 Improving the criminal justice response

It has long been fashionable to look to other jurisdictions, particularly the US, for possible solutions to the difficulties the criminal justice system has had in effectively responding to domestic violence in England and Wales. The pro-arrest approach introduced to England and Wales into the policy statements circulated by the Home Office to the police in the late 1980s and early 1990s was partly based on alleged successes of mandatory arrest policies pioneered in parts of the US a decade earlier. The more recent invocation of 'enhanced' or 'effective' evidence gathering as a solution to the difficulties of victim-based prosecutions similarly draws on the alleged successes of the approach of prosecuting domestic violence without the victim's testimony in parts of US. This trend in looking abroad for solutions to the problem of developing an adequate criminal justice response to domestic violence is continued by the recent development of specialist domestic violence courts in England and Wales. Specialist domestic violence courts are at the core of the government's strategy for improving the handling of domestic violence cases by the criminal justice agencies. The crucial question is whether the specialist court initiative has the ability to deliver the promised improvements.

Background to domestic violence court specialisation

The development of specialist domestic violence courts occurred much earlier in the US than it did in England and Wales. In the US specialist domestic violence courts have been running since the earlier 1980s in some states. A survey carried out in 2001 found that there were over 300 courts in operation in different parts of the US at that time (Kellitz, 2001). The domestic violence courts in the US have developed according to a variety of different models and vary in what they seek to achieve, but at a most basic level most share the objectives of improving victim safety and increasing perpetrator accountability. Many of the courts have been subject to individual evaluations and also feature in overview reports that seek to compare the model and performance of different courts. This literature provided a rich source of data for policy makers in England and Wales seeking to learn from court specialisation in other jurisdictions (Cook et al, 2004; Plotniknoff and Woolfson, 2005).

One of the main differences between the specialist domestic violence courts in the US is the type of cases they handle; some handle only civil matters, some handle only criminal matters and limit their caseload according to the seriousness of the offence, others handle both the civil and criminal components of a domestic violence case on the basis of a 'one family, one court' principle. The approach of some of the specialist domestic violence courts in the US is firmly routed in 'problem solving' or therapeutic justice. This problem solving or therapeutic justice approach conceives a strong role for the judge in working with the other agencies and the defendant in ensuring that the defendant is referred to appropriate treatment programmes and his performance on this programmes is effectively monitored (Berman and Feinblatt, 2005). The potential for any of the models of specialist domestic violence courts operating in the US to be transported to the different cultural and legal context of England and Wales obviously poses some challenges (Walsh, 2001; Burton, 2006). Nevertheless there are arguably valuable lessons to be learned from the US courts.

Brooklyn Felony Domestic Violence court has been highlighted as a 'good practice' example of a criminal only domestic violence court (Cook et al, 2004). The Brooklyn court clusters domestic violence felony cases to a trained dedicated judge and advocacy team. Victims of domestic violence have access to independent advocacy support provided by 'Safe Horizon' and also specialist support from counselling services located within the District Attorney's office. Evaluation of the court found that the provision of specialist support from both within and outside the criminal justice system made it more likely that the victim would remain committed to the prosecution and improved the quality of information available to prosecutors and the court. Specialisation was also found to speed up the processing of cases, reduce the number of hearings required, and increase the percentage of defendants pleading guilty (Newmark et al, 2001). Overall the specialist court did not increase the proportion of convictions, but it did affect the mode of case disposition. There was an increase in the proportion of defendants who, having initially pleaded not guilty, changed their plea to guilty before trial. The researchers concluded that these were cases that were likely to have resulted in conviction if they had reached trial, but were unclear on why more defendants decided to plead guilty rather than go through with a trial. They speculate that there might be greater use of plea bargaining in the court, which they say may perhaps be related to the fact that the victim has more support and this in turn enhances the evidence available. The sentencing practices of the Brooklyn courts did not become significantly more punitive; convicted defendants were only marginally more likely to be imprisoned than was the case before the court came into operation. More surprisingly, the court did not increase the proportion of defendants sentenced to perpetrator programmes. However it did have powers to mandate participation in perpetrator programmes as a condition of pre-release. The researchers hypothesise that the power to require perpetrators to participate in treatment before conviction may explain why there was no increase in treatment based penalties post-conviction (Newmark et al, 2001).

The Brooklyn Felony Domestic Violence offers an interesting comparator for specialist courts in England and Wales. As a criminal only court it is closest in model terms to the first domestic violence courts developed here, yet it also has distinctive features that are not replicated in the UK system, both in terms of its institutional context and the powers available to the court. It remains significant because it highlights the limitations of a single justice system approach to court specialisation. Although the Brooklyn court, as with many other criminal only specialist domestic violence courts in the US, does bring some improvements to the criminal justice response to domestic violence (see also Kellitz, 2001), it does not address the issues of overlapping civil or family law matters that may be pending in relation to the same family. In some parts of the US specialist civil-only domestic violence courts have been developed to address the problems that the civil/family courts have in adequately responding to domestic violence. The need for cases to be effectively prioritised and for victims to receive advice and assistance in completing paperwork to obtain restraining orders has been addressed through court specialisation in Quincy District Court, Massachusetts (Salzman, 1994). Although the Quincy court does have links with the criminal courts insofar as they refer women to daily briefing sessions at the District Attorney's Office where there are staff to advise them on their rights and services available when making a criminal complaint, the civil and criminal aspects of a case are not fully integrated.

In parts of the US efforts have been made to develop integrated domestic violence courts that handle both the criminal and civil/family law matters arising out of domestic violence. There is not a single model or template of a combined or integrated domestic violence court; courts looked at the limitations of a single system approach and devised a number of different ways for improving the interface between the civil and criminal jurisdictions. The Clark County Domestic Violence Court, Vancouver, Washington provides victims of domestic violence with a 'one-stop shop' where they can obtain redress under the criminal law and remedies under the civil law from one judge knowledgeable in domestic violence matters (Fritzler and Simon, 2000). Although there were some teething troubles in conferring the civil jurisdiction upon judges who had traditionally only dealt with criminal matters these were overcome and the court was set up with minimal funding. One of the key benefits of the integrated approach is that it avoids inconsistent orders which might previously have been made in the separate systems and which caused much frustration to victims. The court is not only innovative in integrating the justice systems, it is also committed to the problem solving approach mentioned above.

Convicted defendants in the Clark County Domestic Violence Court are nearly always given intensive supervision by probation and/or frequent court reviews when they are sentenced. The treatment and monitoring of domestic violence offenders is regarded as an important aspect of the goals of the court. In this sense the Clark County court and others like it, for example the District of Columbia Domestic Violence Court (Steketee et al, 2000), depart from the traditional adversarial model of criminal justice that is a feature of both the US and England and Wales (Sanders and Young, 2006). Whereas in the traditional adversarial model the judge's role ends upon sentencing, the problem-solving approach requires the judge to undertake a significant ongoing role in monitoring compliance with the court orders and encouraging the defendant to change his behaviour. Whether problem-solving approaches work and are an appropriate response to domestic violence is a matter of ongoing evaluation and debate. There is some research which suggests that judicial monitoring does have benefits which outweigh its disadvantages (Gondolf, 2000; Steketee et al, 2000; Burton, 2006). For example Gondolf's research suggests that monitoring reduces the rate of non-completion of treatment programmes and in turn reduces the rate of recidivism. Supporters of courts adopting an integrated and problem-solving-approach to domestic violence assert that they represent a levelling of the playing field that has long been tilted against victims of domestic violence (Berman and Feinblatt, 2005). Arguments such as these formed the impetus for seeking to import some of the core values and components of successful specialist domestic violence courts in the US (Sacks, 2002; Mazur and Aldrich, 2002) to England and Wales.

Domestic violence courts in England and Wales

The first specialist domestic violence court was set up in Leeds in 1999. The court operates in the criminal summary jurisdiction only and clusters domestic violence cases so that pre-trial hearings (except first remand) are all heard on the same day each week by a specially trained magistrates (Grundy, 2000). The clustering of cases facilitates the provision of support by independent advocates for those women who wish to take up the services provided by the Help Advice and Law Team (HALT). Specialist domestic violence police officers and representatives of HALT are always available for the court hearings. The introduction of the specialist court was found to improve the information exchanged between the agencies, speed up the processing of cases, and increase the training of participants in the court and their recognition of the seriousness of domestic violence. Similar successes were reported from early evaluations of specialist cluster courts set up in West London (Standing Together, 2002; 2003) and Wolverhampton (Cook, 2003) in 2002. A different model of 'fast tracking' domestic violence cases was adopted in Cardiff in 2001, again resulting in a number of reported improvements to the criminal justice process (Robinson, 2003). The Government were keen to establish what could be learned from the performance of these first domestic violence courts and commissioned an evaluation of the four courts mentioned above and Derby specialist domestic violence court, again a criminal-only cluster court operating in the magistrates' jurisdiction, which opened for business in May 2003. The evaluation was to inform a decision about whether to roll specialist domestic violence courts out across the whole of England and Wales (Cook et al, 2004)

The research carried out by Cook et al (2004) drew upon the existing evaluations in all five sites, in particular to establish baseline data, where possible, for what was happening in the area before the specialist courts came into being. The baseline data was however far from complete and so new data were gathered though observations and interviews at all five sites and analysis of a sample of 216 case files completed in a three-month period towards the end of 2003. The qualitative data collected focused on practitioners and victims' perspectives on the implementation and the impact of the specialist domestic violence courts. The case file data was analysed quantitatively to chart the progress and outcomes, including sentencing practices, of the sample of cases and identify any significant characteristics related to outcome.

Through the qualitative data the researchers were able to provide detailed portraits of the models of specialisation in operation in each site, highlighting the similarities and differences. Although there were variations in the arrangements some common features were found. Perhaps the most significant shared feature was the provision of independent advocacy support and/ or specialist domestic violence police officers present at court to advise and support victims. This feature, combined with the provision of specialist training for practitioners and effective multi-agency working arrangements, seemed to be crucial to the success of the courts. The process evaluation found a high level of commitment from individuals working in the specialist courts and good working relationships between the agencies.

The success of the courts in terms of meeting traditional criminal justice targets, such as speeding up cases and reducing the number of court hearings, was found to be somewhat patchy. Some sites did provide evidence the number of court hearings had reduced, for example Leeds and West London, but often defence lawyers were blamed for requesting adjournments that necessitated more hearings and slowed down the progress of the case. This reinforces the advice promulgated in the good practice guidance devised in the US (Sacks, 2002) to try to involve defence lawyers at the outset and ensure that they are familiar with the approach and requirements of the specialist court. Specialist domestic violence officers being present at court can help to speed up the processing of cases because they can facilitate access to information on the spot. However this should not be allowed to conflict with the best approach to dealing with victim retraction, which may actually require an adjournment to ensure that the victim's views are being properly ascertained and assessed in relation to the decision as to whether or not to continue the prosecution.

The specialist courts did not have any impact on the level of victim retraction; about half of all victims in the case file sample retracted their complaint at some point in the proceedings. This confirmed practitioners' views that specialisation did not reduce victim withdrawal, which from the point of criminal justice targets could be viewed as disappointing. Practitioners within the specialist courts disagreed on the reasons why victims retracted their complaints; voluntary sector respondents thought it was partly due to lack of information about the case, which was not something that the criminal justice practitioners highlighted. Although retractions might be classed as 'failures', the voluntary sector support agencies were more flexible in their interpretation. If the victim receives appropriate advice and support, and despite this feels that the right decision is not to go ahead, that 'supported retraction' is much better than decision to withdraw taken in isolation. Viewed from this perspective, reduction in the proportion of victim retractions is not an appropriate measure of the success of domestic violence courts (Robinson and Cook, 2006). A better measure of success is to look at how the specialist courts handle the retraction process. Court specialisation is beneficial because it facilitates the provision of independent advocacy support that underpins the supported retraction process.

It was noted in the last chapter that the police have been encouraged in recent years to adopt the policy of effective evidence gathering and the CPS are expected to consider evidence other than that of the victim for taking forward prosecutions in cases where the victim remains committed and when she does not. The available empirical evidence suggests that these policy initiatives are poorly implemented in general, thus it is interesting to know whether court specialisation has any influence on improving police and CPS performance in these respects. Cook et al (2004) found that the specialist domestic violence courts acted as a focus for enhanced or effective evidence gathering. The existence of the specialist court and the associated training for practitioners reinforced the policy message that gathering evidence other than the victim's statement was important in all domestic violence cases. Nevertheless, even in the context of specialist domestic violence courts there is much room for improvement in implementing the effective evidence gathering policy in practice. Although practitioners interviewed tended to believe that the quality of evidence collected had improved since the introduction of the specialist domestic violence court, the case file analysis showed that police and prosecutors were still reliant predominately on the victim's testimony and there were missed opportunities for a wider range of evidence to be gathered. Whilst practitioners acknowledged that photographic evidence of the scene and the victim's injuries could be a powerful evidential tool, the research found that case exhibits, which were mainly photographs, were only present in 30 per cent, of cases despite the fact that 78 per cent of victims suffered injuries. Issuing the police with a set of prompts to assist in the evidence gathering process, as was done during the 2006 Enforcement Campaigns, could potentially yield improvements in the evidence available to specialist domestic violence courts. Court specialisation on its own is not enough to significantly improve the evidence-gathering process, although later evaluation of the Croydon specialist domestic violence court (see below) did find a dramatic improvement in evidence gathering once a specialist court was introduced in combination with a set of prompts for investigating officers.

Good evidence has the potential to increase the proportion of guilty pleas. Many practitioners in the five-site evaluation felt that defendants still delayed pleading guilty to the last moment, testing the commitment of the victim to the day of trial. From the criminal justice perspective this again represents a failure because it misses the target of encouraging early guilty pleas and reducing the number of cracked trials. It may also represent a failure for the victim in that she has to bear the stress and uncertainty of waiting for the trial and the trauma of attending court on the day of trial. This depends in part on how well the victim is supported through the process; some may feel that there is more protection and support for them whilst the case is ongoing than there is once a conclusion is reached. The case file evaluation found wide variation in the proportion of guilty pleas in the specialist courts and the timing of those pleas. This perhaps suggests that local cultures are more influential than the existence of specialist courts *per se*. There was also significant variation in the use of bindovers across the five sites; some courts using them very frequently and others hardly at all. The fact that there is little evidence that the domestic violence courts increased the proportion of defendants convicted overall could clearly be viewed as a failure when one the goals of the courts, at least from the government's perspective, is to bring more perpetrators to justice. Cook et al (2004) argue however that the comparatively low numbers of discontinuances up to trial could shed a different light on this finding; suggesting that every attempt is made within the specialist courts to hold perpetrators to account by continuing the cases right up to the point of trial.

The success of specialist domestic violence courts needs to be measured in terms of the process as well as the outcome, however the key outcome which is often used to assess the performance of the courts is their sentencing practices. The sentencing of domestic violence has long been troubled territory. As discussed in Chapter 5, there is now more formal guidance on the appropriate penalties and what should be taken into account as aggravating and mitigating factors (SGC, 2006). The five sites were evaluated before this guidance came into effect, and also at a time when the provision of perpetrator programmes was patchy both nationally and across the sites evaluated. In this sense the findings of Cook et al are dated and represent a snapshot of practice in the early days of the courts. Nevertheless the sentencing outcomes in the five sites were perhaps somewhat surprising. The practitioners interviewed expressed strong views that the sentencing practices of the courts improved with specialisation. Respondents from both the criminal justice agencies and the voluntary sector support agencies both believed that the magistrates' attitudes towards appropriate penalties for domestic violence had changed and they were much less likely to accept the view that it was 'just a domestic' and adopt victim blaming approaches. Despite claims that attitudes of the magistrates had undergone a sea change, looking at the actual penalties imposed in the case file study the most common penalty was a conditional discharge followed by a fine. Nevertheless nearly one-third of convicted offenders did receive a community rehabilitation order, some of which included referral to a perpetrator programme. Given the overall context of limited guidance on appropriate sentencing and limited availability of perpetrator programmes this is a fairly positive finding. Now that the national availability of perpetrator programmes has greatly improved, the sentencing options available to the courts have been expanded and the guidance more clearly delineated, one would expect to see further improvement in the sentencing practices of the specialist courts if the initial assessment that attitudinal factors are not a barrier to appropriate sentencing outcomes is correct.

None of the first five specialist domestic violence courts in England and Wales was able to meet the criticism of a lack of communication between the criminal and civil justice systems in cases where a family experiencing domestic violence were involved in both systems. This is not a purely hypothetical problem; the lack of integration has proved problematic in cases which have reached the appellate courts (see Burton, 2004). Not only were the five courts based solely in the criminal justice system, Cook et al also found that the arrangements for sharing information were very poorly developed. Only one of the courts, West London, kept a log of cases in the civil courts which it used to cross-check for cases appearing in the specialist court. Most of the courts were entirely reliant on the victim and her advocate making them aware of any ongoing proceedings in the civil/family courts. Awareness is of course only part of the problem, the fact that the criminal courts know that matters are also being dealt with elsewhere does not necessarily mean that they can provide a seamless response to domestic violence or cut down on the demands that the legal system places on the victim in seeking effective redress against domestic violence.

The first steps are now being taken towards an integrated domestic violence court in England and Wales. Croydon specialist domestic violence court aspires to be the forerunner in this area and after starting life as a criminal-only cluster court is now evolving to the combined court model. Croydon specialist domestic violence court is also distinctive in modelling itself more closely on the problem-solving approach evident in some of the US courts described above. This is perhaps not surprising given that the New York Center for Court Innovation was instrumental in the formulation of the policies and templates for the court (Mazur and Aldrich, 2002).

Croydon court was evaluated alongside a project in Caerphilly as part of a follow-up project to the five-site evaluation discussed above. A similar methodology comprising both qualitative and quantitative data was adopted, in this instance taking a sample of 291 cases from the two courts over a 15-month period to the end of 2004 (Vallely et al, 2005). The Croydon domestic violence court has had notable success in encouraging the implementation of the policy of effective evidence gathering; the proportion of cases with case exhibits and medical statements almost doubled after the specialist court was introduced. The impact of better evidence gathering was seen in an increase in the number of defendants convicted in Croydon as a result of being found guilty following trial. The sentencing practices of the magistrates also improved significantly post-specialisation; the use of financial penalties dropped and referrals to perpetrator programmes increased markedly. Croydon is also unique in being the first court to introduce a procedure whereby the defendant's compliance with community rehabilitation orders, now replaced by community orders, is reviewed by the court after three months. Practitioners interviewed by Vallely et al (2005) all agreed that the introduction of 'compliance hearings' in the style of some of the problem-solving courts in the US was a significant feature and benefit of the court. Compliance hearings were thought to benefit both the magistrates, who get feedback on the effectiveness of the penalties they impose, and the defendant, who receives feedback on his compliance with the order and ongoing encouragement/admonishment, if necessary, to complete the course. The victims with cases going through the specialist domestic violence court at Croydon do have access to independent advocacy support, and generally this helps them in getting their voices heard. At the time of the evaluation there was no opportunity for the victims to be involved in the compliance hearings, but research suggests that victims want to be involved in supervision and monitoring (Lewis, 2004) and this represents good practice.

The evidence suggests that the Croydon model may well be pointing the way ahead for other specialist domestic violence courts. The Government has reaffirmed its commitment to support the expansion of specialist domestic violence courts. The Home Office implemented plans for 25 new specialist domestic violence courts in 2005–6 and by April 2007 there were 64 specialist domestic violence courts in operation in England and Wales. Whilst initially many of these courts will exist as criminal cluster courts only, there is potential for them to evolve to combined courts, or for new courts to start from scratch with the combined model.

Do specialist courts benefit victims?

Much of the evidence on the 'success' of domestic violence courts discussed above relates to their performance from the perspectives of the criminal justice agencies and measures success according to targets devised for the criminal justice system. Whilst success in these terms is important to criminal justice policy makers it nevertheless begs the question of whether specialist domestic violence courts really benefit victims. In the past it has been rare for public sector services to look at the perspectives of victims of domestic violence on their experiences of the services provided to them. Hague et al (2003) assert that victims of domestic violence have rarely been 'regarded as competent participants in the policy making process' (p 46). In recent years more effort has been made to include victims of domestic violence in the policy-making process and to access their perspectives through empirical research.

In the final chapter the findings of this research will be examined in more detail, but in this section the focus will be upon victims' perspectives of their experiences in the specialist domestic violence court setting.

One of the first specialist domestic violence courts in England and Wales, the court at West London, has been identified as a forerunner in empowering women to get their voices heard in the design and implementation of innovative multi-agency responses to domestic violence (Hague et al, 2003). The specialist domestic violence court at West London magistrates' court is coordinated by the Standing Together Against Domestic Violence multi-agency partnership. Standing Together has carried out a number of consultations with 'survivors' of domestic violence to provide a framework for monitoring and improving how the agencies respond. Consultations with victims or survivors of domestic violence are a core component of how the court at West London evaluates its success. Standing Together does not ignore other measures of success but the voice of the victim is central to what it is seeking to achieve.

The founding principle of Standing Together is putting the survivor at the centre of the process (Standing Together, 2003). Consultations with survivors before the specialist court was introduced revealed a range of problems with the courts and other criminal justice agencies (Standing Together, 2002b). Generally the women consulted felt that magistrates' attitudes about domestic violence needed to improve and that women needed more information and support to make it through the court process. Many women had fears about facing the defendant at court; they wanted to know what was going to happen and be better prepared for cross-examination. The women were keen on other witnesses and evidence being used to support the case more frequently. In terms of sentencing they endorsed perpetrator programmes and in general wanted penalties that effectively conveyed the seriousness of what the defendant had done and helped to make them safer, although they had mixed views about the effectiveness of restraining orders (Standing Together, 2002b). A consultation carried out with survivors of domestic violence one year after the introduction of the specialist court found that women welcomed the introduction of a dedicated court and felt that the awareness of judges and prosecutors was greatly improved. Magistrates were perceived to be well trained and taking domestic violence seriously, although women did express concerns about the layout of the court, the proximity to the defendant and the lack of special measures such as screens. The presence of independent advocates helped women to feel safer and they were generally very impressed with the advocacy services provided by ADVANCE (Standing Together, 2003).

The research evaluating the first five specialist domestic violence courts and two courts in a follow-up evaluation also accessed victims' perspectives on their experiences at all seven sites (Cook et al, 2004; Vallely et al, 2005). In the five-site evaluation victims perspectives could only be accessed indirectly due to the time frame of the research, but in Croydon and Caerphilly in-depth interviews were carried out with 11 victims at each site. These interviews sought to establish victims' perspectives on their experiences of the specialist domestic violence court and the agencies involved in the work of the court. Insofar as victims had experiences of the criminal justice process prior to specialisation the interviews also sought their opinions on whether specialisation had improved the process and outcomes for them.

As might be expected there is variation in the experiences of victims using the specialist domestic violence courts; not all received a consistently good response from all the agencies involved or felt that their experiences were much better than pre-specialisation. Despite this, positive evaluations of the specialist court process were fairly common and victims discerned improvements in the response of key agencies such as the police and CPS. The majority (16/22) of victims rated their interactions with the police positively and in Caerphilly five victims noted that there was a marked improvement upon how the police had responded when compared to a previous domestic violence incident. One of the sticking points remains the provision of adequate information about the progression of the case, in particular details of bail conditions and release of the defendant from custody. Victims need this information to make arrangements to ensure their own safety. Thus inadequate police performance in this respect undermines one of the key goals of the victim in calling the police; to keep themselves and their children safe (Hoyle and Sanders, 2000).

The specialist court research found that victims' confidence in the criminal justice system was closely related to the gathering of evidence. Victims believed that their cases need to be based on as much evidence as possible and were therefore frustrated when opportunities to gather evidence were missed. As the research found that the criminal justice agencies did miss numerous opportunities for effective or enhanced evidence gathering, it is unsurprising that negative views came through from the victims on evidence gathering. Some victims were upset that photographic evidence of their injuries was not taken, others were disappointed with the quality of the images, which they believed were so poor they did not reflect the true extent of the injury sustained. One victim commented on the photographs taken by the police in her case as follows: 'They were taken at the police station . . . they were hopeless because they were taken so far away that you couldn't see anything. The injuries did not look as serious as they were. My daughter ended up taking some the next day and the bruises were so much clearer, and showed his fingerprints which was important because he said that I had fallen' (Vallely et al, 2005, p 65). Good images have the potential to increase the victims' confidence that the harm sustained will be effectively conveyed to the magistrates.

In about half the cases the victim stated that there were witnesses to the assault, usually children but the police rarely pursued statements from them. The victims themselves were ambivalent about the use of children as witnesses; some were keen, others were not, but there is evidence that those who had reservations did not understand the special procedures in place for taking children's statements and the hearing of children's evidence at court. This is consistent with the findings of other research which suggest the police do not always effectively communicate information about special measures to potential child witnesses and their carers (Burton et al, 2006).

It is clear that even within specialist domestic violence courts there is scope for improving the police response to domestic violence from the victim's perspective. Victim satisfaction with the specialist domestic violence courts tends to stem not so much from their interaction with the criminal justice agencies but from the support that they receive from the independent advocacy services. The majority of victims who had contact with Project SAFF in Caerphilly and CDVAS in Croydon were very happy with the services they received. Both advocacy services provided practical help and emotional support to the victims, and were often able to fill in some of the gaps in information about the progress of the case through the criminal justice system. Thus one victim remarked the advocacy service 'were fantastic . . . my main contact. They made me feel reassured' (p 42), another stated 'They called me a lot and changed my locks. They have kept me updated, brilliant really' (p 66). It is important to recognise that not all victims had positive experiences of the advocacy services, particularly where the roles and responsibilities of the various agencies offering support were not clearly defined; however this cannot undermine the overwhelmingly positive response to advocacy provision. This finding is consistent with other research which suggests the high value of advocacy services to victims of domestic violence (Hester and Westmarland, 2005).

It was noted above that victim advocates often had a different perspective on the significance of victim retraction compared to the criminal justice agencies. The research examined victims' perspectives on the significance of retraction and how they felt that the process had been managed. In many cases the victims stated that they decided not to retract their complaints, partly due to the support provided by the advocacy service. One victim stated: 'I didn't retract this time. I had done lots of times before but I think that was because I didn't feel anyone was taking me seriously and I thought that I was just being left to do things. This time round it was totally different. To be honest I think that the only reason I kept going this time was because of the advocate support' (p 43). Another said: 'The support to me was vital, I don't think that I would have gone to court without it' (p 67). Advocacy support appears then to have the potential to reduce retractions, although overall the retraction rate remains high in specialist courts. Of the victims who did withdraw, one felt further disempowered when the case was continued without her, another saw the witness summons as a welcome relief; removing the decision from her hands and curtailing the prospect of potential recriminations. These polarised views replicate the theoretical debates about whether it is beneficial to prosecute domestic violence when the victim withdraws (Hanna, 1996; Mills, 2003).

Victims' experiences of their appearances at court were influenced by their views on the facilities and how safe they felt. Most felt that the amount of time they spent waiting was okay but some felt the facilities could have been improved and more could have been done to make them feel protected in the courtroom. Some victims lamented not being told about screens or other measures which they might have found helpful. Since both courts were equipped with special measures it may be that the discretionary criteria to be applied in domestic violence cases works against their effective deployment (Burton et al, 2006), in particular the CPS may be overly cautious in applying for special measures in domestic violence cases. Although about half the victims interviewed were satisfied with the CPS performance overall, as with the police, this indicates that even within the specialist court setting there is room for considerable improvement in the response of the criminal justice agencies to domestic violence. Victims want the prosecutor to make an effort to introduce themselves and explain court procedure. If lawyers do not speak to victims or appear to have little knowledge of their case this significantly undermines victim confidence and satisfaction with the CPS.

The CPS does have an important role in conveying information about the victim's experiences to the court. As was noted in the last chapter the narrative of the prosecutor does not always match the victim's experience (Cammiss, 2006). There is limited potential for victims to be directly involved in making their voice heard at court. The victim's advocate can try to ensure that greater regard is played to the victim's perspective through their communications with the criminal justice agencies, but while this is appreciated by victims it is not a direct voice. One opportunity for a victim's own words to be directly heard is through the Victim Impact Statement. The practice of affording the victim an opportunity to make a VIS varies across the specialist courts, but the take-up is generally low. Many victims are not aware that they can make a statement and even if they are they may be confused about what the purposes of the statement are and how it will be used. The potential for confusion and raised expectations was highlighted by Sanders et al (2001), and can have serious consequences in domestic violence cases. One victim felt that the statement may have created an impression for the defendant that she had more 'say' in the outcome than she actually did, posing a danger for her safety: 'I wasn't very secure in what I was being told. His family told me it was the VIS that nearly had him put into prison. I didn't know how it was different and I needed to know because me and my family have to deal with the repercussions' (Vallely et al, 2005, p 66).

In addition to asking victims about their experiences of the process in the specialist domestic violence court, the researchers also asked victims for their views on the outcome of their cases. Levels of satisfaction with outcome were quite low, either because the victim felt that the sentence was not severe enough or that the defendant did not get the help that he needed. Research into the sentencing preferences of victims of domestic violence tends to suggest that they are not overly punitive and show a preference for treatment over custody (Cretney and Davis, 1997); similar findings emerged in the specialist court research. A custodial sentence, whilst scoring positively as a measure of how seriously the criminal justice system views domestic violence, may not be what the victim actually wants. As one victim remarked: 'I was very pleased. He didn't deserve to go to prison. He has problems and they were recognised—he got a fine, probation and a perpetrator programme'. Another victim whose partner was sent to prison remarked: 'they didn't properly assess what he needed. He should have been taken to a hospital rather than prison. He has alcohol problems and they haven't been addressed' (Vallely et al, 2005, p 46). Fines as a penalty on their own were poorly rated, especially when the victims felt that the defendant's financial circumstances had not been adequately investigated. Inadequate or inappropriate penalties have the potential to leave victims with a profound sense of injustice and significantly undermine their feelings of safety. In cases where the courts imposed a restraining order following convictions for offences under the Protection from Harassment Act 1997, victims were generally satisfied. This potentially bodes well for the extension, under the Domestic Violence Crime and Victims Act 2004, of the courts powers to impose restraining orders upon conviction for a much wider range of offences.

Conclusion

Recent initiatives like the domestic violence court specialisation programme do bring incremental improvements to the criminal justice response to domestic violence, but many challenges in effectively meeting the needs of victims and holding perpetrators to account remain. The fit between the aims and objectives of the criminal justice and those of victims remains rather loose. Measuring victim satisfaction is in some ways more problematic than measuring performance against criminal justice targets. Victims of domestic violence are a heterogeneous group and although they share the experience of an abusive relationship they come from diverse backgrounds and may have very different needs. Victims' perspectives on specialist domestic violence courts suggest that they experience the process in similar ways to the non-specialist court, except crucially for the support of the advocate. It should be remembered that it is the clustering of cases to a specialist court which facilitates the provision of advocacy support, and thus the significance of court specialisation in improving criminal justice responses to victims of domestic violence should not be undermined.

Implementing good policy into practice poses challenges even in specialist court settings where the multi-agency framework is well developed and the commitment and training of individuals is strong. The police and the CPS still receive negative feedback on their performance in gathering and presenting evidence, although this is mixed in with increasingly positive assessments of the attitudes displayed by the criminal justice personnel. The criminal justice system still has some way to go in achieving its full potential for effectively responding to domestic violence, but domestic violence courts seem like a step in the right direction.

8   Are legal interventions effective?

When criminal justice agencies conceptualise an improved legal response to domestic violence this often means to them, more arrests, more prosecutions and more convictions. Even on their measures of success the criminal justice response to domestic violence is not always effective. Viewed from the victim's perspective the criminal justice response to domestic violence is sometimes completely at odds with their expectations, and on occasions can be counter productive in the victim's search for a solution to make them feel safer. Likewise the civil justice system frequently fails to deliver what victims of domestic violence want and need to ensure their safety and that of any children affected by the violence. In this chapter the perspectives of victims of domestic violence on the response that they receive from the legal system will be examined. The legal system cannot be totally driven by victims' perspectives and account must also be taken of perpetrators' perspectives, not least in terms of how effective they feel various interventions are in achieving particular outcomes.

Research examining perpetrators' perspectives tends to be even more scarce than research that takes into account victims' perspectives on legal interventions. This concluding chapter will draw on research which takes into account both victims' and perpetrators' assessments of the effectiveness of legal interventions.

Victims' perspectives

The importance of examining what victims of domestic violence think about the services provided to them and whether they feel that various agencies, including those responsible for delivering legal remedies, are meeting their needs has only recently been given serious attention (Hague et al, 2003). In particular the Government has become more interested in listening to what victims of domestic violence have to say about proposed policy innovations and legal reforms. In this respect it commissioned research to examine the views of 'survivors' of domestic violence on the proposals in Safety and Justice (WNC, 2003). The proposals were based on a three-pronged approach for responding to domestic violence; prevention, protection and justice, and support (Home Office, 2003). In this book some of the strategies for improving protection and justice, for example improving the way the law of homicide works in domestic violence cases, have been examined in detail. However victims' views on protection and justice have not yet been analysed in great depth.

The choice of the word 'victim' might in itself be controversial with some groups who want to give women who have experienced domestic violence more of a voice. The term 'survivor' is often used in the literature which examines abused women's perspectives (Mullender and Hague, 2001; Hague et al, 2003; WNC, 2003). 'Survivor' does perhaps have more positive connotations than 'victim'; it is suggestive of the many ways that women cope with domestic violence and the strength they show in resisting it (Kelly, 1988; Hoff, 1990) rather than of theories of 'learned helplessness' (Walker, 1984) which have now come under sustained criticism (Gondolf and Fisher, 1988). For some the construction of 'victimhood' is one of the problems with legal intervention in domestic violence cases (Mills, 2003). In the context of sexual violence Kelly observes 'the focus on coping, resistance and survival reflects the experiences of women interviewed . . . the word "victim" refers to someone who has been killed or destroyed or has suffered a loss' (Kelly, 1988, p 163). In the context of domestic violence Humphreys and Thiara (2002) observe that their data showed that women do not act passively in the face of abuse but seek help from a range of different services. Whilst many women do speak of the ways in which they 'survive' domestic violence it is important to acknowledge that the experiences of abused women are not homogeneous and some will feel more passive than others and may speak of ways in which their self-confidence has been destroyed and how they have suffered a loss. Whilst understanding and supporting the preference for the term survivor, Lewis observes 'many women do not feel like survivors at points in their lives, and . . . some do not survive men's violence' (Lewis, 2004, p 204). Using the terms 'survivor' and 'victim' interchangeably therefore seems like a more accurate reflection of the variety of different experiences. This book has tended to use the term victim because it is the term which is normally used by law enforcement agencies. Its adoption was not intended to downplay the many ways that women try to stop the violence that they have experienced, both through their own resources and calling on the support of outside agencies.

Victims' perspectives on the criminal justice system

Research examining victims' perspectives on the responses of the police has concluded: 'The key problem in the relationship between women and the police is not lack of contact but an inability to hear what the "other side" is saying' (WNC, 2002, p 8). The study, which examined the experiences of so called 'hard to reach' groups, such as ethnic minorities, found that they were 'not "hard to reach" but "hard to hear" '. One of the factors that makes them difficult to hear is pressures from within their own communities, but this is compounded by unhelpful attitudes of the police. The experience will often then become self-reinforcing; women feel unable to trust the police because of previous poor experience and are reluctant to effectively engage with them. However, like many other studies, the WNC (2002) research reported that women's experiences of the police varied according to whether their contact was with specialist domestic violence officers or frontline police. The efforts made to establish domestic violence units were much praised and women reported that they had improved their experience of the police response to domestic violence. However the experience of the frontline operational officers was on the whole much poorer:

> The contrast between these very effective units and individuals and the inadequacy of approaches of frontline officers in these areas leads to an inconsistent experience for women: on the one hand they get practical help from the specialists they encounter during ongoing problems, and on the other a reactive and poorly informed response from the uniformed officers at a time of crisis.
>
> (WNC, 2002, p 9)

One of the perceptions that victims had of specialist domestic violence units was that there were under-resourced and 'low status' in the hierarchy of police work. Thus although individuals within the police were seen as committed to tackling domestic violence effectively, women questioned the strength behind the policy commitment overall. As the study highlighted, poor responses by frontline officers has considerable potential to undermine the good work done by specialist domestic violence officers, for example by not ensuring a speedy enough response to emergency domestic violence calls.

Hague et al (2003) note the crucial role that the police have in meeting the needs of abused women and their children, but also observe that despite 'the major improvements in policing policy which we have witnessed over the last decade . . . in some localities, women continue to report little change' (Hague et al, 2003, p 52). Some local initiatives have received positive feedback from victims, such as the 'Domestic Violence Matters' project evaluated by Kelly (1999). But even in projects such as these the feedback is not universally positive and victims still encounter police officers who fail to take assertive action against perpetrators of domestic violence. There is also a danger when the police become involved in multi-agency responses to domestic violence that their efforts get side-tracked into arrangements which become little more than a 'talking shop' with no real input from victims themselves (Hague et al, 1996; Hague, 2001; Radford and Gill, 2006). In theory partnership working gives 'an opportunity for women's voices on crime prevention to be heard and for unhelpful thinking and practice about domestic violence to be challenged' (Radford and Gill, 2006, p 373) but it can be difficult to get any outcome or agreement from partners who may be unwilling to take on extra work, or lack the authority in their agency to make the commitments necessary.

In this context, the findings of the WNC consultation on survivors' perspectives on the protection and justice proposals in safety and justice are unsurprising. Workshops involving one hundred women who had experience of domestic violence found that women felt the police were more likely to believe the perpetrator of the violence. This was perceived to be a general problem but a particular issue where the man was in a position of status and authority in his public life, when women reported that the police seemed to find it difficult to accept the mismatch in his public persona and his 'private' behaviour. Women themselves were frequently distressed when they called the police and felt that this hindered their ability to effectively communicate with the police. They still reported being made to feel like the guilty party, for example being asked what they had done to provoke their partner. However to concentrate purely on these negative experiences would be to belie the fact that some women did receive a sympathetic and helpful response from the police. Again specialist domestic violence officers were singled out for praise, and women commented on their desire for uniformed frontline police officers to be better trained and more sensitive.

Humphreys and Thiara's (2002) study of women's help-seeking strategies found, consistent with other surveys, that a large proportion in their sample contacted the police. The range of experiences varied from the extremely positive to extremely negative, but overall two-thirds either found them very helpful or fairly helpful. This still leaves a significant proportion of women (30.5 per cent) who said that the police were unhelpful. Women were positive about the police when they responded quickly to their call, but negative when there was significant delay. They were positive about being given accurate information and advice, negative about not being kept informed. They were positive about officers who took a professional approach and acted with understanding, belief and sympathy, but negative about officers who dismissed their concerns and showed indifference to their safety.

Qualitative analysis of the data revealed that those who had negative experiences were often from 'hard to reach' groups. As in some of the studies mentioned above, some women who were abused by men in positions of authority did not feel that their situations were adequately understood and provided for. Whilst a high percentage of women, almost half, had experienced the perpetrator being arrested at some point, many had probably called the police on numerous occasions given the duration of the abuse. About half of the cases where an arrest was made resulted in action being taken by the police or CPS, although women were not always happy with the action taken. Humphreys and Thiara (2002) observe that the Protection from Harassment Act 1997 is underutilised, which supports earlier (Edwards, 2001a) and subsequent (HMCPSI and HMIC, 2004) research discussed in Chapter 6.

Strong action by the police, for example arresting the perpetrator, was welcomed—which supports the analysis of Hoyle and Sanders (2000)—

although some women found that the threshold for intervention was too high. Many women reported poor practice in relation to evidence gathering, which suggests, from their perspective, that much more could be done to implement Circular 19/2000 and policies for enhanced or effective evidence gathering. Overall however the women surveyed by Humphreys and Thiara reported improvements in the police response, although again a lot of the praise was reserved for specialist domestic violence officers. Some victims felt that the police were still making moral evaluations about whether they deserved to be helped, for example one commented ' "just because you have been in trouble it doesn't mean you shouldn't be looked after" ' (Humphreys and Thiara, 2002, p 61).

Victims' perspectives on the CPS and the courts are not as comprehensively reported as their perspectives of policing. However, the research evidence that does exist suggests that their experiences of these agencies are as patchy as those with the police. Women in the WNC (2002) study reported a lack of practical help and protection at court. They commented on the lack of facilities, in particular separate waiting areas, or on occasions where separate rooms were provided they were small and inadequately equipped. For some women this communicated ambiguous messages about who the 'guilty party' was (WNC, 2002, p 15), which reinforces the findings of Burton et al (2006) that sometimes special measures leave victims feeling they are being punished or treated as if they are at fault. As was highlighted in the last chapter specialist domestic violence courts can go a considerable way to improving the experience of the court process by being more alert to the safety issues at court and providing adequate facilities.

Criticisms of the CPS included not being kept informed about what was going on and prosecutors not taking time to introduce themselves at court and explain the procedure. Some victims were critical about the level of knowledge that prosecutors had of their case, perceiving them to be unprepared and undermining the evidence that the police had gathered to support the case (WNC, 2002, p 15). These findings support the research discussed in Chapter 6, which showed that the CPS did not always present a case which the victim could recognise as her own experience. Whilst this hampers the magistrates, women also perceived attitudinal barriers to their effective recognition of their experiences by magistrates. Again the specialist domestic violence courts, which involve domestic violence awareness training for magistrates, may go some way to addressing concerns that victims have expressed in these respects.

In terms of outcomes, women in the WNC study stated that they wanted 'heavier and more consistent sentencing' (WNC, 2002, p 20). The sanctions imposed by the courts were felt to not adequately reflect the serious nature of the conduct. One woman singled out an incident where her partner received a small financial penalty for an assault during which he strangled her unconscious (WNC, 2002, p 21). It is clear that the question of appropriate sentencing of domestic violence is not fully resolved so far as victims are concerned, even in the specialist court setting, but some courts are reporting a reduction in the use of fines and the process, if not the outcome, in the specialist court setting does seem to be better for some women.

The capacity of the criminal justice system to meet the needs of victims of domestic violence is limited. What victims want most is to be safe: arrest, prosecution and conviction on their own do not necessarily achieve safety (Hoyle and Sanders, 2000). A successful outcome for the criminal justice system is not necessarily a successful outcome for the victim. As the criminal justice system cannot necessarily deliver what the victim wants, it perhaps makes better sense to focus on evaluating the process rather than concentrating exclusively on outcomes. Although satisfaction with the process is linked to the outcome victims do distinguish between the two; they have a sense of being treated well even if the outcome is not what they wanted, or a sense of being treated badly even if the outcome is what they wanted. It has long become trite to comment, in relation to a defendant's experience of the criminal justice process, that the 'process is the punishment' (Feeley, 1979). It is worth remembering that the process can also be a punishment for the victim. The research on victims' perspectives outlined above suggests that the criminal justice agencies need to double their efforts to ensure that victims feel that the criminal justice process is not a punishment for themselves, and so that more victims feel that both the process and outcome have contributed to their safety.

Victims' perspectives on the civil justice response

It is important to remember that victims do not always clearly distinguish between the civil and criminal justice response; where they have taken one or both routes they may confuse them with each other. Humphreys and Thiara (2003) found that women 'tended to conflate their experiences of law enforcement and court proceedings' (p 203). This confusion is likely to continue to increase with the blurring of the boundaries between the civil and criminal law responses to domestic violence discussed in Chapter 4.

In Chapter 3 the important role of solicitors in facilitating access to the civil justice remedies was described. It was also noted that solicitors sometimes hindered their clients own quest for safety by encouraging or pressuring them to accept lesser remedies, for example undertakings in lieu of court orders, or persuading them it was pointless in contesting a case for contact which the victim felt was unsafe for her and her children. Like the early research examined in Chapter 2 (Barron, 1990), later research reports victims' disappointment with the service provided by their own solicitors. One study found: 'Many women felt let down by their solicitors. Some had good experiences but it was evident that the services that women got from solicitors was patchy and they were unsure how to access solicitors who specialised in domestic violence . . . [One woman said] . . . "If they were sloppy you can feel more at risk and more vulnerable" '(WNC, 2002, p 14).

Humphreys and Thiara (2002) found that the women in their study were quite poorly informed about the civil remedies available to them. Whilst over two-thirds had been told about non-molestation orders, only a third said they had been told about occupation orders. The authors conclude that this represents either a significant failing in outreach services, or more likely, underlines that women may need to have information about civil orders repeated to them at several stages. In their study 43 per cent of women had used civil protection orders, and just over a third said that they were helpful and the abuse stopped; a further 40 per cent reported that they were of some help (Humphreys and Thiara, 2002, p 53). This suggests, the authors argue, that women's experiences of the civil remedies have improved after the implementation of the Family Law Act 1996, but, consistent with the practitioners' perspectives examined in Chapter 3, the costs of obtaining a remedy and the enforcement of orders remained significant issues for victims from their perspective. One woman stated, for example: ' "The abuse didn't stop because the courts did not deal with the breach of the order" ' (Humphreys and Thiara, 2002, p 54).

Given the conflation of the civil and the criminal court experience it is difficult to untangle which criticisms relate to the judiciary in their criminal law capacity and which relate to the civil courts, however some comments specifically relate to the civil courts and the lenient approaches of judges in this context (WNC, 2002, p 16). The WNC study found that women wanted protective orders of a longer duration, although there was considerable scepticism about their ability to protect. When it comes to post separation violence there is some evidence that women find non-molestation and occupation orders effective—but for women suffering chronic violence they are of little help (Humphreys and Thiara, 2003). Child contact arrangements were found to be the most significant element undermining victims' efforts to keep their children and themselves safe. Women reported that they found the first six months after separation the most dangerous. Very few who had post separation contact arrangements reported no further problems. Humphreys and Thiara (2003) confirm the research which shows some of the problems that women encounter relate to their own solicitors. Arrangements are negotiated in the shadow of the solicitor's representation of the likely outcome of court proceedings and women agreed to arrangements their solicitor negotiated. A few women who resisted court-ordered contact were threatened with imprisonment for contempt. Humphreys and Thiara (2003) observe: 'The initiation of contact proceedings and associated court orders were effectively closing down re-location as a major safety strategy for many women . . . contact arrangements provided several abusers with the leverage they needed to violate the separation' (p 208). It is clear that the practices of law are resistant to change in this area and many women feel that their legitimate concerns are being ignored by solicitors and the courts. Humphreys and Thiara conclude that this area of law 'facilitated the man's capacity to continue abuse rather than curtailing it'.

The WNC (2003) found that even men who were in prison for domestic violence were allowed contact with their children; their mothers were forced to take them to visit for fear of being held in contempt of court themselves. Although they were afraid of the effect that contact with their father might be having, and the mental and physical abuse that might occur, they felt that the man would appear credible to outside agencies and had little expectation that their concerns would be recognised. In this respect victims of domestic violence have low expectations of the law. Are they right to expect so little? Can the limitations of the legal response to domestic violence highlighted by victims' perspectives in this chapter and evident in the content and practices of law discussed throughout this book ever be adequately addressed?

Are legal interventions changing violent men?

It is clear from the research evidence discussed in this chapter that victims of domestic violence do not experience legal interventions in the same way; some women do receive some benefit from legal interventions, others feel let down by their contact with the law enforcement agencies, and others feel that their contact with the legal system has left them more unsafe. It should not be assumed that all legal innovations are likely to improve the position of victims of domestic violence, even when they are motivated by an express political commitment to that objective. The unintended consequences of legal reforms may reduce the capacity of victims to keep themselves safe. However a number of innovative approaches to tackling domestic violence have reported successes with enhancing perpetrator accountability and victim safety, for example specialist domestic violence courts. It is mainly innovative projects such as these which led Lewis (2004) to conclude that 'legal interventions can be effective and play a vital part in protecting women and challenging men' (p 205). Victim's experiences of the legal process however need to be complemented by research evidence on how effectively legal interventions challenge violent men. As Lewis (2004) observes the research evidence on men's experiences of the legal process and outcomes is more limited than that on victims' experiences.

A recent study by Hester and Westmarland (2006) has examined service provision for perpetrators of domestic violence. The authors note the dearth of research evidence on perpetrators' perspectives and designed the study to complement Hester's earlier research on attrition (Hester et al, 2003). Whilst acknowledging the importance of looking at services for women, Hester and Westmarland (2006) observe that provision of adequate services for violent men is vital to stop them re-offending in the future. The research used a multi-method approach which including looking at the profiles of a large number of perpetrators reported to the police. The majority of the perpetrators were men and had wide-ranging experiences of legal interventions. A high proportion of offenders in the study were arrested by the police, most commonly for breach of the peace, but the men interviewed for the study described a number of strategies they used to avoid arrest and prosecution, including absenting themselves from the house and pressurising their partner to withdraw complaints. Even when men were arrested it sometimes had little effect upon them, despite being held in custody overnight: 'It led them to think that the police did not take their violent behaviour seriously, and reinforced the men's minimisation of the incident' (Hester and Westmarland, 2006, p 2). The attrition rate in this study was consistent with other research; only 5 per cent of incidents resulted in a conviction, and the majority of those convicted received financial penalties. Fifty per cent of the men were involved in a further domestic violence incident within a three-year follow-up period, a significant proportion (18 per cent) against a different partner. Those who had been convicted for an earlier incident of domestic violence were involved in fewer incidents over time but were more likely to be convicted again. Hester and Westmarland (2006) found that some perpetrators did not acknowledge that their behaviour was a problem and did not want to change, but men who did want to change most frequently asked their GP for help and positioned themselves as in need of medical care or treatment, rather than accepting responsibility for their behaviour. Hester and Westmarland (2006) question the effectiveness of this approach, noting it 'can be dangerous', and given the research evidence about the causes of domestic violence this seems appropriate. Whilst some men may have accompanying problems such as alcoholism or depression these are not the root causes of domestic violence (Smith, 1989; Yllo and Bograd, 1988) and interventions with violent men are unlikely to be successful if they focus exclusively on these issues and fail to address male attitudes to women and the acceptability of violence more generally. Some of the perpetrators in Hester and Westmarland's study did have experience of perpetrator programmes (prison, probation or voluntary/community) and these had impacted on the ways they managed their interpersonal relationships, but they were critical of the inclusion of elements related to sex.

There is a growing body of research which relates to men's experiences of perpetrator programmes (Dobash et al, 2000; Mullender and Burton, 2001; Bowen et al, 2002). The efficacy of these programmes has been subject to much debate and the methodology of some studies has been seriously questioned. However Lewis (2004) concludes that we should be cautiously optimistic about perpetrator programmes because they do seem to work for some men and improve the quality of life and safety of some women. Perpetrator programmes do not stop all violent men and court mandated programmes only capture a small proportion of the men who might benefit because of the high attrition rate and the traditional problems with availability of perpetrator programmes. Nevertheless Lewis (2004) argues sanctions which include referral to perpetrator programme are more effective than fines or prison in stopping violence. In her study 33 per cent of men sentenced to complete a perpetrator programme committed a subsequent violent act against their partner within 12 months of sentencing compared to 70 per cent who received a traditional penalty. Men who participated in the perpetrator programmes indicated a growing awareness of their own behaviour and became more aware of its impact. Most of the men had previous experience of some kind of intervention, commonly from the police, but few had experienced any intervention which challenged their abusive behaviour. Discussions of power and control and jealously helped them to understand their behaviour. Lewis (2004) concludes that it is increased understanding of their behaviour which makes the programme successful for some men, rather than the threat of further legal intervention. However for some men deterrence does play an important role in legal interventions and can be effective, albeit in a short term and limited way. There is an element of resistance to perpetrator programmes which is reflected in some of the comments made by their partners, but women also expressed reservations about the effectiveness of traditional sanctions.

The issue of what violent men need to change their behaviour is likely to continue to be a matter of debate. Hester and Westmarland (2006) indicate that men are most likely to seek help at points of crisis, for example separation, but this is also when they are most dangerous. Agencies seeking to help violent men always need to be aware of the safety of women and children. Some men will be seeking a response which does not require them to accept responsibility for their behaviour, but violent men need to accept responsibility and learn new responses to feelings such as jealousy. Legal interventions can perform an important role in motivating men to seek help to change, and accredited perpetrator programmes, which comply with RESPECT guidelines (Mullender and Burton, 2001) also have a role to play.

Conclusion

It would be naïve and unrealistic to expect the law to end domestic violence but it is within the power of law to offer victims of domestic violence a measure of protection and to challenge the attitudes of violent men. The law could do more than it currently does to protect victims and challenge perpetrators—at the moment it often fails to do either adequately. Sometimes the failings are in law, other times in its implementation. However the research evidence surveyed in this book supports, in the author's view, the position of the 'sceptical reformist' (Lewis, et al, 2001). The sceptical reformist sees value in legal reform but at the same time does not expect too much from it. Committing to an alternative 'absentionist' view, that it is inappropriate to try to change the law and legal practices because there is no real benefit to victims or offenders, is not viable on the empirical evidence that some victims and perpetrators do benefit from some legal interventions.

Some commentators have suggested that domestic violence should be taken out of the legal system and dealt with in a rehabilitative framework, for example Mills (2003) suggests community intervention based on a Truth and Reconciliation Commission model. For Mills state intervention replicates domestic abuse; it undermines women's agency and conceptualises them as victims. She argues mediation would give women more control and choice. However the dangers of mediation approaches have been highlighted by others (Lerman, 1984) and should not be seen as an alternative to legal intervention. The power dynamics of abusive relationships fundamentally undermine the victim's position in mediation. Stark (2004) rightly criticises Mills for divorcing choice from its social and structural context, which effectively constrains the choices available to women.

Abandoning legal interventions in domestic violence is not practically or ethically justifiable. The state has obligations to protect victims of domestic violence and these obligations are strengthened by the Human Rights Act 1998. If the legal system fails to provide effective remedies for domestic violence then the state may breach Article 2, the right to life, and Article 3, the right to be free from inhuman and degrading treatment (Choudry and Herring, 2006). It is not sustainable to argue that the right to privacy in Article 8 shields the perpetrator from intervention in his family life. The right to privacy is a qualified right and does not provide absolute protection from unwanted intrusion; consideration must be given to the rights of competing individuals and society as a whole. The victim's right to privacy and a family life arguably supports intervention (Choudry and Herring, 2006). We must therefore concentrate on improving both the process and the outcome of legal interventions if we are serious about complying with human rights law and making legal interventions relating to domestic violence 'hit home'.

Bibliography

Abrahams, C (1994) *The Hidden Victims: Children and Domestic Abuse*, London: NCH Action For Children

ACPO and CENTREX (2004) *Guidance on Investigating Domestic Violence*, CENTREX

Adler, Z (1987) *Rape on Trial*, London: Routledge

Alexander, R (2002) *Domestic Violence in Australia: The Legal Response*, 3rd edn, Leicchhardt, NSW: The Federation Press

Allen, M (1999) 'Provocation's Reasonable Man: A Plea for Self Control', *The Journal of Criminal Law*, 63: 216–244

Aris, R, Harrison, C and Humphreys, C (2002) *Safety and Contact: An Analysis of the Role of Child Contact Centres in the Context of Domestic Violence and Child Welfare Concerns*, London: Lord Chancellor's Department

Attorney General (2005) *Attorney General's Guidelines on the Acceptance of Pleas and the Role of the Prosecutor's Role in the Sentencing Exercise*

Ashworth, A (2005) *Sentencing and Criminal Justice*, 4th edn, Cambridge: Cambridge University Press

Ashworth, A (2006) *Principles of Criminal Law*, 5th edn, Oxford: Oxford University Press

Ashworth, A and Fionda, J (1994) 'Prosecution, Accountability and the Public Interest: The New CPS Code', *Criminal Law Review*, 894–903

Bainham, A (2003) 'Contact as a right and obligation' in Bainham, A, Lindley, B, Richards, M, and Trinder, L (eds), *Children and Their Families: Contact, Rights and Welfare*, Oxford: Hart Publishing

Baldwin, J (1987) 'Understanding Judge Ordered and Directed Acquittals in the Crown Court', *Criminal Law Review*, 536–555

Barron, J (1990) *'Not Worth the Paper . . .?' The Effectiveness of Legal Protection for Women and Children Experiencing Domestic Violence*, Bristol: Women's Aid Federation England

Barron, J. (2002) *Five Years On: A Review of Legal Protection from Domestic Violence*, Bristol: Women's Aid Federation England

Berman, G and Feinblatt, J (2005) *Good Courts: The Case for Problem Solving Justice*, New York: New Press

Bird, R (2006) *Domestic Violence: Law and Practice*, 5th edn, Bristol: Jordan Publishing

Bourlet, A (1990) *Police Intervention in Marital Violence*, Milton Keynes: Open University Press

Bowen, E, Brown, L and Gilchrist, E (2002) 'Evaluating probation based offender programmes for domestic violence perpetrators: A pro-feminist approach', *The Howard Journal*, 41(3): 221–236

Brereton, D (1997) 'How different are rape trials? A comparison of the cross-examination of complainants in rape and assault trials', *British Journal of Criminology*, 37(2): 242–262

Brookman, F and Maguire, M (2003) *Reducing Homicide: A Review of the Possibilities*, Home Office Online Report, 03/2003

Brownlee, I (2004) 'The Statutory Charging Scheme in England and Wales: Towards a Unified Prosecution System', *Criminal Law Review*, 896–907

Burton, M. (2000) 'Prosecution decisions in cases of domestic violence involving children', *Journal of Social Welfare and Family Law*, 22(2): 175–191

Burton, M (2001a) 'Intimate Homicide and the Provocation Defence—Endangering Women? R v Smith' *Feminist Legal Studies*, 9(3): 247–258

Burton, M (2001b) 'Reviewing CPS decisions not to prosecute', *Criminal Law Review*, 374–384

Burton, M (2003a) 'Third Party Applications for protection orders in England and Wales: service provider's views on implementing Section 60 of the Family Law Act 1996, *Journal of Social Welfare and Family Law*, 25(2): 137–150

Burton, M (2003b) 'Criminalising civil orders for protection from domestic violence', *Criminal Law Review*, 301–313

Burton, M (2003c) 'Sentencing Domestic Homicide Upon Provocation: Still "Getting Away with Murder" ' *Feminist Legal Studies*, 11(3): 279–289

Burton, M (2004) 'Lomas v Parle—Coherent and effective remedies for victims of domestic violence: time for an integrated domestic violence court?' *Child and Family Law Quarterly*, 16(3): 317–329

Burton, M (2006) 'Judicial Monitoring of Compliance: Introducing "Problem Solving" Approaches to Domestic Violence Courts in England and Wales', *International Journal of Law, Policy and the Family*, 20(3): 366–378

Burton, M (forthcoming) 'R (on the application of Christopher Rabess) v Commissioner of police for the Metropolis—"Scream Quietly or the Neighbours will Hear"; Domestic violence, "nuisance neighbours" and the public/private dichotomy revisited' *Child and Family Law Quarterly*, 20(1)

Burton, M, Evans, R and Sanders, A (2006) *Are Special Measures Working? Evidence from the criminal justice agencies*, Home Office Online Report 01/06

Burton, M, McCrory, A and Buck, T (2002) *The civil remedies for domestic violence under the Family Law Act 1996: Is section 60 the way forward?*, Unpublished report, submitted to the Lord Chancellor's Department, October 2002

Burton, S, Regan, L and Kelly, L (1998) *Supporting Women and Challenging Men: Lessons from the Domestic Violence Intervention Project*, Bristol: Policy Press

Buzawa, E and Buzawa, C (1996) *Do Arrests and Restraining Orders Work?* Thousand Oaks, CA: Sage

Cahn, N (1991) 'Civil images of battered women: The impact of domestic violence on child custody decisions', *Vanderbilt Law Review*, 44(5): 1041–97

Cammiss, S (2006) 'The Management of Domestic Violence Cases in the Mode of Trial Hearing: Prosecutorial Control and Marginalizing Victims' *British Journal of Criminology*, 46: 704–718

Campbell, S (2002) *A Review of Anti-Social Behaviour Orders*, Home Office Research Study 236, London: Home Office

Cavanagh, K, Emerson, R, Dobash, R, Dobash, R and Lewis, R (2002) *Homicide in Britain: Risk Factors, Situational Contexts and Lethal Intentions* (Interviews with Women), Research Bulletin No. 3, Department of Applied Social Science, University of Manchester

Chalmers, J, Duff, P and Leverick, F (2007) 'Victim Impact Statements: can work, do work (for those who bother to make them)', *Criminal Law Review*, 360–379

Chatterton, M (1983) 'Police Work and Assault Charges' in Punch, M (ed), *Control in the Police Organisation*, Cambridge, Massachusetts: MIT Press

Children Act Sub-Committee of the Lord Chancellor's Advisory Board on Family Law (2002) *Guidelines for Good Practice on Parental Contact in Cases where there is Domestic Violence*, London: Lord Chancellor's Department

Choudry, S and Herring, J (2006) 'Domestic Violence and the Human Rights Act 1998: A New Means of Legal Intervention', *Public Law*, 752–784

Clarke, A, Moran Ellis, K and Sleney, J (2002) *Attitudes to Date Rape and Relationship Rape: A Qualitative Study*, Sentencing Advisory Panel

Clarkson, C, Cunningham, S and Keating, H (2007) *Criminal Law*, London: Sweet and Maxwell

Coleman, K, Hird, C and Povey, D (2006) *Violent Crime Overview, Homicide and Gun Crime 2004/5*, Home Office Statistical Bulletin 02/06

Collinson, A (2004) *Tough Love: A Critique of the Domestic Violence Crime and Victims Bill 2003*, London: Policy Exchange

Cook, D (2003) *Evaluation of Wolverhampton Specialist Domestic Violence Court*, Regional Research Institute, University of Wolverhampton

Cook, D, Burton, M, Robinson, R and Vallely, C (2004) *Evaluation of Specialist Domestic Violence Courts/Fast-Track Systems*, Crown Prosecution Service and Department for Constitutional Affairs

Cownie, F, Bradney, A and Burton, M (2007) *English Legal System in Context*, 4th edn, Oxford: Oxford University Press

Cretney, A and Davis, G (1995) *Punishing Violence*, London: Routledge

Cretney, A and Davis, G (1996) 'Prosecution "domestic" assault', *Criminal Law Review*, 162–174

Cretney, A and Davis, G (1997a) 'The significance of compellability in the prosecution of domestic assault', *British Journal of Criminology*, 37(1): 75–89

Cretney, A and Davis, G (1997b) 'Prosecuting domestic assault: Victims failing courts or courts failing victims?' *Howard Journal*, 32(2): 146–157

Crown Prosecution Service (2004) *The Code for Crown Prosecutors*, London: CPS

Crown Prosecution Service (2005) *Policy for Prosecuting Cases of Domestic Violence*, London: CPS

Crown Prosecution Service (2005) *CPS Domestic Violence: Good practice guidance*, London: CPS

Crown Prosecution Service (2006) *Domestic violence monitoring snapshot: Cases finalised in December 2006*, London: CPS

Darbyshire, P (1997) 'An Essay on the Importance and Neglect of the Magistracy', *Criminal Law Review*, 627–643

Dobash, RE and Dobash, RP (1979) *Violence Against Wives: A Case Against the Patriarchy*, London: Open Books

Dobash, RE and Dobash, RP (1992) *Women, Violence and Social Change*, London: Routledge

Dobash, RE and Dobash, RP, Cavanagh, K and Lewis, R (2000) *Changing Violent Men*, London: Sage

Dobash RE, Dobash, RP, Wilson, M and Daly, M (1992) 'The myth of sexual symmetry in marital violence', *Social Problems*, 39(1): 71–91

Dobash, RP and Dobash, RE (2004) 'Women's Violence to Men in Intimate Relationships: Working on a Puzzle', *British Journal of Criminology*, 44: 324–349

Dobash, RP, Dobash, RE, Cavanagh, K and Lewis, R (2004) 'Not an Ordinary Killer, Just an Ordinary Guy: When Men Murder an Intimate Woman Partner', *Violence Against Women*, 10: 577–605

Dobash, RP, Dobash, RE, Cavanagh, K and Lewis, R (1999) 'A research evaluation of British programmes for violent men', *Journal of Social Policy*, 205–233

Donovan, C (2007) *Comparing Love and Domestic Violence In Heterosexual and Same Sex Relationships: Full Research Report*, ESRC End of Award Report, RES-000-23-0650. Swindon: ESRC

Douglas, G and Lowe, N (1998) *Bromley's Family Law*, London: Butterworths

Edwards. S. (1987) ' "Provoking her own demise": From Common Assault to Homicide' in Hanmer, J and Maynard, M (eds), *Women, Violence and Social Control*, London: Macmillan

Edwards, S. (1989) *Policing 'Domestic' Violence: Women, the Law and the State*, London: Sage Publications

Edwards, S. (1996) *Sex and Gender in the Legal Process*, London: Blackstone

Edwards, S (2001a) 'Domestic violence and harassment: An assessment of the civil remedies', in Taylor-Browne, J (ed), *What Works in Reducing Domestic Violence? A Comprehensive Guide for Professionals*, London: Whiting Birch

Edwards, S. (2001b) 'New directions in prosecution', in Taylor-Browne, J (ed), *What Works in Reducing Domestic Violence? A Comprehensive Guide for Professionals*, London: Whiting Birch

Edwards, S (2004) 'Abolishing Provocation and Reframing Self-Defence—the Law Commission's options for reform, *Criminal Law Review*, 181–197

Ellison, L (2001) *The Adversarial Process and the Vulnerable Witness*, Oxford: Oxford University Press

Ellison, L (2002) 'Prosecuting domestic violence without victim participation', *Modern Law Review*, 65(6): 834–858

Ellison, L (2003) 'Responding to victim withdrawal in domestic violence prosecutions', *Criminal Law Review*, 760–772

Ellison, L (2007) 'Witness Preparation and the Prosecution of Rape', *Legal Studies* 27: 171–187

Emerson, R (1991) 'Case Processing and Interorganizational Knowledge: Detecting the "Real Reasons" for Referrals', *Social Problems*, 38(2): 198–212

Emerson, R and Paley, B (1992) 'Organizational Horizons and Complaint Filing', in Hawkins, K (ed), *The Uses of Discretion*, Oxford: Clarendon Press

Estrich, S (1987) *Real Rape: How the Legal System Victimizes Women Who Say No*, Boston: Harvard University Press

Faragher, T (1985) 'The police response to violence against women in the home' in Pahl, J (ed), *Private Violence and Public Policy*, London: Routledge and Kegan Paul

Feeley, M (1979) *The Process is the Punishment*, New York: Russell Sage Foundation

Fenwick, H (1997) 'Procedural rights of victims of crime: Public or private ordering of criminal justice process?' *Modern Law Review*, 60: 317–333

Fineman, M and Myktuik, R (eds) (1994) *The Public Nature of Private Violence*, London: Routledge.

Finkelhor, D and Yllo, K (1985) *License to Rape: Sexual Abuse of Wives*, New York: Free Press

Finney, A (2006) *Domestic Violence, Sexual Assault and Stalking: Findings from the 2004/5 British Crime Survey*, Home Office Online Report 12/06

Ford, D (1991) 'Prosecution as a victim power resource: A note on empowering women in violent conjugal relationships', *Law and Society Review*, 25(2): 313–334

Ford, D and Regoli, M (1993) 'Criminal prosecution of wife assaulters: Process, problems and effects' in Hilton, Z (ed), *Legal Responses to Wife Assault: Current Trends and Evaluation*, Newbury Park: Sage

Freeman, M (1984) *State, Law and the Family*, Cambridge: Cambridge University Press

Fritzler, R and Simon, L (2000) 'The development of a specialized domestic violence court in Vancouver Washington utilizing innovative judicial paradigms', *University of Missouri Law Review*, 69–153

Geldof, B (2003) 'The Real Love that Dare not Speak its Name: A sometimes coherent rant', in Bainham, A, Lindley, B, Richards, M, and Trinder, L (eds), *Children and Their Families: Contact, Rights and Welfare*, Oxford: Hart Publishing

Gelles, R and Loseke, D (1993) *Current Controversies on Family Violence*, California: Sage

Genders, E (1999) 'Reform of Offences Against the Person', *Criminal Law Review* 689

Gilchrist, E and Blissett, J (2002) 'Magistrates' attitudes to domestic violence and sentencing options', *The Howard Journal*, 41(4): 348–363

Glass, D (1995) *All My Fault: Why Women Don't Leave Abusive Men*, London: Virago

Gondolf, E (2000) 'Mandatory Court Review and Batterer Programme Compliance', *Journal of Interpersonal Violence*, 15(4): 428–437.

Gondolf, E and Fisher, E (1988) *Battered Women as Survivors: An Alternative to Learned Helplessness*, Lexington, MA: Lexington Books

Grace, S (1995) *Policing Domestic Violence in the 1990s*, Home Office Research Study 139, London: Home Office

Grady, A (2002) 'Female on Male Domestic Violence: Uncommon or Ignored?' in Hoyle, C and Young, R (eds), *New Visions of Crime Victims*, Oxford: Hart Publishing

Gregory, J and Lees, S (1999) *Policing Sexual Assault*, London: Routledge

Grundy, M (2000) *Final Evaluation Report of Leeds Domestic Violence Cluster Court*, University of Huddersfield

Hague, G. (2001) 'Multi-agency initiatives', in Taylor-Browne, J (ed), *What Works in Reducing Domestic Violence? A Comprehensive Guide for Professionals*, London: Whiting Birch

Hague, G, Malos, E and Dear, W (1996) *Inter-agency Approaches to Domestic Violence*, Bristol: University of Bristol, School for Policy Studies

Hague, G, Mullender, A and Aris, R (2001) *Is Anyone Listening? Accountability and women survivors of domestic violence*, London: Routledge

Hayes, M (2005) 'Criminal Trials Where a Child is the Victim: Extra Protection or a Missed Opportunity?' *Child and Family Law Quarterly*, 17(3): 307–327

Hanmer, J and Griffiths, S (1998) *Domestic Violence and Repeat Victimisation*, Police Research Group Briefing Note 1/98, London: Home Office

Hanmer, J and Griffiths, S (2001) 'Effective policing', in Taylor-Browne, J (ed), *What*

Works in Reducing Domestic Violence? A Comprehensive Guide for Professionals, London: Whiting Birch

Hanmer, J, Griffiths, S and Jerwood, D (1999) *Arresting Evidence: Domestic Violence and Repeat Victimisation*, Police Research Series Paper 104, London: Home Office

Hanna, C (1996) 'No right to choose: Mandated victim participation in domestic violence prosecutions', *Harvard Law Review*, 109: 1850–1910

Hansard (Committees) House of Commons (1993) *Memoranda of Evidence to the Home Affairs Committee on Domestic Violence*, London: HMSO

Harris, J (2000) *The Evaluation of the Use and Effectiveness of the Protection from Harassment Act 1997*, Home Office Research Study No. 203, London: Home Office

Harris, J and Grace, S (1999) *A Question of Evidence: Investigating and Prosecuting Rape in the 1990s*, London: Home Office

Harwin, N and Barron, J (2000) 'Domestic violence and social policy', in Hanmer, J and Itzin, C (eds), *Home Truths about Domestic Violence: Feminist Influences in Policy and Practice: A Reader*, London: Routledge

Hawkins, K (1992) 'The Use of Legal Discretion' in Hawkins, K (ed), *The Uses of Discretion*, Oxford: Clarendon Press

Herbert, A (2003) 'Mode of Trial and Magistrates' Sentencing Powers; Will increased powers inevitably lead to a reduction in the committal rate?, *Criminal Law Review*, 314–325

Herbert, A (2004) 'Mode of Trial and the Influence of Local Justice', *Howard Journal of Criminal Justice*, 43: 65–78

Herring, J (2007) 'Mum's Not the Word: An Analysis of Section 5 of the Domestic Violence, Crimes and Victim Act 2004', Homicide Conference Proceedings, University of Leicester, April 2007

Hester, M (2005) 'Making it through the Criminal Justice System: Attrition and Domestic Violence', *Social Policy and Society*, 5(1): 79–90

Hester, M, Hanmer, J, Coulson, S, Morahan, M and Razak, A (2003) *Domestic Violence: Making it Through the Criminal Justice System*, University of Sunderland, Northern Rock Foundation and International Centre for the Study of Violence and Abuse

Hester, M, Pearson, C, Harwin, N and Abrahams, H (2007) *Making an Impact: Children and Domestic Violence: A Reader*, 2nd edn, London: Jessica Kingsley

Hester, M and Radford, L (1992) 'Domestic Violence and Access Arrangements for Children in Denmark and Britain', *Journal of Social Welfare and Family Law*, 11: 57–70

Hester, M and Radford, L (1996) *Domestic Violence and Child Contact Arrangements in England and Denmark*, Bristol: Policy Press

Hester, M and Westmarland, N (2005) *Tackling Domestic Violence: Effective Interventions and Approaches*, Home Officer Research Study 290, London: Home Office

Hester, M and Westmarland, N (2006) *Service Provision for Perpetrators of Domestic Violence*, Bristol: University of Bristol

Hilton, N (1991) 'Mediating wife assault: Battered women and the new family', *Canadian Journal of Family Law*, 9: 29–53

Hitchings, E (2005) 'A Consequence of Blurring the Boundaries—Less Choice for the Victims of Domestic Violence?' *Social Policy and Society*, 5(1): 91–101

HMCPSI (1998) *The Inspectorate's Report on Cases Involving Domestic Violence* Crown Prosecution Service Inspectorate, Thematic Report 2/1998

HMCPSI (2007) *Without Consent: A report on the joint review of the investigation and prosecution of rape offences*, Crown Prosecution Service Inspectorate

HMCPSI and HMIC (2004) *Violence at Home: Joint Thematic Inspection of the Investigation and Prosecution of Cases Involving Domestic Violence*, Crown Prosecution Service Inspectorate and HM Inspectorate of Constabulary

HMICA (2005) *Domestic Violence, Safety and Family Proceedings*. Thematic review of the handling of domestic violence issues by the Children and Family Court Advisory and Support Service (CAFCASS) and the administration of family courts in Her Majesty's Courts Service (HMCS), London, HMICS.

Hoff, L (1990) *Battered Women as Survivors*, London: Routledge

Home Office (1990) Home Office Circular 60/1990, *Domestic Violence*, London: Home Office

Home Office (1998) *Living Without Fear: An Integrated Approach to Tackling Violence Against Women*, London: Home Office

Home Office (2000) Home Office Circular 19/2000, *Domestic Violence*, London: Home Office

Home Office (2000b) *Setting the Boundaries: Reforming the law on sex offences*, London: Home Office

Home Office (2002) *Justice For All*, London: Home Office

Home Office (2003) *Safety and Justice: The Government's proposals on Domestic Violence*, London: Home Office

Home Office (2005) *Domestic Violence: National Plan*, London: Home Office

Home Office (2006) *Lessons Learned from the DV Enforcement Campaigns 2006*, London: Home Office

Horder, J (1992) *Provocation and Responsibility*, Oxford: Oxford University Press

Horder, J (1994) 'Rethinking Non-Fatal Offences against the Person', *Oxford Journal of Legal Studies*, 335

Horder, J (1999) 'Between Provocation and Diminished Responsibility', *King's College Law Journal*, 143–166

Horder, J and McGowan (2006) 'Manslaughter by Causing Another's Suicide' *Criminal Law Review*, 1035

Hoyle, C (1998) *Negotiating Domestic Violence: Police, Criminal Justice and Victims*, Oxford: Clarendon Press

Hoyle, C and Sanders, A (2000) 'Police response to domestic violence: From victim choice to victim empowerment', *British Journal of Criminology*, 40: 14–36

Hucklesby, A (1994) 'The Use and Abuse of Conditional Bail', *Howard Journal of Criminal Justice*, 33: 258–270

Humphreys, C and Harrison, C (2003) 'Focusing on safety: domestic violence and the role of child contact centres', *Child and Family Law Quarterly*, 15(3): 237–254

Humphreys, C and Kaye, M (1997) 'Third-party applications for protection orders: Opportunities, ambiguities and traps', *Journal of Social Welfare and Family Law*, 19(4): 403–421

Humphreys, C and Stanley, N (2006) *Domestic violence and child protection: Directions for good practice*, London: Jessica Kinsgley

Humphreys, C and Thiara, R K (2003) 'Neither Justice nor Protection: Women's Experiences of Post-separation Violence, *Journal of Social Welfare and Family Law*, 25: 195–214

Humphreys, C and Thiara, T (2002) *Routes to Safety: Protection Issues Facing Abused*

Women and Children and the Role of Outreach Services, Bristol: Women's Aid Federation England

Humphreys, C, Hester, M, Hague, G, Mullender, A, Abrahams, H and Lowe, P (2000) *From Good Intentions to Good Practice: Mapping Services Working with Families where there is Domestic Violence*, Bristol: Policy Press

Kaganas, F (1999) 'Occupation Orders under the Family Law Act 1996' *Child and Family Law Quarterly*, 11(2): 193–203

Kaganas, F (2000) 'Contact and Domestic Violence' *Child and Family Law Quarterly*, 12(3): 311–324

Kaganas, F and Day Sclater, S (2004) 'Contact Disputes: Narrative Constructions of "Good Parents"' *Feminist Legal Studies*, 12: 1–27

Kay, R (2001) 'Guidelines on Sanctions for Breach: Hale v Tanner' *Modern Law Review*, 64: 595–602

Kellitz, S (2001) *Specialization of Domestic Violence Case Management in the Courts: A National Survey*, Virginia: National Center for State Courts

Kelly, L (1988) *Surviving Sexual Violence*, Oxford: Polity Press

Kelly, L (2002) 'Limited progress? Reflections on recent developments in domestic violence legislation in Europe', Paper prepared for ESF Seminar, Leiden, Netherlands

Kelly, L (1999) *Domestic Violence Matters: An Evaluation of a Development Project*. Home Research Study 193, London: Home Office

Kelly, L and Humhreys, C (2001) 'Supporting women and children in their communities: Outreach and advocacy approaches to domestic violence', in Taylor-Browne, J (ed), *What Works in Reducing Domestic Violence? A Comprehensive Guide for Professionals*, London: Whiting Birch

Kelly, L, Lovett, J and Regan, L (2005) *A Gap or a Chasm? Attrition in Reported Rape Cases*, Home Office Research Study 293, London: Home Office

Kelly, L, Temkin, J and Griffiths, S (2006) *Section 41: An Evaluation of New Legislation Limiting Sexual History Evidence in Rape Trials*, Home Office Online Report 20/06

Kewley, A. (1996) 'Pragmatism before principle: The limitations of civil law remedies for the victims of domestic violence', *Journal of Social Welfare and Family Law*, 18(1): 1–10

Kewley, A (2000) 'Double jeopardy: Race and Domestic Violence', in Murphy, J. (2000) *Ethnic Minorities, Their Families and the Law*, Oxford: Hart Publishing

Lacey, N (1998) *Unspeakable Subjects*, Oxford: Hart Publishing

Law Commission (1992) Report (No 207) *Domestic Violence and Occupation of the Family Home*, London: HMSO

Law Commission (1992b) Report (No 205) *Rape Within Marriage*, London: HMSO

Law Commission (2003) Consultation Paper (No 173) *Partial Defences to Murder*, London: Law Commission

Law Commission (2005) Consultation Paper (No 177) *A New Homicide Act for England and Wales?* London: Law Commission

Law Commission (2006) Report (No 304) *Murder, Manslaughter and Infanticide*, London: TSO

Lees, S (1992) ' "Naggers, Whores and Libbers": provoking Men to Kill', in Radford, J and Russell, D (eds), *Femicide: The Politics of Woman Killing*, Buckingham: Open University Press

Lees, S (1996) *Carnal Knowledge: Rape on Trial*, London: Hamish Hamilton

Lerman, L (1984) 'Mediation of wife abuse cases: The adverse impact of informal dispute resolution on women', *Harvard Women's Law Journal*, 7: 57–113

Lerman, L (1992) 'The decontextualisation of domestic violence', *Journal of Criminal Law and Criminology*, 83(1): 217–235

Levison, D and Harwin, N (2001) '*Accommodation Provision*', in Taylor-Browne, J (ed), *What Works in Reducing Domestic Violence? A Comprehensive Guide for Professionals*, London: Whiting Birch

Lewis, R (2004) 'Making Justice Work: Effective Legal Interventions for Domestic Violence, *British Journal of Criminology*, 44(2): 204–224

Lewis, R, Dobash, R P, Dobash, R E and Cavanagh, K (2001), 'Law's Progressive Potential: The Value of Engagement with the Law for Domestic Violence', *Social and Legal Studies*, 10: 105–130

Lloyd, S, Farrell, G and Pease, K (1994) *Preventing Repeated Domestic Violence: A Demonstration Project on Merseyside*, Police Research Group, Crime Prevention Unit Series Paper 49, London: Home Office

Lockton, D and Ward, R (1997) *Domestic Violence*, London: Cavendish

Lord Chancellors Department (2003) *Domestic Violence: A Guide to Civil Remedies and Criminal Sanctions*, London: Lord Chancellor's Department

Macdonald, S (2003) 'The nature of the anti-social behaviour order—R v (McCann and others) v Manchester Crown Court', *Modern Law Review*, 64: 630–639

Mackay, R and Mitchell, B (2005) 'But is this Provocation? Some Thoughts on the Law Commission's Report on Partial Defences to Murder', *Criminal Law Review*, 44–55

Mackinnon, K (2005) *Women's Lives; Men's Laws*, Cambridge, MA: Harvard University Press

Macklem, T and Gardner, J (2001) 'Compassion Without Respect: Nine Fallacies in R v Smith', *Criminal Law Review*, 623–635

Madden Dempsey, M (2006) 'What counts as domestic violence? A conceptual analysis', *William and Mary Journal of Women and the Law*, 12: 301–333

Mahoney, M (1991) 'Legal images of battered women: Redefining the issue of separation', *Michigan Law Review*, 90: 1–94

Maguire, M (2002) 'Crime Statistics: The 'Data Explosion' and its Implications' in Maguire, M, Morgan, R and Reiner, R (eds), *The Oxford Handbook of Criminology*, 3rd edn, Oxford; Oxford University Press

Mama, A (1989) *The Hidden Struggle: Statutory and Voluntary Sector Responses to Violence Against Black Women in the Home*, London: London Race and Housing Research Unit

Mazur, A and Aldrich, L (2002) *What Makes a Domestic Violence Court Work?* New York: Center For Court Innovation.

McCann, K (1985) 'Battered women and the law: Limits of the legislation', in Brophy, J and Smart, C (1985) *Women in Law*, Boston: Routledge and Kegan Paul

McColgan, A (1993) 'In Defence of Battered Women Who Kill' *Oxford Journal of Legal Studies*, 13: 508–529

McConville, M, Sanders, A and Leng, R (1991) *The Case for the Prosecution*, London: Routledge

McGee, C (2000) *Childhood Experiences of Domestic Violence*, London: Jessica Kinsgley

Mills, L (2003) *Insult to Injury*, New York: Springer Publishing

Mills, L (2005) 'Intimacy and Terror: Making Peace with My Critics', *Violence Against Women*, 11: 1536–1543

Ministry of Justice (2007) *Domestic violence: A guide to the civil remedies and criminal sanctions*, London: MOJ

Mirrlees-Black, C (1999) *Domestic Violence: Findings from a New British Crime Survey Self-completion Questionnaire*, Home Office Research Study 191, London: Home Office

Mitchell, B and Cunningham, S (2006) Defences to Murder, Annex C, Law Commission (2006) Report (No 304) *Murder, Manslaughter and Infanticide*, London: TSO

Morgan, J (1997) 'Provocation Law and Facts: Dead Women Tell No Tales, Tales Are Told About Them', *Melbourne University Law Review*, 21(1): 237–276

Mullender, A (2000) 'Meeting the Needs of Children', in Taylor-Browne, J (ed), *What Works in Reducing Domestic Violence? A Comprehensive Guide for Professionals*, London: Whiting Birch

Mullender, A and Burton, S (2001) 'Dealing with perpetrators', in Taylor-Browne, J (ed), *What Works in Reducing Domestic Violence? A Comprehensive Guide for Professionals*, London: Whiting Birch

Mullender, A and Hague, G (2001) 'Women Survivors' Views', in Taylor-Browne, J (ed), *What Works in Reducing Domestic Violence? A Comprehensive Guide for Professionals*, London: Whiting Birch

Mullender, A and Morley, R (1994) *Children Living with Domestic Violence: Putting Men's Abuse of Women on the Child Care Agenda*, London: Whiting and Birch

Mullender, A, Hague, G, Imam, U, Kelly, L, Malos, E and Regan, L (2002) *Children's Perspectives on Domestic Violence*, London: Sage

Murphy, J (1996) 'Domestic Violence: The New Law', *Modern Law Review*, 59: 845

Newmark, L, Rempel, M, Diffily, K and Kane, K (2001) *Specialized Felony Domestic Violence Courts: Lessons on Implementation and Impacts from the Kings County Experience*, Washington DC: Urban Institute of Justice Policy Center

Nicolson, D and Sanghvi, R (1993) 'Battered Women and Provocation: The Implications of R v Ahluwalia', *Criminal Law Review*, 728–738

Norrie, A (2001) 'The Structure of Provocation', *Current Legal Problems*, 307–346

Nourse, V (1997) 'Passions Progress: Modern Law Reform and the Provocation Defence', *The Yale Law Journal*, 106: 1331–1406

Olsen, F (1983) 'The Family and the Market: A Study of Ideology and Legel Reform', *Harvard Law Review*, 96: 1497–1578

Painter, K (1991) *Wife Rape, Marriage and the Law: Survey Report: Key Findings and Recommendations*, Manchester: Faculty of Economic and Social Studies, University of Manchester

Paradine, K and Wilkinson, J (2004) *Protection and Accountability: The Reporting, Investigation and Prosecution of Domestic Violence Cases*, London: HMIC

Perry, A (2006) 'Safety first? Contact and family violence in New Zealand' *Child and Family Law Quarterly*, 18(1): 1–21

Plotnikoff, J and Woolfson, R (1998) *Policing Domestic Violence: Effective Organisational Structures*, Police Research Series Paper 100, London: Home Office

Plotnikoff, J and Woolfson, R (2005) *Review of the effectiveness of specialist courts in other jurisdictions*, London: Department for Constitutional Affairs.

Quick, O and Wells, C (2006) 'Getting tough with defences' *Criminal Law Review*, 514–525

Radford, J (1992) 'Womanslaughter: A Licence to Kill? The Killing of Jane Asher' in Radford, J and Russell, D (eds), *Femicide: The Politics of Woman Killing*, Buckingham: Open University Press

Radford, J (2003) 'Professionalising responses to domestic violence in the UK: Definitional difficulties', 2(1) *Community Safety Journal*, 32–39

Radford, J, Hester, M and Kelly, L (1996) *Women, Violence and Male Power*, Buckingham: Open University Press

Radford, L (1985) *The Law and Domestic Violence Against Women*, Unpublished PhD Thesis, University of Bradford

Radford, L (1987) 'Legalising Woman Abuse' in Hanmer, J and Maynard, M (eds), *Women, Violence and Social Control*, London: Macmillan

Radford, L (1988) *The Law and Domestic Violence Against Women*, PhD Thesis, University of Bradford, Department of Applied Social Sciences

Radford, L and Gill, A (2006) 'Losing the Plot? Researching Community Safety Partnership Work Against Domestic Violence', *Howard Journal of Criminal Justice*, 45(4): 369–387

Radford, L and Hester, M (2006) *Mothering Through Domestic Violence*, London: Jessica Kingsley

Radford, L, Sayer, S and Aid for Mothers Involved in Contact Action (AMICA) (1999) *Unreasonable Fears? Child Contact in the Context of Domestic Violence: A Survey of Mother's Perceptions of Harm*, Bristol: Women's Aid Federation England

Redmayne, M (1999) 'Standards of Proof in Civil Litigation, *Modern Law Review*, 62: 167–195

Reece, H (2006) 'The End of Domestic Violence', *Modern Law Review*, 69: 770–791

Rights of Women (2005) *Rights of Women Response to Law Commission Consultation Paper (No. 177) A New Homicide Act for England and Wales?*

Robinson, A (2003) *The Cardiff Women's Safety Unit: A Multi-Agency Approach to Domestic Violence*, Cardiff: Cardiff University, School of Social Sciences

Robinson, A (2004) *Domestic Violence MARACs (Multi-Agency Risk Assessment Conferences) for Very High-Risk Victims in Cardiff*, Cardiff: Cardiff University, School of Social Sciences

Robinson, A and Cook, D (2006) 'Understanding Victim Retraction in Cases of Domestic Violence: Specialist Courts, Government Policy and Victim-Centred Justice', *Contemporary Justice Review*, 9(2): 189–213.

Rock, P (1993) *The Social World of an English Crown Court*, Oxford: Clarendon Press

Rumney, P (2003) 'Progress at a Price: The Construction of Non-Stranger Rape in the Millberry Sentencing Guidelines', *Modern Law Review*, 66: 870–884

Rumney, P (1999) 'When rape isn't rape: Court of Appeal sentencing practice in cases of marital and relationship rape', *Oxford Journal of Legal Studies*, 19(2): 243–269

Russell, D (1990) *Rape in Marriage*, Indianapolis: Indiana University Press

Sacks, E (2002) *Creating a Domestic Violence Court: Guidelines and Best Practice*. San Francisco: Family Violence Prevention Fund

Salzman, E (1994) 'The Quincy District Court Domestic Violence Prevention Program: A Model Framework for Domestic Violence Intervention, *BCL Review*, 74: 329

Sanders, A (1986) 'An Independent Crown Prosecution Service?' *Criminal Law Review*, 16–27

Sanders, A (1988) 'Personal Violence and Public Order: Prosecution of domestic violence in England and Wales', International Journal of Sociology of Law, 16(3): 359–382

Sanders, A and Young, R (2006) *Criminal Justice*, 3rd edn, Oxford: Oxford University Press

Sanders A, Hoyle, C, Morgan, R and Cape, E (2001) 'Victim Impact Statements: Don't work, can't work', *Criminal Law Review*, 447–548

Saunders, H (2002) *Making Contact Worse? Report of a National Survey of Domestic Violence Refuge Services into the Enforcement of Contact Orders*, Bristol: Women's Aid Federation England

Saunders, H (2004) 'Twenty-Nine Child Homicides: Lessons Still to be Learnt on Domestic Violence and Child Protection', Bristol: WAFE

Saunders, H and Barron, J (2003) *Failure to Protect? Domestic violence and the experiences of abused women and children in the family courts*, Bristol: WAFE

Schneider, E (2000) *Battered Women and Feminist Lawmaking*, New Haven and London: Yale University Press

Sentencing Advisory Panel (2002) *Advice to the Court of Appeal—Rape*, London: SAP

Sentencing Advisory Panel (2006) *Domestic Violence: The Panel's Advice to the Sentencing Guidelines Council*, London: SAP

Sentencing Guidelines Council (2005) *Manslaughter by Reason of Provocation: Guideline*, SGC

Sentencing Guidelines Council (2006a) *Overarching Principles: Domestic Violence*, SGC

Sentencing Guidelines Council (2006b) *Breach of a Protective Order: Definitive Guideline*, SGC

Sherman, L (1993) *Policing Domestic Violence: Experiments and Dilemmas*, New York: Free Press

Sherman, L and Berk, R (1984) 'The specific deterrent effects of arrest for domestic assault', *American Sociological Review*, 49: 261–272

Smart, C (1989) *Feminism and the Power of Law*, London: Routledge

Smith, L (1989) *Domestic Violence: An Overview of the Literature*, Home Office Research Study, No. 107, London: Home Office

Standing Together (2002) *First Soundings From a Specialist Domestic Violence Court*, London: Standing Together Against Domestic Violence

Standing Together (2002b) *Survivors Speak: A report on the findings of consultations with survivors of domestic violence 2001–2002*, London: Standing Together Against Domestic Violence

Standing Together (2003) *Heard Not Judged: Consultation with survivors of domestic violence in the London Borough of Hammersmith and Fulham 2002–2003*, London: Standing Together Against Domestic Violence

Stanko, E (2001) 'The Day to Count: Reflections on a methodology to raise awareness about the impact of domestic violence in the UK', *Criminal Justice*, 1(2): 215–226

Stark, E (2004) 'Insults, Injury and Injustice: Rethinking state intervention in domestic violence cases', *Violence Against Women*, 10: 1302–1330

Steketee, M, Levey, L and Kellitz, S (2000) *Implementing an Integrated Domestic Violence Court: Systemic Change in the District of Columbia*, Williamsburg, Virginia: National Center for State Courts

Tadros, V (2005) 'The Distinctiveness of Domestic Abuse: A Freedom Based Account', in Duff, A and Green, S (eds), *Defining Crimes*, Oxford: Oxford University Press

Tadros, V (2006) 'The Homicide Ladder', *Modern Law Review*, 69: 601–618

Temkin, J (2000) 'Prosecuting and defending rape: Perspectives from the bar', *Journal of Law and Society*, 27(2): 219–248

Thornton, M (1995) *Public and Private: Feminist Legal Debates*, Oxford: Oxford University Press

Vallely, C, Robinson, A, Burton, M and Tredidga, J (2005) *Evaluation of Domestic Violence Pilot Sites at Caerphilly (Gwent) and Croydon*, London: Crown Prosecution Service

Waddington, P (1999) 'Police (Canteen) Sub-Culture: An Appreciation', *British Journal of Criminology*, 39(2): 286–309

Walby, S (2004) *The Cost of Domestic Violence*, London: DTI

Walby, S and Allen, J (2004) *Domestic Violence, Sexual Assault and Stalking: Findings from the British Crime Survey*, Home Office Research Study 276, London: Home Office

Walby, S and Myhill, A (2001) 'New survey methodologies in researching violence against women', *British Journal of Criminology*, 41: 502–522

Walby, S and Myhill, A (2001b) 'Assessing and managing risk' in Taylor-Browne, J (ed), *What Works in Reducing Domestic Violence? A Comprehensive Guide for Professionals*, London: Whiting Birch

Walker, L (1984) *The Battered Woman Syndrome*, New York: Springer

Walker, A, Kershaw, C and Nicholas, S (2006) *Crime in England and Wales 2005/06*, Home Office Statistical Bulletin, London: Home Office

Wall, Lord Justice (2006) 'A report to the president of the Family Division on the publication by the Women's Aid Federation of England entitled Twenty-Nine Child Homicides: Lessons Still to be Learnt on Domestic Violence and Child Protection with particular reference to the five cases in which there was judicial involvement', London: Royal Courts of Justice

Walsh, C (2001) 'The trend towards specialisation: West Yorkshire innovations in drugs and domestic violence courts', *The Howard Journal*, 40(1): 26–38

Warner, K (2000) 'Sentencing in cases of marital rape: Towards changing the male imagination, *Legal Studies*, 20: 592

Wells, C (1997) 'Stalking: The criminal law response' *Criminal Law Review*, 463–470

Wells, C (2000) 'Provocation: the paradigm principle' in Ashworth, A and Mitchell, B (eds), *Rethinking English Homicide Law*, Oxford: Oxford University Press

Williams, G (1991) 'The problem of domestic rape' *New Law Journal*, 206 and 246

WNC (2002) *Seen but not heard—women's experience of the police*, Women's National Commission

WNC (2003) *Unlocking the secret: Women Open the Door on Domestic Violence*, Women's National Commission

WNC (2004) *Violence Against Women Working Group response to the consultation paper on domestic violence and sentencing*, Submission to the Sentencing Advisory Panel.

WNC (2006) *Making The Grade?* Women's National Commission

Yllo, K and Bograd, M (1988) *Feminist Perspectives on Wife Abuse*, California: Sage

Index

abuse of trust/power 63, 70
actual bodily harm (ABH) 12, 60
ADVANCE 118
advocacy services 120
aiding and abetting 56
Anti Social Behaviour Orders (ASBOs) 54, 55–6
arrests: mandatory policy in US 96; purpose of 92–3; *see also* powers of arrest
assault 60
associated persons 2, 14; categories of 16–18
attention seeking 78–9
attrition 94, 104, 107–8
Australia 48, 52, 56, 106

bail 103
balance of harm test 21, 22, 24, 25; incorrect application of 23
Barron, J 34–5, 37–8
battered women 74, 77, 81, 85
battered women syndrome 78–9, 80, 81, 83
best interests, childs 30
Blunkett, D 57
bodily harm: extension of meaning 61
boyfriend/girlfriend relationships 19, 39
Brandon, Lord 13
breach of orders 28, 41, 62, 66
British Crime Survey 4–5; methodological issues 4–5
Brooklyn Felony Domestic Violence Court 110–11
Brown, Sir Stephen 16
Butler Sloss, LJ 22

cameras, use of by police 95, 96
case construction 34

child abuse 42–3; risk assessment of 43
child contact 42–4; father's rights 44
children: affected by domestic violence 42–4, 64, 65, 100–1; deaths of 43, 74; exposure to domestic violence 64; evidence of 119–20; FLA applications by 16; needs of under MHA 1983 13
Children Act Sub Committee 30
Children and Adoption Act 2006 44
Children and Family Court Advisory and Support Service (CAFCASS) 43–4
civil orders: evidential requirements for obtaining 55
civil partners 16, 20–1; *see also* same sex partners/relationships
civil partnerships, agreement to enter 17
civil remedies 34, 39, 57
Clark County Domestic Violence Court 111–12
Clyde, Lord 80, 81
cohabitants 13; non-entitled 26
cohabitation: definition of 16, 20; indicators of 18
Collinson, A 57
committal proceedings 28, 36, 53
common assault 60, 69
community based penalties 53–4
community rehabilitation orders 117
compliance hearings 117
conduct of parties 13, 14, 21
contact 42–4; and domestic violence 30–2, 64, 129–30
contact orders 29; compliance with 44
contact proceedings 29–30
contempt of court 28, 41
contempt proceedings 54
County Courts 11, 35; power of arrest 12; power to grant injunctions 12

Court of Appeal: committal proceedings 28–9; domestic violence and contact 30–2; marital rape 70, 72; and occupation orders 24

courts: facilities at 120–1, 127; integrated domestic violence 57; and post-separation violence 43; response to breach of orders 41; role of 8; specialist domestic violence 104, 109–22

criminal prosecutions 62; cost of 63

criminalisation of breach of non-molestation orders 52–3; sentencing 53

Crown Court 57, 60; mode of trial 105–6

Crown Prosecution Service (CPS) 2, 3, 54, 57, 86, 89, 97–104; bail decisions 103; enhanced role 104; establishment of 97; obstacles to protection 59; policy statement 98; practice 99–104; preserving the family 100–1; prosecution policy 98–9; victims' persectives of 127; victim withdrawal 99–100, 102–3; voice of victim 121

Croydon specialist domestic violence court 116–17

custodial sentences 54

custody disputes 36

diminished responsibility 83

Diplock, Lord 77

discretionary test 21

disempowerment of women 48–9

Dobash, R E and R P 6, 89

domestic violence: aggravating factors 63–4; civil/criminal boundaries blurred 50, 53, 56, 128; criminal law offences applying to 59; criminal statistics 4; definition 1–4, 60; different for women than men 5; female on male 5; financial cost of 47–8; judicial statistics 4–5; legal recognition of 6; mitigating factors 64; multiple definitions 2; other jurisdictions 1; penalties 65–6; self-definition limited 5; specialist police units 91–2, 125; special criminal offence of 66–8

Domestic Violence, Crime and Victims Act 2004 (DVCVA) 53; missed opportunity 57

Donaldson, Lord 15

emotional abuse 60

empathy 33, 89

engagements 17, 18

entitled applicants 20, 21

ethnic minorities 6, 124–5

evidence 55–6, 67; effective gathering 94, 95, 98, 114–15, 116–17, 119, 127; hearsay 101; sexual history 108

exclusion orders 12, 13, 35, 36, 37

family courts 106, 111, 116; bad practice 45

Family Law Act 1996: single set of remedies 47; third party aplications 39

fear of violence 62–3

feminist law making 6

fines 41, 53, 106, 122, 128, 131

gender bias 81, 85

good character 64, 73

grandparents 16

grievous bodily harm (GBH) 60, 66

Hailsham, Lord 13

harassment 15, 16, 17, 59, 62–3

harm: child abuse 29; definition 21, 30

hearsay evidence 101, 102

Help Advice and Law Team (HALT) 112

Her Majesty's Crown Prosecution Service Inspectorate (MHCPSI) 94–5, 101

Her Majesty's Inspectorate of Constabulary (HMIC) 94–5

Her Majesty's Inspectorate of Court Administration (HMICA) 43–4

High Court: jurisdiction to grant injunctions 11

Hirst, Lord 78

Hoffman, Lord 80, 81

Home Office 2–3, 91, 94

homelessness 22, 24, 90

homicide 74–86; cooling off period 75–6, 77; sentencing 85–6; slow burn effect 76; three tier structure 83

homicide statistics, gendered nature of 4

House of Lords 8, 13, 61, 69, 77, 80

housing needs 21, 22, 24

Hoyle, C 1, 92–3, 95, 101, 119, 126, 128

Human Rights Act 1998 133

immaturity 79

imprisonment 28–9, 36, 41, 53, 62, 70–3, 85–6; contempt proceedings 28

indecent assault: length of sentence 71–2

independent advocacy support 48, 49, 110, 113, 114, 117, 120, 122 infidelity 75, 82, 86; allegations of 35–6, 85

injunctions 34; breach of 36; enforcement of 36; financial cost of 37; not irrevocable 34; powers of courts 11–12

intimidation 15, 48, 50, 100

intoxication; mitigation for rape 71, 73

Islington, civilian intervention in 93

jealousy 70, 80, 81–2, 83, 84, 86, 132

judges 8, 35–6, 40; and contact proceedings 31; monitoring of orders 112; religious sensitivity 31

judicial interpretation 11

judiciary; attitudes of senior 59; and rape cases 69–70; response in contact proceedings 30

juries 57, 75, 77, 78–84

Justice for All 52

Keith, Lord 69

Killingbeck, graded response in 93

Lane, Lord 68–9

law: gendered 8; role of 7, 8

Law Commission 13–14, 21, 27, 82; partial defences to murder 82; and powers of arrest 27; review of law of murder 83; third party applications 51

legal aid 63

legal language 40

Legal Services Commission 40

Lord Chancellor's Department 39

magistrates' courts 2, 35, 40, 56–7, 60, 104–7; power to grant orders of protection 12; sentencing 106–7; training 127

malicious wounding 60

matrimonial home rights 20–1

matrimonial homes 12

mediation 132–3; by police 91

medical diagnosis of psychiatric harm 61–2

mens rea 60

mental conditions 79, 80, 83

Merseyside 93

Millberry guidelines 70–4

Millett, Lord 81

miscarriages of justice 56

mode of trial 105

molestation, interpretation of 15–16

multi-agency working arrangements 113, 125–6

murder: defence of provocation 59; review of the law 83–4; *see also* homicide

neurotic disorders 61

Nicholls, Lord 82, 83

non-molestation orders 14, 15–16, 36; associated persons and 16; courts' discretion to grant 19; criminalisation of breach 28, 52–6; duration of 19–20; sentences for breach 28; without notice orders 26–7

non-physical abuse 39–40

Northern Ireland 52–3

NSPCC 39

occupation orders 14, 20–9; declaratory orders 21; difficulty obtaining 41; and divorce proceedings 25; increase in number 36–7; as last resort 24; regulatory orders 21, 22, 23, 25; without notice 26–7, 38, 41

occupation rights order 25; criteria for non entitled applicants 25–6; draconian solution 32; duration of 26; regulatory orders 25–6

offences: ranking of 66–7

Offences Against the Persons Act 1861 (OAPA) 60

other jurisdictions 42, 44, 47, 48, 68, 98, 109

ouster orders 12, 21, 23, 36

pendant alarms 93

perpetrator programmes 53, 65, 66, 110–11, 115, 116, 117, 118, 131, 132

photographs 119

police 2, 8, 59; call handlers 95, 96; early failings 89–90; enforcing powers of arrest 41; gatekeepers to criminal justice 89; obstacles of 59; priorities 54; third party applications 51; training package 96; use of arrests 91–2; victims views of 125–7

post traumatic stress disorder (PTSD) 78, 80, 81

Potter, Sir Mark 43

powers of arrest 12, 27, 36, 38, 41; increase in number 37; occupation orders 29; police enforcement of 41; regional variations 37; shorter than order 27; without notice orders 27

Privy Council 80, 82
property rights 20; men's 23
prosecutors 98–104, 105, 114, 127;
    specialist 108
Protection from Harassment Act 1997
    55–6, 57, 60; new criminal offences
    created by 62
provocation 32, 64; medieval roots 75;
    as mitigating factor 64; murder
    defence 59
provocation defence 75–85; call for
    abolition 84–5; concept become too
    loose 84; development of 75; gender
    bias 85; objective component 77–83;
    statutory definition 75; subjective
    component 75–7
public funding 37, 40, 52
public funds 47
public/private dichotomy 7, 51, 90
psychiatric injury 61–2
psychological abuse 60
psychological bullying 64, 86
public interest test 98, 99, 101–2

Quincy District Court 111

rape 68–74; credibility of complainant
    73; criminal justice response 107–8;
    intoxication and 71; length of
    sentence 71–2; marital 4, 59, 68–74;
    relationship 71
reasonable (wo)man 77–81
Refuge 39, 98
refuges, women's 37–8, 51
rehabilitation 54, 65
relative, definition of 16
relevant child 14, 21, 23
reprisals 50
residence orders 29–30
RESPECT guidelines 65, 132
restraining orders 62; cost of 63; in
    criminal proceedings 56–7; under
    PHA 62, 63
rights of occupation 12
risk assessment 43–4, 99

Safety and Justice 52, 68, 82, 123
same sex partners/relationships 6, 16, 20
sanctions for civil contempt 54
sceptical reformists 132
self control, standard of 77, 78, 79, 80, 83
self defence 6, 85
sentences, maximum for contempt 29
sentencing: breach and substantive

offences 54–5; custodial sentences 65;
    domestic homicide 85–6; magistrates'
    courts 106–7; preference of victims
    121–2; purpose of 53; rape cases 70;
    specialised courts 115; victims'
    perspectives 127–8
Sentencing Advisory Panel (SAP) 64, 70,
    82, 85, 86
sentencing guidelines 59–60, 72
Sentencing Guidelines Council (SHC)
    53, 54–5, 63–5, 66, 86
sexual offences 69
significant harm 21, 23–4
silent phone calls 60–1
Slynn, Lord 80
social workers 47, 48
solicitors: contact matters 44; financial
    costs of 47; gatekeeper to civil
    protection 34, 40; good family law 42;
    relationship with client 33–5, 39–40,
    45, 128, 129
Southhall Black Sisters 97–8
stalkers 62
stalking 5, 60, 62, 63
standard of proof 55–6
Standing Together 118
supervised access 44
Sweden 68

Tadros, V 67–8
Taylor, Lord 78
third party applications 39, 47–52;
    paternalistic 48; support for
    implementation of 48; victim's consent
    for 50
threats to kill 60
traditional family values 14
transient relationships 18

undertakings 27, 35, 40, 41; breach of 36;
    continued use of 37, 40–1
United States 6, 45; mandatory
    prosecutions 104; prosecuting
    authorities 97; specialist courts 109–10
unsympathetic treatment of women 34, 35

Victim Support 39, 98
victims: choices 54; credibility 106;
    families of 86; Impact Statement 121;
    not uniform 49; protection of 38;
    specialist domestic courts 117–22;
    stereotypical behaviour 66; use of term
    124; voice drowned out 108;
    vulnerability of 63; wishes in

sentencing 65; withdrawal/retraction 66, 90, 99–100, 101, 102, 103, 104, 113, 114, 120
violence: definition of 3; degrees of 66–7; exclusion orders 12
violent men: legal interventions and 130–2
voluntary support agencies 37, 38–9; third party applications 51–2

Wall, Lord Justice 32, 43
warranted excuse 85
weapons, use of 86
welfare checklist 30
without notice orders 26–7
Women's Aid of England (WAFE) 37, 39, 43, 44, 62–3, 97, 98
Women's National Commission (WNC) 64, 65, 104